Journalism and New Media

9-6-01

Journalism and New Media

John V. Pavlik

COLUMBIA UNIVERSITY PRESS   NEW YORK

COLUMBIA UNIVERSITY PRESS
Publishers Since 1893
New York   Chichester, West Sussex
Copyright © 2001 Columbia University Press
All rights reserved

Library of Congress Cataloging-in-Publication Data

Pavlik, John Vernon.
    Journalism and new media / John V. Pavlik.
        p. cm.
    Includes bibliographical references and index.
    ISBN 0–231–11482–6 (cloth)—ISBN 0–231–11483–4 (paper)
        1. Electronic news gathering   2. Journalism—Data processing   3.
    Journalism—Computer network resources   4. Journalism—Technological
    innovations   I. Title.

PN4784.E53 P38 2001
070.4'0285—dc21
∞   00–065710

c   10   9   8   7   6   5   4   3   2   1
p   10   9   8   7   6   5   4   3   2   1

Contents

Foreword

John Pavlik has provided us with a comprehensive and invaluable guide to understanding and utilizing new media in journalism. In exploring the potential of contextualized journalism, with its use of new digital capabilities in video and audio, Professor Pavlik argues convincingly that these techniques offer opportunities for the practice of better journalism, which will bolster public faith in the media. In practical terms he tells us how journalists in their reporting and storytelling as well as the business practices of their managers will have to adapt to an increasingly networked world. He does not minimize the enormous problems ahead in managing the Internet, certifying what is reliable, and maintaining standards as media Web sites compete in continuous news coverage. While his book serves as a very useful reference on everything from organizing a New Age newsroom to job hunting in new media, the general reader may be most impressed by Professor Pavlik's evocative passages on the positive and negative forces that will shape journalism in the digital age. He believes that on balance journalism, with the tools of new media, can play a larger and more useful role in our society. The wealth of information and analysis Professor Pavlik brings to bear in his impressive book reassures us that his optimism is not misplaced.

—Seymour Topping, administrator of the Pulitzer Prizes and professor of International Journalism at the Graduate School of Journalism of Columbia University

Acknowledgments

I offer my sincerest thanks to all those who helped me in writing *Journalism and New Media*. Ann Miller, my editor at Columbia University Press, offered more than three years of editorial guidance and encouragement in the development and evolution of the book. I am deeply indebted to the anonymous reviewers commissioned by Columbia University Press to comment on earlier drafts; their comments and insights were of tremendous value in shaping and refining my ideas and my analysis of the changing new media landscape and its impact on journalism. Adam Clayton Powell III, vice president of Technology for the Freedom Forum, offered a critique of the early drafts of the book that were of extraordinary value in making it clear in its focus. Seymour Topping, administrator of the Pulitzer Prizes and professor of International Journalism at the Graduate School of Journalism of Columbia University, has contributed immeasurably to the book, both through his editorial suggestions and with an eloquent foreword. My Columbia students, Pamela L. D. Peeters, cofounder of the Unit for Environmental Education, Columbia University, and Reuben Abraham provided valuable research assistance. Finally, my wife, Jackie, and daughters, Tristan Mariana and Orianna Magdalena, deserve special thanks for their love and support during the writing and editing of the book, especially during the late nights and early mornings when I headed off in the darkness to my computer.

Introduction: Understanding the Impact of New Media on Journalism

Journalism is undergoing a fundamental transformation, perhaps the most fundamental since the rise of the penny press of the mid-nineteenth century. In the twilight of the twentieth century and the dawn of the twenty-first, there is emerging a new form of journalism whose distinguishing qualities include ubiquitous news, global information access, instantaneous reporting, interactivity, multimedia content, and extreme content customization. In many ways this represents a potentially better form of journalism because it can reengage an increasingly distrusting and alienated audience. At the same time, it presents many threats to the most cherished values and standards of journalism. Authenticity of content, source verification, accuracy, and truth are all suspect in a medium where anyone with a computer and a modem can become a global publisher.

Although the easy answer is to point to the Internet, the reasons for the transformation of journalism are neither simple nor one-dimensional. Rather, a set of economic, regulatory, and cultural forces, driven by technological change, are converging to bring about a massive shift in the nature of journalism at the millennium.

The growth of a global economic system, made up of regional economies, all interrelated (witness the volatility in the world's financial markets in August 1998, when drops in Asian and Russian markets triggered drops in European and U.S. markets) and increasingly controlled by multinational corporate behemoths, has rewritten the financial basis for journalism and the media in general. Deregulation, as outlined in the U.S. Telecommunications Act of 1996 and played out in like fashion in many other parts of the world (where privatization of telecommunications has been a driving force), has spawned increasingly powerful competitive forces in journalism and communications. The end of the cold war has unleashed a variety of pent-up cultural and political forces that have yet to stabilize. Together, these forces have created an environment of uncertainty for journalism as it enters this new age in which the alignment of superpowers has been fundamentally altered, shareholders are the most important stakeholders, and competition is more likely to come from a software company based in Redmond, Washington, than from the cross-town newspaper or broadcaster.

Fueling this changing environment has been the emergence of the first and perhaps most powerful medium of global interactive communications. As James Carey writes, "The Internet should be understood as the first instance of a global communication system. That system, in turn, is displacing a national system of communications which came into existence at the end of the nineteenth century as a result of the railroad and telegraph, and was 'perfected' in subsequent innovations through television in the network era."[1]

But in many ways the Internet is merely a product, or symptom, of a more fundamental technological change that has been under way for the past half-century and only now is beginning to crystallize: the convergence of telecommunications, computing, and traditional media. Together, this new media system embraces all forms of human communication in a digital format where the rules and constraints of the analog world no longer apply. Some would question whether this convergence is actually occurring. They would point to the fact that most people around the world in 2000 still do not have a computer in the home and that in most homes that do have a computer, the TV set and the computer are still separate devices. They would note that even in the United States in 2000 most TV sets do not connect to a telephone line or any other medium of "upstream" communication capability (i.e., the ability for the audience member to send information as well as receive it).

The trend toward convergence is undeniable, however, if not yet complete. By 2000 more than eight million U.S. households as well as millions more in Japan and many other parts of the world had subscribed to digital broadcasting services such as DirecTV, which links TV sets to a system of digital video (i.e., computerized) and a telephone line (which is required for the DBS to operate) for ordering pay-per-view programs and the like. Moreover, more than twenty million individuals subscribe to America Online (AOL) and more than seven times that number are connected to the Internet through home, work, or school, reflecting a growing connectivity between computer and telecommunications.

Not only is the technology coming together, but convergence is also occurring in the realm of media ownership. Hundreds of billions of dollars worth of mergers and acquisitions occurred in the Internet and digital networks domain during the final three years of the twentieth century. AT&T purchased TCI, which is the parent of @Home, a primary broadband service provider (i.e., cable modem). America Online purchased Netscape, a leading Internet Web browser, and is merging with Time Warner. And the list is growing every day.

If there is no denying that convergence is occurring, other assumptions about convergence are worth addressing. Paramount is the frequently held, techno-utopian assumption that convergence is a good thing and inevitable. If this were so, there would be little need for a book or any other analysis of convergence and its effects. In this book, however, I propose that although convergence is happening, it is neither inevitable nor necessarily good. I do not offer a technologically deterministic view of new media. Rather, I assert that convergence merely holds the promise of a better, more efficient, more democratic medium for journalism and the public in the twenty-first century. But serious problems also plague civilization in the digital age, among them, enormous threats to privacy, increasing concentration of ownership, a shrinking diversity of voices, an ever-escalating race to report the news more rapidly, and inequitable access to information technology and digital journalism.

This book posits that new media are transforming journalism in four ways. First, the nature of news content is inexorably changing as a result of emerging new media technology. Second, the way journalists do their work is being retooled in the digital age. Third, the structure of the newsroom and news industry is undergoing a fundamental transformation. And, fourth, new media are bringing about a realignment of the relationships between and among news organizations, journalists, and their many publics, including audiences, sources, competitors, advertisers, and governments.

Each of these effects is the focus of a major section of the book, with individual chapters examining the impact of new media in detail. The book opens with a consideration of the effect of new media on news content, because that is perhaps the area of most visible impact. I propose that developments in new media are giving rise to the development of new storytelling techniques that engage the audience in more contextualized and navigable news reporting. This storytelling embraces a wider range of communication modalities (e.g., text, images, video, graphics); nonlinear writing, or hypermedia (i.e., links); extraordinary customization; and heightened audience involvement. Moreover, news is becoming much more fluid. In the old world of analog media, a story was typically published by a newspaper or covered on the evening television news and then perhaps updated the next day. Today, news is in a constant state of flux. Updates are made continuously. When visiting a Web site, one of the first things a viewer checks is when the site was last updated and, if this hasn't occurred recently, he or she moves on to another site. Software robots even automatically alert "netizens" (citizens of the Internet) when a favorite news site or story has been updated.

The second section of the book examines how new media are transforming the work of journalists. Digital tools for news gathering, communication, editing, and production have become increasingly portable, inexpensive, and powerful, giving journalists in the field the same capability as those in a hard-wired central newsroom. Together, these tools give journalists increasingly effective techniques for finding diverse and reliable sources, checking facts, and meeting deadlines. They also make plagiarism increasingly simple and tempting and raise a serious threat to good old shoe-leather reporting.

The third part of the book looks at the structural implications of new media. The traditional newsroom is organized along the lines almost of a military unit, with a strong publisher, editor, or news director overseeing a relatively rigid hierarchical organization. Decisions follow a strong chain of command. Online newsrooms tend to be increasingly decentralized and flexible, especially those that are original to the Internet, and they reflect a more experimental and adaptable entrepreneurial culture. Staffs are much more likely to include large numbers of freelance contributors. Although this gives the online newsroom an adaptable design, it also makes it more difficult to instill and maintain a strong newsroom culture of traditional news values. The boundary between advertising and editorial sometimes blurs.

The structure of the news industry is also evolving. Competition comes from many corners, and news providers are not just the traditional newspapers, magazines, and broadcasters. Rather, the World Wide Web furnishes a low-cost global forum for anyone with a message, especially corporate, not-for-profit, and government enterprises, whose voices formerly filtered through a news media gatekeeper.

The fourth section of the book argues that new media are transforming the relationships that exist among news organizations, journalists, and their many publics, including audiences, advertisers, and sources. The traditional news provider typically has served a well-defined geographic community. Local newspapers and local broadcasters served their local city, town, suburb, or regional market. National news providers served primarily a single country or extended region.

Today's online news operations may continue to serve local communities, but those that hope for eventual financial viability are retooling to serve much larger and geographically diverse communities of interest that may include local citizenry but also larger numbers who live well beyond the local or even national boundary. This shift brings with it profound implications not just for commerce and culture but for democracy, which in the United States has traditionally been based on geographic boundaries, with a corresponding news media system among whose primary responsibilities was the creation of a well-informed electorate.

I provide evidence to support these four effects in two forms. First, I have conducted original, collaborative, interdisciplinary research linking journalism and computer science. This research has primarily involved two multi-year projects involving the development of a Mobile Journalist Workstation and omnidirectional imaging for news gathering and storytelling. I discuss both of these research projects in detail.

Second, a synthesis of both published research on trends in online journalism and case studies of how individual news organizations have covered specific stories is used to critically analyze the transformation of journalism from an analog to a digital media system.

The fifth and final section of the book speculates on the future of journalism and journalism education in the context of emerging technology. It suggests that the changes in journalism are only beginning and that regulatory changes and emerging artificial intelligence tools will exert subtle but profound influences on the nature of journalism in the twenty-first century. Leadership must come from both the industry and the academy if the fourth estate — journalism — is to continue to serve democracy effectively. Finally, an afterword offers speculation on the evolving role of the journalist in an age of ubiquitous information provided by a wide-ranging set of news and content providers, many of whom may be seeking influence in the court of public opinion but may be largely indistinguishable to the public.

Together, these and other new media technologies examined throughout the book present a unique opportunity for storytellers, especially journalists, to create much more engaging, navigable, contextualized reports that tell the day's events more accurately, fully, and dynamically. At least, that is the potential. They are also producing a glut of information that threatens to overwhelm the public in a sea of information of frequently dubious quality and origin. This book considers the implications of these emerging tools of the information age and speculates on their likely adoption, evolution, and impact on news and society in the next millennium, examining both the positive and negative forces that will shape the face of journalism in a digital age. Each potentially positive development is placed into a critical perspective to evaluate more fully whether journalism will ultimately see an improvement and whether society will likely benefit as a result.

Journalism and New Media

Part I

Altering News Content

The first part of this book examines the impact of new media on news content. I propose that developments in new media are leading to the development of new storytelling techniques that engage the audience in more contextualized and navigable news reporting. This interactive storytelling embraces a wide range of communication modalities (e.g., text, images, video, graphics), including nonlinear writing—or hypermedia (i.e., links)—and offers possibilities for extraordinary customization and heightened audience involvement. Moreover, news is becoming much more fluid than in the past. In the old world of analog media, a story was typically published by a newspaper or on the evening television news and then perhaps updated the next day. In 2000, news is in constant flux. Updates are continuous. When visiting a Web site, a viewer often first checks when a site was last updated and, if this hasn't occurred recently, moves on to another site. Software robots even automatically alert "netizens" (citizens of the Internet) when a favorite news site or story has been modified. Chapter 1 examines the changes occurring in storytelling in journalism, and chapter 2 offers an assessment of the state of online journalism in the United States and around the world.

1 Transforming Storytelling: From Omnidirectional Imaging to Augmented Reality

You're immersed in the evening news of 2010. A ninety-second video bulletin reports an important extraterrestrial discovery on Europa, Jupiter's largest moon. Using your head-worn display, you look around the surface simply by turning your head. You look at the left-hand portion of the three-dimensional omnivideo (your gaze acts as a mouse would today) and say "select," and a second window in your immersive environment plasma display reveals a special video inset with detailed animation showing how life began under Europa's frozen hydrogen crust. A special commentary from Arthur C. Clarke, the inventor of the communications satellite and the man who once posited that life might exist on at least one of Jupiter's four Galilean moons, explains what it all means for life on earth.

A Journalist's Medium

It has been said that newspapers are an editor's medium and that broadcasting is a producer's medium. To the extent that either of these statements is true, today it can be said that the Internet is a journalist's medium. The Internet not only embraces all the capabilities of the older media (text, images, graphics, animation, audio, video, real-time delivery) but offers a broad spectrum of new capabilities, including interactivity, on-demand access, user control, and customization. Thus using the new media tools available via the Internet, online journalists can tell stories using whatever mo-

dalities and communication features are needed and appropriate for a particular story. Moreover, each audience member can receive personalized
news that places each story into a context meaningful to her or him. The
only real limits on the Internet as a journalistic medium are bandwidth,
connectivity, and credibility of content. All three of these are likely to become much less constraining over time, as bandwidth and connectivity increase (i.e., as transmission speeds increase, allowing for easier access to
quality multimedia content, and as the number of citizens connected to the
Internet increases) and as citizens become more familiar with the Internet
and develop new media literacy skills that allow them to recognize reliable,
authentic online sources. Bandwidth and related network congestion are
periodically a heightened problem for all online news providers whenever
there is a breaking story of particularly great audience interest. In August
1998 Hurricane Bonnie drew such widespread audience demand for updated information that many weather-related sites experienced record demand (e.g., the Weather Channel's Web site drew its largest audience ever),
and the National Hurricane Center had to shut down its informational site
because the volume of traffic (estimated at a million hits a day) was inter-
fering with data flow over the network used by meteorologists.[1]

Contextualized Journalism

This chapter examines the fundamental nature of the storytelling transformation of journalism in an online, electronic environment and argues
that a new form of news is emerging, perhaps best described as contextualized journalism. Contextualized journalism has five basic dimensions or
aspects: (1) breadth of communication modalities; (2) hypermedia; (3)
heightened audience involvement; (4) dynamic content; and (5) customization.

Communication Modalities

First, and most obviously, news in this new media environment can take
advantage of the full range of communication modalities, including text,
audio, video, graphics, and animation, as well as emerging capabilities such
as 360-degree video. These capabilities enable the journalist to tell each

story in a way uniquely suited to it, no longer constrained by the limited modalities available in previous analog media. A variety of fixed media publishing enterprises have demonstrated the value of the enriched storytelling capabilities of multimedia. One noteworthy example is Voyager, a company founded by Bob Stein, whose electronic publishing produced a series of highly acclaimed digital products, such as *Poetry in Motion*, featuring a rich multimedia presentation of the work of poet Amiri Baraka (formerly known as LeRoi Jones), *Starry Night*, which explores Van Gogh's remarkable painting, and *First Person: Mumia Abu-Jamal*, a report on the black journalist convicted of murder and sentenced to death in a sensational case involving racial and political cross-currents in Philadelphia. Each of the Voyager titles involves not only extensive textual content but a dynamic blend of audio and video that brings each subject to life in a highly contextualized and engaging fashion.[2] Stein and some of his colleagues from Voyager are now embarking on a new venture called Night Kitchen that brings simple-to-use multimedia authoring tools to the desktop in a product called TK3, which will enable journalists and authors in general to create electronic documents similar in style to the Voyager titles, without the need for a highly trained programmer.[3]

Unfortunately, online journalism has only slowly begun to incorporate many of these multimedia capabilities. There are several reasons for this. First, except for many television network–based sites, most online news operations (with a parent newspaper or other print operations) do not have extensive traditions in creating multimedia content; neither do they have a culture or set of resources to begin producing such multimedia content easily. Some innovative sites are beginning to produce more original multimedia content, however, and this will grow in the months and years ahead. Second, some news operations tend to view online reporting as merely an extension of their existing activities, and if they are print based, they tend to not view video and audio as terribly relevant. Third, many operations do not have staff with multimedia capabilities and backgrounds and are likely to hire reporters similar to those who have worked for the parent print operations, where the emphasis is on the written word; graphics, images, audio, and video are not part of their training.

A *room with an omnidirectional view*.   Dating to the work of the Lumière brothers in 1890s' Paris, the constraints of limited-field-of-view photography have provided the fundamental structure of visual storytelling, especially news and entertainment on television and film. Video- and photojournalists, cinematographers, and other videographers have used the frame of the photographic lens to define the linear narrative of visual storytelling. Now, three fundamental developments have made possible a paradigmatic shift in visual storytelling. First, digital video, although not new, has matured and is set to become important not just in production but also in storytelling, as viewers at home and elsewhere will have direct access to video in digital form. Second, a new generation of image and sound acquisition devices (e.g., new 3-D cameras and microphones, high-resolution remote sensing satellite imagery, etc.) will open up the possibilities available to those creating images and video, offering options ranging from panoramic views to three-dimensional immersive environments. Third, the growth of networked media, including today's Internet and tomorrow's digital television, will furnish a wide range of creative and interactive alternatives to visual storytellers.

The following discussion examines in detail the nature of a new video system capable of shooting and recording 360-degree views of events, locations, and people. Although the implications of this particular new media technology are significant for journalism, I examine it in depth here as an example of the wide spectrum of new tools that may be influencing the practice and content of journalism in the years to come. It is not my intention to imply that 360-degree imaging is necessarily the most important new media development for journalism; rather, it is illustrative of the coming transformation of news in the digital age.

Bentham's panopticon.   Columbia computer science professor Shree Nayar has invented a camera with an unusually large field of view. Nayar's invention captures a 360-degree field of vision through a single photographic lens and involves no moving or mechanical parts. The so-called omnidirectional camera employs a CCD camera (a camera with a charge-coupled device) and a standard lens but records light gathered from the surface of a specially crafted parabolic mirror, based in part on principles derived from telescopes of the 1950s designed to permit astronomers to observe the entire night sky through a single lens.

Imagine a sphere encased in a mirror; then cut that mirror in half. Looking into such a highly curved mirror, you would see an entire hemisphere of vision, but the image would be distorted much as an image reflected in a mirror in the house of illusions at a carnival. Processing the omnivideo through software written by Professor Nayar and his doctoral student, Venkat Peri, removes the distortion in the video image and can display the video either as a wide-screen panoramic view or as discrete portions within the overall field of view (i.e., as twelve software "cameras," each containing 30 percent of the total 360-degree space, can be displayed on a computer monitor).[4] Professor Nayar has also developed an omnicamera formatted for the World Wide Web and accompanied by a Java applet that permits multiple viewers simultaneously to pan, tilt, or zoom anywhere in the field of view. This is possible because Nayar's omnicamera involves no mechanical or moving parts; the view is controlled by software. Columbia University licensed a start-up company called Remote Reality in Silicon Alley (an area of Manhattan south of Forty-first Street) to manufacture and sell the camera in two versions, the ParaShot, which shoots still images, and the ParaMax, which shoots full-motion 360-degree video. Other omnidirectional imaging devices and systems are also available on the commercial market, including Internet Pictures Corporation, or iPIX, based in Oak Ridge, Tennessee; i-Move, based in Portland, Oregon; and Be Here,[5] of Palo Alto, California. iPIX is a widely used commercial 360-degree still imaging system, described in promotional materials as an "interactive photography technique [that] allows the user to be immersed inside a 360 degree digital image representing any environment that can be photographed. The user, via a mouse or keyboard input, is able to navigate in any desired direction in the interactive photograph, magnifying or exploring any part of the image."[6]

Possible applications of omnidirectional imaging are substantial and wide ranging. Surveillance and security systems will be profoundly altered by the introduction of 360-degree video. An omniview camera can survey an entire scene with virtually no blind spots. Supplanting robotic mechanisms and controls, an omnicamera permits multiple viewers to survey different parts of a scene. Professor Nayar is even developing an omnicamera that could be suspended from the belly of a drone surveillance helicopter. In collaboration with Hagen Schempf's group at Carnegie Mellon University, Nayar's research group has developed another called the Cyclops, a six-inch-diameter deployable omnicamera.[7] It involves a miniature 360-degree camera mounted on a gyroscope and encased in a plexiglass sphere. The sphere, which also contains a microphone for capturing sound and batteries for power, can be rolled into areas unsafe for a person to enter, such as a nuclear power plant where there has been a radiation leak, or a burning building, or even a hostage or terrorist situation. The camera can then transmit a 360-

degree video of the location via a wireless transmitter. Another version of the Cyclops has a motor and system of locomotion that allows an operator in a remote location to steer it around objects or corners. The implications for firefighters, police, or even journalists are profound, since such devices would enable safe remote observation of hazardous or inaccessible areas.

Of course, the omnicamera challenges our conventional notions of privacy, as well. In New York City, Mayor Rudolph Giuliani granted Police Commissioner Howard Safir permission to install surveillance video cameras throughout Manhattan, especially in high-crime areas. Imagine the implications if Commissioner Safir installed omnicameras throughout the city. Most people understand that a camera may be watching them when the lens is pointed at them. An omnicamera, however, is watching no matter where it is pointed.

The omnicamera also promises to transform video conferencing, distance learning, and a variety of other applications. For example, consider the potential of an omnicamera installed in a daycare center. When linked to the World Wide Web, parents anywhere in the world with Web access could monitor their children's activity.

Perhaps more interesting is the use of the omnicamera in journalism. At least two applications spring to mind. First, the omnicamera could allow journalists to do what they already do in a new and perhaps improved way. Today, a one-person news crew on assignment for Time Warner's twenty-four-hour local cable news operation in New York City must find the story, interview the subject, ask the right questions, and get all the right video. If she's pointing the camera in one direction and something important happens somewhere else, she must quickly pan the camera or miss an important event. With an omnicamera, the reporter would automatically get all the video, enabling her to concentrate on asking the right questions. This might seem like a small step toward better journalism, but one-person news crews are increasingly common and increasingly pressured to produce broadcast-quality video without much concern about the quality of the journalism. Even a small incremental improvement in the quality of the journalism would be a significant reversal of a decade-long slide in the overall quality of broadcast reporting, especially at the local level. Most local news crews, one person or two (i.e., a reporter with a camera operator), are expected to produce several stories a day, and, given the time needed to get to and from the scene of an event, there is precious little time left either to prepare for an interview or to digest it afterward. And during a breaking news event most reporters, especially if they are expected to broadcast live from the scene, are more occupied with getting a good shot than with getting the story exactly right. If an omnicamera can help even slightly, it will be a worthwhile improvement. An omnicamera could also eliminate the need for cutaway shots of the reporter interviewing the source, which are commonly staged after the fact.

If any of this strikes you as unlikely, think back to the 1993 tragedy in Waco, Texas. The story began on February 28 when agents of the Bureau of Alcohol, Tobacco and Firearms (ATF) attempted to execute arrest and search warrants against David Koresh and the Branch Davidian compound. Gunfire broke out, four ATF agents were killed and sixteen wounded, and an undetermined number of Davidians were killed or injured. The siege lasted nearly two months until April 19, when more than eighty Branch Davidians inside the compound were killed in a raging fire that started after ATF agents launched tear gas canisters into the compound in an attempt to end the siege. Despite its presence during the entire siege, CNN missed videotaping the moment the fire erupted because its cameras were momentarily pointed away from the compound. Had CNN been operating even a single omnidirectional camera, it would not have missed recording this critical event.

The real risk in the deployment of omnidirectional technology is that the omnicamera will become little more than a technological gimmick employed by local (or network) news operations that will be showcased for its own sake rather than as an enhancement to storytelling. There is little to prevent this from happening; indeed, it already has happened with various preceding technologies, such as live transmissions from remote locations, helicopters, and infrared cameras. In a business driven more by commercial interests than the public interest, perhaps the only two things that could help ensure the appropriate use of omnidirectional cameras or any other new media tool would be (1) a clear set of standards for the appropriate use of new media tools articulated by leaders in journalism and the news industry (and adopted by the leading news organizations, such as the Radio Television News Directors Association); and (2) media news startups to a certain degree free of the constraints and traditions of long-standing news organizations and thus able to define their news standards in a fresh manner that could serve as a competitive advantage.

The omnicamera could also be a valuable tool for journalists who find themselves in hazardous zones, such as in a military conflict. Rather than

stand up and pan the camera around the battlefield, putting himself at serious risk of injury or death from enemy or friendly fire, a reporter could
simply set an omnicamera on a tripod and crouch down. If you doubt the
value of such a device to journalists reporting from a war zone, consider the
alarming statistics reported by the Committee to Protect Journalists.[8] Since
1988, 474 journalists have been killed in the line of work, many while covering armed conflicts around the world. In one case, January 10, 1999, three
Associated Press journalists, Ian Stewart (West African bureau chief), Miles
Tierney (television producer), and David Guttenfelder (photographer) were
fired on by rebels in downtown Freetown, Sierra Leone. Tierney was shot
and killed instantly, while the others were wounded. Stewart was shot in the
head and injured critically, while Guttenfelder received minor injuries from
flying glass.[9] An omnidirectional camera would not have saved them, but
any device that might provide reporters with even modestly greater safety is
worthwhile.

Consider the case of Radio B92 journalist D. Bukumirovic reporting from
Serbia. On August 28 and 29, 1998, Bukumirovic was part of a crew of fifty
journalists who entered the village of Klecka in Kosovo. Bukumirovic wanted
to document the carnage taking place in the conflict between Ushtria Cli-
rimtare E Kosoves (UCK) and Serbian troops. As Bukumirovic reported, "The
destruction left after the fighting is clearly visible. There are many burnt and
damaged buildings, including the mosque in the village of Crnoljevo, holes
and tank tracks in the road and pits left by explosions. The convoy of journalists was escorted by police who showed us many positions which had
been held by the UCK, bunkers and kilometers of trenches with a clear view
of the entire region. . . . The police announced that 22 kidnapped Serbs
had been tortured and killed and their bodies burnt in a lime pit in Klecka."[10]
Unfortunately, the police would not allow any journalists with cameras, especially video cameras, to record the scene. So, under the advice of Radio
B92 Internet coordinator Drazen Pantic, Bukumirovic entered the region
with a small digital video camcorder, which he inserted in his rolled-up shirt
sleeve, and videotaped his visit without anyone realizing. If they had seen
his camera, the police or military might not only have taken away his equipment but perhaps arrested Bukumirovic, or worse. A compact omnidirectional camera (experimental applications of a small, head-worn unit have
been tested and a unit just seven millimeters in size is being developed by
Remote Reality) might have recorded even more of the scene without drawing the attention of the military. Radio B92 then took the digital video and

posted it on its Kosovo Web page, where it could be viewed from anywhere in the world.[11]

Even outside a war zone, omnidirectional technology might have important uses, say, at live events, such as protests, political rallies, sporting events, or busy traffic intersections. Or imagine putting an omnicamera on the dashboard of a police cruiser. News reports have sometimes provided dramatic video of a suspect and police officer captured by a dashboard camera, only to have the suspect move to the side of the squad car and a critical moment pass unrecorded. With an omnicamera on the dash, nothing would be lost from view. Of course, police also traditionally use cameras to document interactions between officers and suspects, in an attempt to record the actual events and protect police from allegations of abuse or torture of prisoners. Many prisoners allege they are beaten outside the field of view of the camera. This problem would be addressed by an omnidirectional camera.

The single-lens omnicamera's most significant technical limitation today is its limited image resolution. Because it relies on today's video camera technology and only a fixed amount of information is captured through a single lens, the single-lens omnicamera parses that information into video streams containing only a portion of the information in the original video image. But this technical limitation will be improved upon very quickly as higher-resolution cameras, more powerful processors, and greater bandwidth become available. Remote Reality is in early 2000 testing a version of the ParaShot parabolic mirror that attaches to a 35 mm camera, giving the captured images even higher resolution. Various alternative omnicamera configurations obtain additional resolution by seaming together video feeds from multiple cameras. The main drawbacks to such high-resolution approaches are the cost of multiple cameras and greater bulk and bandwidth requirements. Moreover, most of the 360-degree systems require the viewer first to download a software player to see the omnidirectional image. An exception is the ParaShot, which is server based and therefore does not require the client, or news consumer, to install a software player to view the omnidirectional images or video. A more fundamental challenge, however, is developing the appropriate paradigm for effectively and ethically using omnidirectional imaging.

A second broad application of the omnidirectional camera involves the transformation of storytelling. In many ways, omnidirectional video represents a changing imaging paradigm, one fundamentally different from the achievement a century ago of the Lumière brothers, who invented the first motion picture camera and projected the first motion picture documenting scenes from daily life (*Man Hammering Wall* was among the Lumière brothers' first films and evokes the documentary model of modern television journalism).

Consider this in the context of the historical roots of omnidirectional imaging. The concept is derived from seventeenth- and eighteenth-century panoramas or panoramic paintings and murals depicting scenes, often found in the castles and palaces of Europe.

The panorama, frequently a full 360° cyclorama like this one, was the brainchild of the English artist Robert Barker, who developed the correct perspective approaches to give the appearance of all-around vision. He was granted a patent for his process in 1787. The first exhibition space was not large enough to hold the full 360° painting, which was not displayed in its entirety until 1793 when the first purpose-built panorama building in the world was constructed in Leicester Square. Panoramas became all the rage for the rest of the century and well into the 19th.[12]

A few years later the panorama made its way to the New World. Steamboat skipper Robert Fulton introduced the panorama to Paris in 1799 and shortly thereafter to the United States. John Vanderlyn's 1819 panoramic depiction of the Versailles gardens is on exhibit in the Metropolitan Museum of Art in New York. Panoramic images were also used in reporting the Civil War. One famous three-camera photograph was taken in 1864, just after the Union Army had captured the city of Chattanooga, Tennessee, from Confederate forces. Almost two centuries later the first digital panorama appeared on the *Star Trek* CD-ROM, which allowed circular tours of the chambers of the starship *Enterprise*.

Often, technologies are invented for explicit purposes and applications, in the case of journalism, to improve the efficiency, accuracy, and speed of some aspect of communication. And as important as these intended effects are, the unintended or unexpected consequences are often more significant. The panorama is such a case. When King George III visited one of London's first panoramas in 1794, he was intrigued by the imagery surrounding him, a detailed painting of a naval fleet moored near the Isle of Wight. The reaction of his wife, Queen Charlotte, was somewhat more visceral: she became mildly seasick, which may explain why the work was retitled the *Nausorama* when it was displayed in Hamburg, Germany, a few years later.

Cultural Resistance

One of the biggest factors causing relatively limited use of omnidirectional imaging among news organizations through 2000 has been the slow development of a new storytelling paradigm suited to 360-degree images. Taking a good omnidirectional image is even more complex than taking a good conventional still image (because one must consider the entire field of view). Moreover, most news organizations that have used the technology successfully, such as the *New York Times on the Web*, *CNN.com*, or *MSNBC.com*, have provided interesting-looking 360-degree views of news events, frequently for features, but rarely have they used the images to tell a story. Instead they use them as novel complements to accompanying text reports. A development that may advance the storytelling of omnidirectional imaging is the incorporation of object-oriented video or hot spots (hypertext links), as well the addition of audio tracks to omnidirectional still images. In this second case, the reporter will report accompanying facts and context for the image in an audio narration with ambient sound, while using a Java applet to pan, tilt, or zoom throughout the 360-degree view automatically. In this way, one might tell a story and create a dynamic, moving picture from a single, 360-degree still image, minimizing the bandwidth and processing power for a high-resolution video report.

Although iPIX and the other 360-degree imaging systems are in some news use, most have significant limitations, such as being large and complex to use, thereby limiting their potential in online journalism, especially by freelancers or one-person news crews, or require multiple images that must be stitched together to create the 360-degree effect. From a journalistic perspective, this is a significant problem since breaking news events rarely pause to let the camera operator take multiple pictures so as to create a composite image: it is difficult if not impractical to stop a moving train, a speeding bullet, or a night-stick–wielding police officer. Thus a camera that can capture an entire field of view in a single instant offers significant advantages journalistically, although other devices might be useful in other applications, such as architecture, fashion, or nature photography. This is one of the most important advantages of the ParaShot omnicamera. It takes in the entire field of view through a single lens, whereas most alternative products use multiple cameras, multiple mirrors, and multiple CCDs requiring the user or photographer to piece together the images. In early 2000 iPIX introduced a system using a double-lens system attached to a single camera to create 360-degree images; this enables the iPIX system to see the entire field of view in a single moment.

How have such comprehensive images been used in reporting? In the spring of 1999 West African immigrant Amadou Diallo was slain by four undercover police officers in the Bronx, New York. Diallo was exiting the vestibule of his apartment building late at night when four members of New York's street crime unit arrived, apparently investigating a rape case, and opened fire on the unarmed man. Firing forty-one bullets, the police hit Diallo at least nineteen times, several bullets entering the prone body's feet. Although all news media in the New York area covered the incident, a special report created collaboratively by students at Columbia University's Center for New Media and APBnews (an online news service dedicated to crime coverage) was unique in featuring a 360-degree look at the scene. Visitors to the APBnews site can navigate through the vestibule where Diallo was shot, examining the physical space, the bullet holes, and the messages inscribed on the wall by police investigators and others, as well as the Bronx street where Diallo lived and the police opened fire. Is it better journalism? Perhaps. But it absolutely gives the news consumer more context.

As part of a multiyear research investigation, in 1997 a group of new media reporters at the Center for New Media's News Laboratory developed the first complete news report using an omnicamera. Equipped with the camera, fifty pounds of battery packs, and assorted video recording technology, the interdisciplinary team of student journalists, engineers, and computer scientists reported on the ongoing efforts of the Irish Lesbian and Gay Organization (ILGO) to march in New York City's historic St. Patrick's Day parade. The omnicamera enabled the student news team to capture the dynamic event in a 360-degree field of vision that conventional video technology could not obtain even employing multiple cameras. As the protesters marched into the parade and the police threatened them with arrest, the omnicamera documented the entire scene. A digital version of the omnicamera report is available for viewing at the News Lab's Web site.[13]

Omnidirectional video ultimately gives viewers more control over the news experience, and this can lead to improved credibility for news. By providing viewers with a sense that events are being placed in fuller context, even something as simple as the size of a crowd at a protest can only help to reengage a fragmenting audience. The Integrated Media Systems Center (IMSC) at the University of Southern California, a multiyear engineering research project funded by the National Science Foundation, is also developing related technology for audio news. Omnidirectional or immersive audio may enable storytellers not only to offer news on demand using voice command but also to create sound environments that will allow either fixed or mobile news consumers to experience through sound the compelling sense of being at a news event. Consider how National Public Radio today effectively uses ambient sound to place stories at a remote location in a manner that engages the listener, or consider filmmaker Steven Spielberg's effective use of audio technology in the movie *Saving Private Ryan* to transport the audience to the battlefields of World War II. Imagine using immersive audio technology to engage audio news consumers in a similar fashion via head-worn sound systems or environmental sound systems at home or in a car.

Hypermedia

Stories told online (including via television linked to the Internet or other network-based digital technology) can make connections much more easily than in any other medium. This is done primarily through the use of hyperlinks, or clickable pointers to other online content, although other tools for making such links or associations are now emerging.

Although hyperlinks are familiar to anyone who has ever surfed the Net, there is not a great deal of research on the implications of hyperlinks for journalism. A leading program of research on hyperlinks, and hypermedia in general, in journalism has been developed by Eric S. Fredin and Prabu David at Ohio State University. Fredin and David write, "While the integration of audio, video, graphic, and textual information is often perceived as the exciting benefit of hypermedia over traditional media, the more substantial benefit may be the links between electronic pages, such as the links connecting any one news story to related news stories and other sources of information."[14] Such links are ubiquitous in news stories reported at Internet news sites. Consider, for example, a story on August 25, 1998, on *ABCNews.com*. It examined criticism the U.S. military had begun to receive regarding the effectiveness of the Tomahawk cruise missile attack on suspected terrorist attacks in Afghanistan and a chemical weapons factory in Sudan that the Clinton administration had tied to Osama bin Laden, the Saudi multimillionaire accused of funding the attacks on U.S. embassies in Kenya and Tanzania. As with most online stories, the bin Laden report contained a variety of hyperlinks to other previously published reports and related sites, such as a story on the suspected chemical weapons plant, as well as an interactive map of the two bomb sites that contained additional details explaining why the United States bombed them.

Fredin and David note that such hyperlinks have also been used in other areas of online reporting. "For example, on a Web site such as *CNN.com*, a typical story about the 1996 presidential elections had links to stories on the same topic that were done earlier in the campaign. The earlier stories in turn were linked to candidates' home pages and platform positions. Some news stories were linked to home pages of relevant federal agencies, to home pages of interest groups, or to enormous on-line news archives such as *Lexis/ Nexis*. The result," Fredin and David observe, "is a massive and interconnected information network."

This represents a new form of journalism that places stories in a much richer historical, political, and cultural context. "The fact that massive repositories of information are only a few mouse clicks away offers a richness to hypermedia that set it apart from traditional media," conclude Fredin and David. At the same time, they point out, hypermedia require or at least enable a much more active and participatory audience. (I examine the issue of audience participation in further detail in chapter 8, presenting evidence that younger audiences, who are growing up with hypermedia, not just on the Internet but in all forms of new media, are comfortable with active participation in their media experience and that passive media consumption may not be an inherent preference among audiences but instead a learned behavior.)

A live example of this comes from a new media startup in New York's Silicon Alley called APBnews (available at www.APBnews.com). An Internet-original—or purely online—news product, it has no print or broadcast parent. Started in the fall of 1998, it has rapidly grown to become a major provider of news about crime and criminal justice. Consider how APBnews covered a major news story compared to coverage of the same story in the *New York Times*. The late Frank Sinatra's FBI file became public property on December 10, 1998. News organizations across the United States and internationally noted the release of the report and the accusations it contained, including Sinatra's alleged mob connections, his arrest for "seduction," and the 4F status for psychological instability that made him ineligible for the World War II draft.

The *New York Times* provided a credible journalistic accounting of the thirteen-hundred-page file, examining each of these subjects in an approximately twenty-five-hundred-word account. It did not make the entire file available, either in the paper or on its Web site, most likely because of space limitations (although it must be noted that, to its credit, it did provide this service with the several-hundred-page Starr report). The *Times*'s report, both in print and online form, illustrates how most general-interest newspapers or news magazines approach a story such as this. A primary source publishes information, and news organizations report the release of the report, providing an overview of its contents and pointing out certain notable items.

By contrast, the APBnews report was a uniquely Internet story using a wide range of online media capabilities ranging from text reporting to interactivity, images, and all thirteen hundred pages of the FBI's Sinatra file, complete with annotations and separate sidebars about the most important sections of the report. Because of the overall quality of the APBnews's reporting, the FBI even began referring its own queries to the site's Sinatra posting (so reported the site's executive vice president for content, Mark Sauter, a Columbia Journalism School graduate, class of 1985). In recognition of its groundbreaking reporting, in 1999 APBnews was the first online original-news organization to receive a national journalism award from the Society of Professional Journalists.

The case of APBnews illustrates the potential transformation of news content in a digital age. No longer is news constrained by the technical limitations of analog media, whether print, television, or radio. Instead, all modalities of human communication are available for telling stories in the most compelling, interactive, on-demand, and customized fashion possible. Certain constraints, of course, still apply, including newsroom traditions and training, as well as newsroom economics, and these may ultimately determine whether journalists fully utilize online capabilities to create better, more complete, and contextualized news reports. Nevertheless, the technology makes improved news content possible.

If the Sinatra story seems to lack weight, consider the sometimes-heard criticism that American news media tend to focus on events to the exclusion of broad social, economic, or political processes and trends. The most common explanation for this is that events make better, or at least easier, stories than broad social trends, although the best journalism, of course, uses an event-based story to illustrate a broader trend. Be that as it may, another December 1998 report by APBnews illustrates how new media, especially online news, can make trend reporting more palatable, at least to editors who sometimes shy away from it for fear of boring readers. The site published a story about a newly released FBI national crime report that was flawed in overreporting certain types of crimes and underrporting others. Many news organizations published or broadcast stories about the issuance of the report, while many community news providers did stories looking into the report's data about the local geographic community and perhaps interviewing some local residents or officials as to how they reacted to FBI data showing their communities as either more or less safe than average or other communities in the report. The APBnews story went well beyond this standard news model: it published the entire report online. That meant that users visiting the site could not only get the best available journalistic intelligence about the data in the report but also look up data about any community, county, or state in the United States and evaluate the significance of the data for themselves. Moreover, the site provided reader forums and other means of soliciting reader feedback that then shaped the overall news content the site provided on the crime trends revealed in the FBI report. In 1999 APBnews added an interactive crime map to its site permitting any user to enter any zip code in the United States and get the crime rate for that area. Like some other online news initiatives (e.g., Salon), APBnews faced serious financial diffi-culties in 2000 and, after laying off its staff of 170, filed for bankruptcy protection in July. The following September it was acquired by *Safety-Tips.com*, another Internet enterprise, and has continued its operations.

Object-oriented multimedia. A complementary new media storytelling technique with significant implications for journalism is object-oriented multimedia. Object-oriented multimedia refers to the creation of digital ob-jects in full motion video and audio. Using MPEG-4 or even next-generation Web technology, storytellers can create items that incorporate both linear and multilinear narrative forms by making every image within a video stream a digital object. Each object, such as a person, place, or building, can be encoded with layers of additional content, such as textual description, in-teractive graphics and animation, additional motion video or audio, or links to other sites on the World Wide Web, all retrievable or accessible with a mouse click. Thus a reporter might create a standard two-minute report for the evening news but also encode another hour or more of content accessible to viewers interested in more depth but not forced on viewers who prefer more passive acquisition of news.

Object-oriented multimedia is essentially the extension of digital objects from relatively static Web pages (e.g., clickable hyperlinks) to digital video, which is now entering the market in both the United States and around the world. It permits journalists and other content creators to layer in additional content and create interactive elements and hyperlinks in motion video. Consider another example. Say that a political reporter might produce a story about a candidate for U.S. president. In analog television, a typical report might provide a ninety-second linear narrative that all viewers would watch in similar fashion. Using object-oriented multimedia, a digital video report might contain the same ninety-second linear narrative but also many layers of additional content. These additional layers might include a detailed statistical profile of the candidate's voting record, complete with graphics and animations illustrating the candidate's campaign contributors and their relationships to his or her voting record on various bills, as well as links to the candidate's own Web site. These additional video elements could be accessed by a mouse click, a remote-control click, or even voice command. Not all viewers, however, would obtain this content, only those who were interested. Similar applications could be effectively used in a wide variety of stories, ranging from weather reporting to sports and the arts. All could benefit from the additional context.

Leading research on object-oriented multimedia is under way at both Columbia University and IBM Research. At Columbia, electrical engineering professor Alex Eleftheriadis has developed a software authoring tool known as Zest that extends principles of virtual reality modeling language (VRML is used for creating navigable three-dimensional environments for the Internet) into full-motion video. Because of the flexibility of Eleftheriadis's design, Zest will run on both the Internet and digital television using MPEG-4 technology.

At IBM's T. J. Watson Research Center, Dr. Jeane Chen, manager of Interactive Media Solutions, and others have developed HotVideo, a related software product that enables authors, whether journalists or other content creators, to create hyperlinked motion video.

These techniques represent an important stage in the development of contextualized journalism because they extend hypermedia in at least two important directions. First, they bring it out of the realm of relatively static

Web environments and into the dynamic world of motion video. Second, they introduce it into the leading news delivery system: television.

Audience Involvement

The third aspect of contextualized journalism is audience involvement. Audience involvement is potentially much greater online, since the Internet is an active medium of communication rather than a passive medium like traditional analog print and broadcast media. One way involvement is increasing is through the use of immersive storytelling. Immersive storytelling is largely a new format for presenting and interacting with the news in a three-dimensional environment. Today, most work involves producing three-dimensional representations of actual locations in news stories, which are produced digitally and then transferred back to analog format for distribution on television. But as television converts from analog to digital format in the next decade, three-dimensional news presentations will become common. At *CBS News,* for example, 3-D "extrusions" are routinely used in a variety of news reporting, ranging from stories about conflicts in Iraq to environmental stories set in the Brazilian rain forest to President Clinton's 1999 State of the Union Address (where a 3-D fly-through was created for Washington, D.C.). These three-dimensional animations are far more than virtual environments. They are precisely rendered 3-D representations of actual buildings, cities, and regions based on 2-D images acquired via high-resolution remote sensing satellite imagery and other image acquisition devices and built from precise databases known as geographic information systems (GIS). Recent advances in computer processing power have made it possible to create these 3-D extrusions using desktop computers rather than massive parallel-processing supercomputers. As digital television makes its way across the country, 3-D news reporting will become available to all viewers for their own navigation and interaction. The hypothetical news scenario described in the prologue of this section will become a reporting reality.

An interdisciplinary team of graduate and undergraduate students at Columbia University has developed the first augmented reality application for the delivery of immersive news to a mobile news consumer. When equipped with a mobile augmented reality news system (the system involves a see-through head-worn display as well as other devices that enable the wearer to see computer-generated images and text displayed over a real scene), a news consumer walking on the the the Morningside Heights campus of Columbia University can relive the 1968 Columbia student revolt. An attached global positioning system (GPS) receiver monitors the users' location and a head tracker determines where the user is looking.[15] As the user turns toward Low Library, the main administrative building on campus, the user sees through the head-worn display the name of the building written in semitransparent letters across the Low rotunda. In addition, a news headline appears: "1968 Student Protest." By gazing briefly at the headline, the user selects it. If the user taps on the "video playback" icon on a handheld "personal digital appliance" (PDA), the mobile news system accesses a digital archive of video through a wireless link to the World Wide Web. The viewer then sees and hears about an incident that virtually shut down the campus in 1968, when student demonstrators occupied five campus buildings in protest of university plans to build a new physical fitness facility on a public park located in nearby Harlem. Although the full functionality of the system is limited to the campus today, developments such as Bill Gates and Craig McCaw's Teledesic satellite system will make such a system available on a worldwide basis early in the next decade. Will geographically based news, information, and entertainment find a willing audience? Rent a car with a GPS mapping system and drive to an unfamiliar part of town. The answer is obvious.

Dynamic Content

The fourth aspect of contextualized journalism is dynamic content. News content is much more fluid—dynamic—in an online environment, which enables better representation of events and processes in real life. People want and get their news on demand and in real time. Audiences aren't willing to wait for the evening news or the next day's paper for developments in a breaking story. They want to know right now, and they want their information as current as possible, and via the Internet they can find it. This represents something of a double-edge sword for journalists, who now not only can but must provide continuously updated news for an audience increasingly accustomed to having access to the latest news developments. The journalist A. J. Liebling once observed, "I can write better than anyone who can write faster. And I can write faster than anyone who can write better,"[16] but today's journalist must write both faster *and* better. The problem is that few journalists have time for thoughtful analysis before they issue their reports.

Customization

Finally, news in an electronic, digital environment can be customized, or personalized, in a way not possible in other media. Coupled with the first four dimensions, this personalized nature of online journalism potentially offers audiences a view of the world that is much more contextualized, textured, and multidimensional than stories told in the worlds of print and broadcast analog media. Although some skeptics would argue that personalized media will bring even further audience fragmentation, this is a red herring. While it is true that the so-called multichannel universe has unarguably brought an end to the dominance of the three network newscasts and the Internet is offering a burgeoning array of news choices, this diversity represents more inclusiveness of alternative viewpoints, not an exclusion of them. In fact, early research suggests that younger audiences value the diversity of news perspectives made available via the Internet (I examine this subject in further detail in chapter 8). Personalization as it is manifesting itself on the Internet today is more a matter of obtaining news customized to an individual's life situation than a screening out of important news. For example, many Internet news consumers obtain financial news personalized for their own investment portfolios, sports information targeted to their favorite teams, health news related to their own health situations, and weather for their home communities. Few Internet news consumers use customization features to screen out important news stories of regional, national, or international scope, such as the U.S. bombing of suspected terrorist camps in Afghanistan and Sudan or President Clinton's grand jury testimony during the Monica Lewinsky inquiry. Moreover, just as in the traditional media environment, the news system on the Internet resonates with major stories. Whether one visits the *New York Times* on the Web, the New Zealand *Herald*, or *MyYahoo.com*, it is almost impossible to miss certain stories.

Will It Be a Better Journalism? Will Democracy Be Better Served?

Contextualized journalism can bring a variety of potential benefits to the citizenry and to democracy, including more engaging reporting, more complete information, and news that better reflects the complexities and nuances of an increasingly diverse and pluralistic society. Democracy depends on an informed citizenry. Traditionally, the press, whether online or off, has served as information provider to the citizens of a democracy. Increasingly, however, the press and journalism in all media have slipped in their performance of this vital duty. Consider the following words from Carl Bernstein, the *Washington Post* reporter who, along with Bob Woodward, broke perhaps the greatest news story of the second half of the twentieth century, the break-in of the Democratic headquarters at the Watergate hotel. "[Journalism] is disfigured by celebrity, gossip and sensationalism. I believe it's the role of journalists to challenge people, not just to mindlessly amuse them. In this culture of journalistic titillation, we teach our readers and our viewers that the trivial is important."[17]

The idea of reporting the facts in context is certainly not a new notion; journalists throughout history have sought to place stories into better and more complete context. The problem has been that for the most part the media used to publish journalism have not provided the means to achieve this. The space and time limitations of analog print and broadcast media have foreshortened the news and led to a newsroom culture in which most stories are reported in truncated form, telling each story from a single point of view and providing the audience with reports that purport to be the truth. But despite the claims of many traditional journalists, the truth is not easily encapsulated into a single linear narrative of fifteen hundred words or less in print or three minutes or less of video and audio. Only in an interactive, broadband online medium can context be provided for complex, multidimensional news events where perspective and point of view are centrally important in understanding the complete truth behind the news.

Imagine it is November 22, 1963, and you are in Dallas, Texas, about to document one of the most dramatic acts of terrorism in history. Your name is Abraham Zapruder. Instead of holding an 8 mm Bell and Howell film camera, you are holding an Omnicamera. Instead of producing the most-debated 5.6 seconds of film in history, you use your omnicamera to record not only the assassination of President John F. Kennedy but also the Texas School Book Depository where Lee Harvey Oswald crouched at a sixth-floor window.[18] Panning around the scene, you observe whether a second gunman fired shots from the so-called grassy knoll. Instead of publishing a twenty-six-volume report that theorized Oswald fired from a single gun the shots that killed the president and wounded Texas governor John Connally, the Warren Commission might have had irrefutable evidence as to what actually transpired that day. Perhaps there would have been no lingering conspiracy theories. Oliver Stone probably would not have made his controversial film, *JFK*. Not only would journalism have been changed, but the course of history itself would might have been altered.

Perhaps, however, the introduction of such 360-degree imaging technology would have opened even more questions. Additional information might have revealed the presence of a second gunman. This would no doubt have fueled even more speculation about a conspiracy. The ability to survey the entire scene might have made everyone present a potential suspect. Still, is society not better served by having access to more complete information? Wouldn't a more informed public discourse produce more just democracy? However you answer these questions, developments such as omnidirectional video news will challenge the public and journalists alike to reconsider what journalist Walter Lippmann meant when in 1921 he wrote of the role of the media in shaping the "world outside and the pictures in our heads."[19]

Taken as a whole, these new media developments are transforming the very nature of news content and storytelling. In the twenty-first century, we may see the world through a computer-mediated reality and become empowered participants in the process of contextualized journalism. What is beginning to emerge is a new type of storytelling that moves beyond the romantic but unachievable goal of pure objectivity in journalism. This new style will offer the audience a complex blend of perspectives on news stories and events that will be far more textured than any single point of view could ever achieve.

In early 1999 Trevor Butterworth, associate editor of *Newswatch*, observed, "Traditional journalism, of course, is based on the belief that there *is* an external reality that can be accurately reported on and that the public needs to know. Many older journalists and some venerable institutions, like the *New York Times*, still cherish this ideal, even if it is sometimes victim to bias and inaccuracy."[20] Although objectivity is a laudable goal toward which to strive, much as the pursuit of truth is a worthy endeavor, in most cases it is impossible to obtain or at least impossible to know whether we have achieved it. In almost every case and especially when the story is controversial, no journalist was present when the event (or process) in question occurred. Typically, journalism and any other form of systematic inquiry attempt to derive a version of the truth by gathering information from a variety of sources and reconstructing what most probably occurred. We can never know whether we have revealed it, and mostly we can only hope to approximate it through triangulation, like the best research in either the physical or social sciences. By offering different perspectives on what may or may not have occurred, journalism can facilitate the public's understanding of an event or process by revealing as many verifiable facts as possible. Drawing on those facts, we can each reach our own conclusions about what did or did not happen. "If there is anything I hope people leave here with, it is that the facts are everything," wrote award-winning journalist Michael Gartner, editor of the *Ames (Iowa) Daily Tribune*. "Nobody cares about your opinions. People want facts. Facts and fairness, that's what we teach."[21]

Offering a single perspective necessarily furnishes only a limited view of the reality of what occurred. Thus, whether achievable or not, objectivity and truth can best be pursued through a storytelling medium that supplies the texture and context possible in an online, multimedia, and interactive environment. Because it is impossible for any human being to lay aside completely all his or her personal beliefs and present a culturally and bias-free account of any event, process, or set of facts the best one can do is to reveal to the reader one's biases and provide a balanced accounting of the facts, circumstances, and context surrounding a story. Intelligent readers can then reach their own conclusions as to reality.

Consider the following case. In 1996 Jonathan Katz reported on the drive-by killing of twenty-five-year-old "gansta" rap star Tupac Shakur in Las Vegas, Nevada. Because of greatly increased reader interaction through email, Katz saw his understanding and reporting on Shakur change dramatically over a period of several weeks as different perspectives on Shakur's complex life emerged. Traditional journalism would not accommodate reader feedback in this manner. Katz told the story in his own words at a meeting of journalism educators hosted by the Freedom Forum Pacific Coast Center on February 27, 1999.

When Tupac Shakur was killed, I wrote a column about what a good writer he was and this was not appreciated in the coverage of his death and the way he died. I was pretty nearly roasted alive for this by people saying he was violent and he shot people and how could I say this and it was a dumb column and stupid and thoughtless.

So I wrote a second column saying that, from the response, I really hadn't thought this through as well as I should have. Then I got a wave of email, mostly from black colleges, dumping on me for taking back what I said in the first place, saying, "Why are you so weak-minded about this? You were right in the first place. He was a good writer and he was violent, but you shouldn't be listening to these people." And then I got a third wave of mail from record-industry executives saying, "You've got to understand the music industry and the place of hip hop and the place of rap, and the truth is you were a little bit right in each case but not entirely right in either."

So I ended up writing a third column saying, "Let's pretend that I know now what I should have known three weeks ago and let's go back and do this all over again."

So I had this revelation in my mind. I dropped the idea that I was always right all the time. I really think I'm right at the moment and it's the best I can do when I write something, and then we'll see what happens.[22]

This same experience is being repeated in a growing number of news organizations, even at the *New York Times*. Consider the case of columnist Thomas L. Friedman, who wrote a column about a small-town entrepreneur named Lyle Bowlin who, for about $150 a month, had launched a Web-based competitor to online bookseller *Amazon.com*. Bowlin was both selling books for a lower price than *Amazon* did and was making a profit because of his lower overhead (he operated his business out of a spare bedroom). After his first column Friedman wrote,

Well, the column elicited the usual range of skeptical responses from experts, who argued that Mr. Bowlin's operation was just a fluke, or that he wasn't calculating his costs properly, or that Amazon.com would soon crush him and all other would-be little-guy competitors. Well, to all of you I say: YOU'RE WRONG. You think the Internet is overrated. It's underrated. Here's the email I got from Mr. Bowlin two days after the column ran, both in *The Times* and on line on www.nytimes.com: "Dear Tom, I thought I would just fill you in on the impact the column has had. We had over 142,000 hits between

11 P.M. Thursday night [when the column first appeared on the Web] and 2 P.M. Friday afternoon from 40 different countries, before the software that tracks hits gave up and crashed. I have personally responded to over 1,400 emails." Mr. Bowlin's experience underscores another point: If you think globalization is overrated, you're also wrong. You ain't seen nothin' yet. As Lyle Bowlin can tell you, the minute you start to do business on the Web, you now have to think globally. You have to think about your customers as global, your competitors as global, *your readers as global*, your suppliers as global and your partners as global.[23]

Underscore "your readers as global." Journalists now need to think about a global audience that not only reads what they write and report but can comment, provide perspective, and offer new insight into the complexities of an increasingly global society. This is the essence of the contextualized journalism possible in the digital age.

2   Assessing the State of Online Journalism

Imagine a library that carries the equivalent of 4,925 daily newspapers from all over the globe. Stop imagining: it's here. The Internet provides more news content than that every day, most of it free. So it's not surprising that increasing numbers of the world's estimated 359 million–plus Internet users are going online for their news.[1] Of course, the Internet provides a lot of information of dubious value and origin. Anyone with a computer, a modem, and an axe to grind (or an agenda to promote or a product to sell) can create a credible-looking Web site and publish "news" for a global audience, right alongside the news provided by the world's established news providers (witness the PairGain Technology Internet hoax, which I discuss fully in chapter 8). How can a news consumer tell what's reliable? It's not necessarily easy, and it makes going online potentially hazardous. The first step is to look for recognizable, trusted brands.

The quality of much of the news online is as high as that of leading newspapers, news magazines, or television or radio outlets, because much of it comes from those media. Yet that fact prompts another question: If online journalism is little more than another delivery system for these older media, even a potentially better delivery system, what's all the fuss about? In terms of journalism, what's the point?

For many online journalists, the point is to engage the unengaged. Some of us envision a kind of news that, as it upholds the highest journalistic standards, will allow news consumers to understand the meaning of the day's events in a personalized context that makes better sense to them than traditional media do now. Networked new media can be interactive, on-demand, customizable; they can incorporate new combinations of text, images, moving pictures, and sound; they can build new communities based on shared interests and concerns; and they have almost unlimited space to offer levels of reportorial depth, texture, and context that are impossible in any other medium. With all this to offer, new media can transform journalism.

An example from MSNBC on the Internet nicely illustrates the potential. On February 21, 1997, NBC's *Dateline* ran a piece about dangerous roads in America, zeroing in on three particularly treacherous thoroughfares. The program invited viewers to log onto the MSNBC site to learn about roads in their community. Those who did so could enter their zip code and within seconds, based on federal data, find out how many fatal accidents had occurred in that community between 1992 and 1995 and on which roads.[2] Within twelve hours, MSNBC logged sixty-eight thousand visitors to that feature. I was one of them. My zip code in New York City (Manhattan's Upper West Side, 10027) had had ninety-four fatal accidents, with the most dangerous road being Broadway, with nine fatalities.

Money Online, which received a National Magazine Award for new media in 1997, the first time such online awards were given, illustrates the journalism potential of the online environment.[3] The site's MoneyDaily section, for example, has introduced a wide range of customizable interactive features, including one about the flat tax that allows people to key in their own earnings profiles and then see how the proposed flat tax would affect them. Had the 1996 presidential bid of Steve Forbes sustained longer into the year, such a feature might ultimately have affected many voters' presidential preferences.

Of course, the potential to customize content also means readers may select only the content that appeals to them. Although there is perhaps some merit to this contention, it just deflects attention from the real issue. Some readers, or audience members, will undoubtedly look for information that matches their interests or subscribe to online information sources that most closely fit their preferences. For example, investors will likely prefer news about companies in which they hold stock or that may affect their investment portfolios. Nevertheless, research from the past half century indicates most readers use the media, whether new or old, to connect more broadly to society. One 1945 study by sociologist Bernard Berelson, who examined readers' reactions during a protracted newspaper delivery strike in New York City, found that most readers didn't miss anything in particular, with one exception: the obituaries. Said one respondent, "I just read the headlines and the obituaries. I'm a nurse, so I always look to see if any of my patients have died."[4] Instead, most felt a vague feeling of disconnection from their community.

This is still a primary function of online media. Most people go online to connect with the news of their community, whether geographic or of the mind. They use customization features to supplement their general news appetite with specialized, personal interests in sports, finance, travel, education, the environment, health, or anything else. Rather than fracturing society, online media, with online journalism as a core part of it, are giving people whose time is at an ever higher premium an effective and efficient means to stay connected. Already, there are glimmers of a transformed journalism in some of the good online work that is out there now.

News Online: A Baedeker for 2000

Think of the online news world as a vast virtual newspaper divided into sections: international news, national news, regional news, business and finance, technology, politics/culture/opinion, health, and sports.[5] Within these sections, who is doing the job well? Which sites are beginning to produce a new kind of journalism? Here are some of them.

International Section

Online journalism provides an abundance of international news. Regardless of where you sit, access to international news has never been better. Of course, what constitutes international news depends entirely on where you sit. If you are located outside the United States, international news has always been fairly abundant, although frequently dominated by news from the USA. Although this doesn't completely change in the online environment, access to the *New York Times on the Web* became free in 1998 for anyone anywhere in the world, marking a significant increase in access to the single most reliable (as measured by a number of criteria, including the receipt of the greatest number of Pulitzer Prizes by a single news organization) source of news published by a U.S. media company.

If you are located in the United States, the Internet brings access to a wide variety of notable international online journalism offerings, such as the Spanish-language La Nacion Online of Costa Rica, the Arabic-language *Al-Qds Daily Online* of Lebanon, the English-language *Jerusalem (Israel) Post* or a host of other news sources from all parts of the world. One standout multimedia Web site is published by *Clarin*, the Buenos Aires newspaper, which claims to be the largest circulation Spanish-language newspaper in the world.[6] No U.S. newspaper offers the level or quality of audio and video found on the *Clarin* site. "Frecuencia Web" (Web Frequency) an interactive music department of the site, offers a unique blend of multimedia reporting on popular music in Argentina and around the world.[7] Articles in the section in February 2000 included "La nueva vida digital de Bowie" (the new digital life of Bowie) with text and audio reports, a punk rock festival, and a report on the music of jazz artist Evan Lurie, including audio selections from his compositions, You can't go home again, Funeral, and Wishes becoming madness.

Although these sources are published in a variety of languages, online resources such as Systran make translation simple and free (Systran works with any site available through the *Alta Vista* search engine, and translates into English from any of five different languages, including German, French, Spanish, Portuguese or Italian, or from any of these languages into English). Translation is not perfect, but it does competently translate the basic idea. For example, the English-language headline "Heavy fighting in northern Kosovo as peace efforts continue" translated via Systran into Spanish as "El luchar pesado en Kosovo norteño como esfuerzos de la paz continúa."[8] Translating the Spanish back into English produced this result: "Heavy fighting in northern Kosovo as efforts of La Paz continue." It's not a bad translation (especially for free), with one error.

No longer must readers accept any single point of view as the full story or complete truth. Consider how international news is being transformed in the world of the Internet and why Americans, as well as people around the world, are devouring unprecedented levels of international news, information, and communication about world events and processes.

No longer is the audience passive. It has come alive with activity. People can get their information from literally thousands of news sources around the world. They can get the story from multiple perspectives, placed in rich historical context, and told using a wide variety of communication modalities, not just the one or two available to analog media. For example, audio, video, interactivity, immersive and navigable images, text, hyperlinks, and much more are available online. All of this media richness gives the online audience a more textured and engaging experience and potentially a much fuller understanding of the subtleties and nuances of stories being reported from around the world. They can also access alternative perspectives on the truth, in a fashion reminiscent of the storytelling device employed in Akira Kurosawa's famous film *Rashomon* (based on Ryunosuke Akutagawa's classic text). Audiences online aren't limited to traditional news sources, either. Consider the Kosovo primer assembled by Pennsylvania State University political science professor Zachary Irwin in response to numerous requests for information about the Kosovo conflict. Irwin has assembled a wide-ranging and comprehensive list of online and other resources and put them on a Penn State Web site. Included are a list of Internet sources on the conflict, a chronology of events in Kosovo and the surrounding region, background material from United Nations humanitarian agencies, and details on ways to help Kosovo.[9] Following are ten nontraditional online international news sources drawing increasing traffic from around the world. Each site features a unique voice and perspective in reporting on world events. None is published by people aiming simply to parade their prejudices. Instead, each provides a credible alternative account of world events.

1. *Art Bin on WWW* is a cultural multimedia zine edited by Karl-Erik Tallmo (Sweden).
2. *Bourque Newswatch* offers political news reports and links; it is edited by Pierre Bourque (Canada).
3. *Digital City Amsterdam* is the largest public freenet in the Netherlands. Marleen Stikker (Netherlands) edits the site.
4. *Enredando* is an alternative new media newsletter edited by Luis Angel Fernández Hermana (Spain), a science correspondent for *El Periódico de Catalunya.*
5. *Need to Know* is an information technology newsletter with a critical edge. Dave Green (UK), a reporter, publishes the site.
6. *Not the South China Morning Post* is a satirical zine committed to press freedom. George Adams (Hong Kong) started the zine to protest the sale of the *South China Morning Post* to Robert Kuok Houk Nien, the Malaysian property tycoon with direct connections to Beijing.
7. *Oneworld* offers human rights news from around the world, frequently challenging accepted viewpoints in traditional media (e.g.,

this headline is from April 26, 1999: "NATO raids cause more damage than Nazis"). The site is edited by Anuradha Vittachi (UK).

8. *Out There News* is an Internet-original news site offering nonlinear journalism on international events (e.g., an interactive tour of the conflict in Northern Ireland, an interactive reader poll on the killings in Algeria, and a documentary on the Congo after Mobutu). John West (UK)cofounded the site.

9. *Taste of War* is a Web site providing updates on the war in Kosovo, news from the spy world, links, and more, edited by freelance journalist Mario Profaca (Croatia).

10. *Urban75* offers an alternative view on environmental news, rave reports, drug information, and the law. Mike Slocombe (UK) is the self-described "head honcho" of the site.

The Internet also provides access to news and information otherwise often censored by governments and others in control of traditional communication media. Recall the Serbian government's April 2, 1999, shutdown of Radio B92, the last independent voice of the Balkans. Radio B92 provided multimedia news that two years earlier had played a pivotal role in the daily protests against Slobodon Milosovic's regime. Drazen Pantic, B92's Internet coordinator and founder of *OpenNet* (the only independent Internet service provider in Serbia), relocated to New York and has frequently participated in Columbia University's News Laboratory as a visiting guest. "The latest text dispatches from B92 stringers, through last night," reported Adam Clayton Powell III of the Freedom Forum, "were still posted on the Open Yugoslavia site, operated from the U.S. at California State University at Los Angeles."[10] And in a demonstration of the Net's resistance to censorship, Radio B92's Web site was still on the Internet after the official shutdown, running on Web servers outside the Balkans. At the top of the home page was a boxed message noting "The Sound of B92 Banned." If you clicked on the box, cached B92 audio was launched. Lower on the page, a short news item was headlined, "Radio B92 Closed Down and Sealed Off." Less than two weeks later, the Yugoslav government closed *OpenNet*.

Other organizations, including Western news operations, have also used the Internet to circumvent government restrictions on reporting on the Kosovo situation. *CNN.com* posted a comprehensive list of Balkans information and more than fifty links to news organizations, human rights groups, and governmental agencies. The North Atlantic Treaty Organization (NATO), which coordinated the military action against Milosovic, published in 1999 online news briefings, military information, aerial photographs of the bombing campaign, and videotaped material of attacking aircraft. In response, Serbian officials launched their own Web site, offering Belgrade's views of the bombing. One headline read, "Criminal NATO Air Force hits only civilians." Other Web sites responded to the apparent closing of Radio B92, offering additional Kosovo news. The Kosova Crisis Center offered regular updates and the War Against Yugoslavia site provided a live Web cam of Belgrade. One of the most useful resources, especially to journalists seeking impartial, nongovernmental information on the Kosovo situation, was also among the least well known. The Intelligence Resource Program at the Federation of American Scientists publishes online maps, U2 aerial photos, and military analysis.[11]

Traffic to sites providing news on the Kosovo situation soared during the war. CNN.com reported some of the heaviest traffic in its history, with up to tenfold increases in traffic from the Balkan countries. One Silicon Alley observer reported in early 1999 that international news and communication on the Internet during the war in Kosovo had lead to a new type of international news coverage.

> The era of televised wars may still be far from over, but three weeks into Europe's first multinational armed conflict in 50 years, listservs and Web-based news services are presenting reporters and news hounds with a peek at the new face of war journalism. Pageviews for news sites like CNN.com, ABCNEWS.com and MSNBC.com have all been through the roof. With foreign journalists expelled from Yugoslavia, the Internet has become the only place to get any information from Yugoslavia that is not from either Yugoslav-controlled TV or NATO spokespersons.[12]

Audiences are refusing to remain passive in their responses to what the media report. In contrast to the world of analog journalism, the public in the digital age frequently seeks to publish its own views on world events and how media report on them. Internet technology enables audiences anywhere to participate in a global dialogue about world events and issues. Individuals can come into direct contact with one another, though separated by thousands of miles, mountains and oceans, and political and cultural boundaries.

Perhaps the most compelling voice on the Internet during the Kosovo war was that of Orthodox Christian priest Father Sava Janjic. His words were read by millions around the world via San Francisco-based *eGroups*, an online electronic discussion group. Janjic posted frequent dispatches on *eGroups*, sometimes contradicting NATO claims that only military sites had been targeted and that civilian casualties had been minimal. On one occasion Janjic wrote: "NATO attacks are nothing but barbarous aggression which affects mostly the innocent civilian population, both Serb and Albanian. The statements by the NATO officials that only military targets are attacked in Yugoslavia are not true and they are intended to deceive many peace loving people in the West that their air force is in a 'humanitarian' action."[13]

National News

The best national news providers online are those that, along with their repurposed content, offer original material designed specifically for the Web. The *New York Times on the Web*, for example, which won the 1999 Newspaper Association of America's Best Online Newspaper Site Edgie Award for large markets (circulation more than 150,000), provides extensive original coverage of new media in its Cybertimes section.[14] The news organization has also published on its Web site "Terra: Struggle of the Landless," a photoessay by Sebastiao Salgado documenting the plight of Brazil's Landless Workers Movement. The forty images are accompanied by audio captions by Salgado, news reports, maps, and various archival materials. The *Times* also publishes much original content online in its book review section.

Many national news sites also cover breaking news, and the better sites use their vast reservoirs of space to add depth and texture. The *Washington Post*, for instance, offered thorough coverage of the surprising 1996 Iranian presidential election, adding in-depth coverage on a special Iran page featuring news, reference material, and other online material.[15] The site has its own staff of journalists, which gives it the capability to do its own enterprise reporting. It flexed those muscles in a special 1997 report on public education in the District of Columbia entitled "D.C. Schools—A System in Crisis" that featured original online reporting on the District's collapsing infrastructure, bloated bureaucracy, and failing special-education programs. Although much of the report ran in the newspaper, the Web site provided enhanced coverage, including a comparison of SAT scores in D.C. versus suburban schools, a profile of the board of trustees of the District, and online reader discussion groups.

Time Online did a particularly impressive job with the 1997 Heaven's Gate tragedy, offering visitors detailed reporting from the magazine's online staff as well as the print side, extensive photographic coverage, and even an electronic link to Heaven's Gate's own Web site, which allowed visitors to learn about the cult from its members' own words.[16] The site became an important historical record, with layers of content that the printed product couldn't accommodate.

Similarly, *CNN.com*—which is one of the world's busiest Web sites, with more than 3.5 million page views a day—features extensive original coverage of the environment and ecological issues.[17] And *CNN.com* goes into considerable depth on stories that get only a minute or two of treatment in television. *USAToday.com* and *ABCNews.com* are especially effective at supplementing their repurposed content with original graphics, animations, and interactive features to enhance reader involvement.[18]

Regional News

The *Mercury Center*, the Web site of the San Jose *Mercury News*, which achieved much attention for a flaw—the online presentation of Gary Webb's "Dark Alliance" series that exacerbated the controversy surrounding his discredited investigative report linking the CIA to the cocaine epidemic in the United States—is most well known for its positive contributions to online journalism.[19] It introduced the use of expanded, layered publishing online and has used it on a variety of stories, making documents, in-depth reports, and other original source material available to readers. In one on-going report on executive pay, the site provides readers with a table listing the compensation received by the top one hundred executives at companies making up the Silicon Valley 150, the largest publicly held companies in the area from 1991, up to the most recently completed fiscal year (at the time of this writing, it was 1998). The site is very well designed, featuring a simple and easy-to-use set of navigational tools that allow the reader clickable access to every section and service available at the site. The top of the page offers an index of sections, from Asia Report to Talent Scout, and services, from the Mercury Mall to the Yellow Pages. The Yellow Pages is supported by Zip2, an electronic directory of more than sixteen million businesses nationwide, fully searchable and with map and directions available, all free—a capability no print outlet can match.

The site also features Good Morning Silicon Valley (GMSV), special on-line coverage of the valley's high-tech industry, which is of interest locally as well as around the world. In fact, Patricia Sullivan, editor of the section, notes that 70 percent of the visitors to the site actually come from areas outside Silicon Valley. This is a lesson that other locally based online news sites would do well to absorb: identify the news stories and coverage areas unique to your region, cover them well, promote your coverage, and you will likely find a great deal of Internet traffic not only from your geographic community but from around the nation and the world.

Another site feature at the *Mercury Center* is its vast digital News Library, containing full search capability of more than one million articles, including all stories published in the paper since 1985 as well as from the archives of twenty-four Knight-Ridder newspapers across the United States. Subscribers, or holders of the site's "library card," can run free searches that return a list of headlines and the first paragraph of every story. Beyond that, they pay twenty-five cents per story. Such a service may be worrisome for managers of Reed Elsevier's costly *Nexis* service.

The *Mercury Center*, commonly known as the *Merc Center*, has also innovated original online storytelling. In 1999, for example, the *Merc Center* brought together its coverage of the Microsoft antitrust trial in an interactive virtual courtroom (a computerized version of courtroom no. 2 in the United States District Court for the District of Columbia and the *Merc Center's* coverage of the Microsoft trial). The feature could serve as a primer for anyone interested in better understanding the U.S. federal court system. Visitors to the site encounter a clickable virtual courtroom graphic with interactive portals into ten dimensions of the courtroom and the *Merc Center's* coverage of the trial, including in-depth reporting on the background of the judge (Federal District Judge Thomas Penfield Jackson), the defendant (Microsoft), plaintiffs (the Department of Justice and the attorneys general of twenty states), the evidence, archives, reference materials, the public gallery in the courtroom, the press, and more (including a reader forum).

Illustrating the ability of the Web to provide depth to its coverage, the Chicago *Tribune* used its Web site to pay tribute to one of twentieth century journalism's larger figures, Mike Royko, after he died on April 28, 1998.[20] The interactive tribute includes thirteen news stories about Royko, an electronic message board where by May 26 more than 690 readers had posted messages, and an archive of more than one hundred of Royko's best columns, including his memorable "Millions in His Firing Squad," on the assassination of Dr. Martin Luther King Jr.

The Tribune company has also developed an interactive city-based feature called *Digital City*, which it localizes at Web sites of other newspapers in the chain, such as the *Orlando Sentinel*.[21] Digital City is a direct competitor with Microsoft's *Sidewalk* online city-based service. *Digital City* offers readers an interactive smattering of news and weather, sports, entertainment, community and marketplace information, and services. For instance, in Orlando, the Entertainment service gives readers an on-demand menu of dining, movies, music, and things to do in the Orlando area, along with reviews of restaurants, movies, concerts, and other activities.

Boston.com has set the standard for convergence—the coming together of once-separate media in a digital, networked environment—in online journalism.[22] The site not only provides an electronic window into Boston's arts, weather, and commerce but offers readers access to the online content of seventeen local media, including the *Boston Globe*, *Banker and Tradesman* (Massachusetts business news), and WGBH, Boston's celebrated public broadcaster.

For quality original online news content, the *Nando Times*, the Web site of the *Raleigh News and Observer* (a McClatchy newspaper) has helped to set the standard.[23] One of the sites' hallmarks has been technological innovation. Among its interactive offerings is the Nando News Watcher, which uses "push" technology to feed the latest local, regional, national, and international news developments from around the world continuously throughout the day to a user's computer screen, where it runs in a small window when another application is in use.

Some small-town newspapers are also distinguishing themselves in the online arena. One of the most notable is *Northscape*, the online edition of the flood-battling *Grand Forks Herald*, in North Dakota.[24] The 38,000-circulation daily has used its Web site to publish the news and serve both its local community and a national one after the 1997 flood and subsequent fire wiped out the newspaper's office.

A number of local, regional, and national Web sites include direct access to the *Wire*, the Web site introduced in 1996 by the Associated Press that provides continuously updated breaking news. NJ Online and the *Dallas Morning News* were the first.[25] Of course, the pressure to be first, especially in an online arena where real-time news is the standard, can be a threat to accuracy. This manifested itself during the Clinton-Lewinsky scandal when the *Dallas Morning News* reported online that it had located a secret service agent ready to testify he had witnessed the president and intern together. Later the same day, the paper retracted the report.

Business and Financial

The best financial news sites all offer a combination of straight news reporting and analysis but give the visitor a variety of other features not possible in print or broadcast media. Standards such as *Bloomberg, Reuters,* the *Wall Street Journal Interactive Edition, CBS MarketWatch,* and *CNNfn Interactive,* as well as niche sites such as *TheStreet.com* and *Motley Fool* all provide real-time stock and market performance data displayed graphically and in text format, as well as interactive financial research tools.[26] *CNNfn Interactive* also features an interactive mortgage calculator that anyone buying a home would find of immense value.[27] Lou Dobbs, former executive vice president of *CNNfn Interactive,* notes that not only has this site drawn immense traffic (Rich Zahradnik, vice president of *CNNfn Interactive,* reports page views at the site had increased from about five million a month in early 1996 to some thirty-three million a month in 1998) but the interactive capabilities keep people there longer (it what's called a "sticky" site), a challenge for new media publishers, who find the Net surfer's attention span to be ever shortening.

Business Week Online also has services and material to hold the user's interest, as well as the quality to earn the site a National Magazine Award for new media in 1997.[28] Bob Arnold, its editor, notes that *Business Week Online* includes every word printed anywhere in the world by any of the many *Business Week* news products. No weekly magazine could hope to be this comprehensive. And although *Business Week* is a weekly, its online site publishes a daily briefing culled from Standard and Poors, a sister company, and from news items filed by the *Business Week* staff around the world, primarily enterprise reporting that might not find its way into the magazine for reasons not only of space but of timing. The site also offers a searchable electronic archive of *Business Week* dating to January 1, 1991, and expanded coverage of one of the magazine's content franchises: the ranking of business schools, complete with interactive features. Since technology is an important coverage area of the magazine, *Business Week Online* offers *Maven*, a computer buying guide produced in conjunction with National Software Testing Laboratories, another McGraw-Hill subsidiary. The site has hosted hundreds of online conference and chat sessions on *America Online*, many featuring leading figures from a variety of fields, such as Oracle CEO Larry Ellison. The site publishes the transcripts and had more than one hundred thousand paid downloads (a single item costs two dollars to download, five dollars for ten items, and twenty dollars for fifty) between 1995 and 1997.

Technology

Research shows some of the most popular online journalism is news about information technology, and CNET, the computer network, publishes perhaps the premier Web site on computer developments for the general consumer audience at its *News.com* site.[29] Ziff Davis's ZDNet is geared toward information technology professionals and provides comprehensive online news on information technology.[30] A 1997 special report comprehensively reviews CD-ROM drives of every speed and type. The report offers an interactive viewer that enables readers to see how varying speed drives were tested. Readers can customize the report to obtain a graphical display of the drives either alphabetically or from best to worst in terms of a variety of characteristics, including access time, performance, and installation. The site also offers readers customizable downloads of more than one thousand software packages. ZDNet also covers breaking technology news, such as the FBI sting that netted Carlos Felipe Salgado Jr., who was suspected of hacking into a computer to steal more than one hundred thousand credit card numbers. Those who desire customized news can join ZDNet's online community at no charge and receive by email continuously updated news reports on six subjects, issues, or companies.

TechWeb and *Infoworld*, from CMP Media, offer similarly comprehensive online news for information technology specialists but are weaker on interactive and other site design considerations.[31] A detailed review of Microsoft's ActiveX Web application, a competitor to Java, illustrates the thoroughness of *Infoworld's* product reviews. The review details ActiveX's value in bringing Web sites to life, particularly intranets, but underscores its limitations due to cross-platform and security concerns. In contrast to ZDNet's CD-ROM drive review, however, *Infoworld's* ActiveX review is not customizable or interactive. It is really just an electronic version of a print story.

Culture, Opinion, and Politics

The Web has produced a set of chic and well-traveled destinations for the digital literati, the best of which not only offer insightful and provocative online discourse but engage readers in interactive discussions and push the storytelling envelope. Some are connected to print publications. One of the most-visited sites is *HotWired*, the electronic version of *Wired* magazine, which features commentary on new media issues as well as new media applications, including its popular software search agent, *HotBot*, which makes searching more than fifty million Web documents simple, effective, and fast.[32]

Atlantic Unbound, the online offering of the *Atlantic Monthly*, has offered readers since 1993 an electronic window into politics, society, the arts, and culture, earning a National Magazine Award in new media in 1997.[33] In addition to offering the reader content taken from its print sister, *Atlantic Unbound* offers a variety of interactive features, including *Post and Riposte*, an online conference center where readers discuss the political and culture issues raised in the magazine.

Among those innovative Web publications unconnected to anything on paper is *Netly News*, a *Pathfinder* creation of leading cyberjournalist Josh Quittner.[34] In addition to writing provocatively and critically about the evolution of the Internet, Quittner offers the Digital Sandbox, where visitors are invited to play with new technologies and gain first-hand experience.

Salon not only offers all the traditional intellectual fare of the opinion magazine but features compelling online discussion as well.[35] In Table Talk, participants discuss topics ranging from books to digital culture in a tree-and-branch conversation structure based on a model developed at the *Well*, the first significant online community, born in the spring of 1985. Table Talk instructs visitors to consider the community standards—such as appropriate language, for example—that define its range of acceptable behavior. *Salon* drew national attention when during the Clinton-Lewinsky controversy it published a report detailing the extramarital affair of Senator Henry Hyde, who had been one of the president's sharpest critics. Although other more traditional media refused to publish news about Hyde's sexual dalliance, *Salon* published the report on the basis that it was relevant and underscored the personal hypocrisy of Hyde's position. Once *Salon* published the story, of course, most other media, online and off, jumped on the bandwagon and published news about Hyde's affair, claiming that once the genie was out of the bottle, there was no point ignoring it. So much for standards.

One of the most discussed of the sites in this category is *Slate*, the Microsoft start-up edited by Michael Kinsley.[36] Heavily promoted, *Slate* offers a rich set of articles and commentary on culture and politics, such as David Plotz's assessment,[37] "Ralph Reed's Creed," or "Selling Seals of Approval," John Merline's investigation of how companies get charities to endorse their products. But *Slate* doesn't fully exploit its online capabilities and thus has been under heavy fire in the online community. It has also spawned perhaps the best online literary parodies, among them, *Stale*, which in 1997 traced the "surprising parallels" between changes in wind patterns and Clinton's electoral popularity.[38] *Slate* attempted to offer its zine only to paying subscribers but in 1999 gave up that position and made its site available to all at no cost, hoping to build a business model on advertising, partnerships, e-commerce, and other revenue sources.

Among the most important sites covering politics are CNN/*Time*'s *All-Politics* and *Cloakroom.com*, both of which make effective use of original in-depth reporting and multimedia content.[39] *George Magazine*'s online offering is an interesting alternative look at the political and cultural scene but can be found exclusively on *America Online*.[40]

Sports

The sports sites on the Web may not necessarily raise the journalistic bar, but they are compelling because they so effectively exploit the Web's capabilities.

The best overall sports reporting is at *ESPN.com*, *CBS SportsLine.com*, and *CNNSI.com* (a collaboration between CNN and *Sports Illustrated*), and choosing among the three is largely a matter of personal preference.[41] Each site provides immediate coverage of games, after-game analysis, and much more, from live game statistics to interactive reader polls to video and audio highlights. Most of this content is free, although more specialized coverage is available for small monthly fees.

The *Sports Network* runs a distant second to these premier general-interest sports services and adheres to a more traditional approach to sports reporting with fewer interactive online features.[42] *USAToday* offers good sports coverage as well, but navigation through the site is not as simple as it is in the three premier sites dedicated to sports coverage. Good sports coverage also comes in highly specialized niche offerings online. *Golf.com*, for example, a 1997 winner of a National Magazine Award in the new media category, provides detailed interactive coverage of professional and amateur golf.[43] Not only does the site feature traditional reporting and analysis, but a variety of interactive features allow golfers to get information customized to their game and interests. A variety of other local news providers have created important online sports news sites as well. For instance, the *Mil-*

waukee Journal Sentinel Online has provided a heavily trafficked site covering the Green Bay Packers football team.[44]

The Future

News content on the Internet has been evolving through three stages. In stage one, which still dominates many news sites, online journalists mostly just republish, or "repurpose," content from their motherships. In stage two, which is gaining momentum and characterizes most of the better news sites, the journalists create original content, augmenting it with such additives as hyperlinks (i.e., clickable electronic links) to other Web sites; some interactive capabilities, such as search engines and electronic clickable indexes where the reader uses a mouse to select different content; some multimedia content, such as photos, video, and audio; and some customization of sites and information, where readers create their one own personal news categories, stock listings, and other content.

Stage three is only beginning to emerge, and only a handful of sites have attempted to enter it. This stage is characterized by original news content designed specifically for the Web as a new medium of communication and frequently of increasingly specialized focus (e.g., *APBnews*'s exclusive crime and criminal justice coverage), with full awareness and treatment of the Internet as a legitimate medium of news delivery, a willingness to break news online aggressively and to rethink the nature of a community online (with communities of interest frequently taking precedence over geography), and, most importantly, a willingness to experiment with new forms of storytelling, such as immersive storytelling, which allows the reader to enter and navigate and throughout a news report rather than simply look at it in linear fashion, as is the case with traditional news reporting, still photography, motion video, and audio. Sometimes this storytelling is augmented with new technology. In any event, the result is a more contextualized news report.

Cybertimes (an online offering of the *New York Times on the Web*, *CNN.com*), *MSNBC Online*, and *APBnews* are among the few but growing number of news organizations to experiment with omnidirectional imaging. Emerging technology will allow viewers to navigate through a live or recorded motion video of a news event. Other tools now in experimental laboratories will add three-dimensional depth capability to still and motion news video and audio, as well as other methods to enrich news contextualization.

Most serious news organizations and other content providers are in new media for the long haul and are committed to producing quality products. They know that young people are turning in growing numbers to online media. Research conducted as early as 1996 by the Pew Research Center for the People and the Press (a part of the Pew Charitable Trusts) showed that eighteen- to twenty-nine-year-olds in the United States were increasingly going daily to the Internet for news (10 percent in 1996).[45] Research from a variety of sources since then confirms this trend and points to increasing use of the Internet for news, especially among younger audiences (more than 25 percent in 2000).[46] Moreover, these new digital tools are enabling news organizations to present their news in electronic formats increasingly accessible to people with disabilities. A joint project between researchers at the University of Southern California (including the Annenberg School of Communication's journalism school) and Columbia University (the Graduate School of Journalism's Center for New Media) is exploring the development of a mobile three-dimensional audio technology (called Personal AudioCast, or PAC) that not only would bring customized audio news on demand to mobile news consumers in general but would meet the special audio news requirements of the visually impaired.

Epilogue: Designing for the Digital Age

Digital design for online news is a major subject, and adequate treatment requires a complete book in itself. Several good ones in fact already exist, such as Kevin Featherly's 1998 *Guide to Building a Newsroom Web Site*.[47] Nevertheless, a few quick words about the most important basic elements of effective online news design are in order:

- Easy navigation through a simple menu bar and clickable headlines and graphics is essential: a news site should be transparent to the reader; it should not require a user's guide.
- Fresh news content, updated regularly, is what online news consumers want; the opening screen should draw attention to what's new, whether it's through scrolling text, well-executed information graphics, or some other technique.
- The most important story should be apparent instantly to the reader; the agenda-setting function of journalism is still centrally

important in the new media age and because of the nature of Internet navigation and screen size, it's not possible to display a large number of stories or headlines effectively on the opening screen.

- Customization features should allow the reader easy personalization of the opening screen as well as other content of the site.
- Contextualization is paramount in online news coverage; links, easily accessible background material, and effective search tools should allow the news consumer to find additional material to help place a current story into its historical or other context.

Part II

Transforming How Journalists Do Their Work

Part II of this book examines how new media are transforming the work of journalists. Digital tools for news gathering, communication, editing, and production have become increasingly portable, inexpensive, and powerful, giving journalists in the field the same capability as those in a hard-wired central newsroom. Combined, these tools give journalists increasingly effective techniques for finding diverse and reliable sources, checking facts, and meeting deadlines. They also make plagiarism increasingly simple and tempting and represent a serious threat to good old shoe-leather reporting.

Chapter 3 reviews the new tools for news gathering, and chapter 4 provides a reporter's field guide to the Internet. Chapter 5 offers an examination of the ethical challenges presented by new media in the journalism of the twenty-first century.

3   New Tools for News Gathering

Technology has always played an important part in the news-gathering and production process. Whether scribbling notes on a page, recording an event on videotape, or taping a telephone interview, journalists are accustomed to using a variety of technical tools to acquire the raw data they use to tell their stories.

Advances in new media technology are transforming these technical tools, which offer new ways to process raw news data in all its forms, whether handwritten notes, audio interviews, or video content. This chapter examines three broad areas of new media tools for digital news gathering and production. First, it examines tools for image acquisition and processing in which journalists interact directly with the content of those images. Second, it reviews tools for processing handwritten notes and audio content. And, third, it considers the mobile journalist workstation as an integrated system of news gathering and production for the reporter in the field. This chapter touches only briefly on the implications of the Internet in news gathering, which chapter 4 examines in detail. By and large, the Internet is a tool for secondary data collection (i.e., collecting data from other published sources) and for accessing public transactional records and represents a large enough subject to warrant a chapter of its own.

Interacting Directly with Images

Consider how journalists will soon work with images and video in digital format. Traditionally, images, whether still or moving, analog or digital, have been searchable in two ways; the same is true for audio. One technique is to search the images based on text descriptors someone has written in order to catalog them. This method works well enough but is very limited if you want to find a picture or video that has not been cataloged or was cataloged in a way inconsistent with your search. The problem is growing more severe as the amount of image and video content being produced worldwide grows exponentially with the widespread distribution of low-cost image capture technologies such as still and motion picture digital video cameras. At Time Inc., for example, hundreds of thousands of images are being added each year to an already vast collection.

This leaves the second, older technique for searching stored pictures: looking at all of them. Needless to say, this can be a very time-consuming process, especially when the images may number in the millions or extend over thousands of hours of video. It is especially problematic when a journalist is on deadline.

A number of researchers are developing a new class of storage, search, and retrieval tools to address this vexing problem: Content-based indexing, storage, and retrieval tools enable the viewer to search the actual content of an image or video. How does this work? One current prototype developed by a Columbia University research team is called WebSEEK. Computer science professor Shih-Fu Chang and his doctoral student, John Smith, developed WebSEEK in 1996 as a software tool to enable Web surfers to find images and video easily on the World Wide Web. Using a software agent known as a spider (an intelligent agent, or software robot), WebSEEK has cataloged some 650,000 images and videos on the Web. The spider doesn't completely ignore existing text descriptors when cataloging the images. Rather, it uses keywords, file names, and file types to make initial classifications. Then, users can search for images based on certain low-level features of the images themselves. For example, one way to use WebSEEK is to select a broad category of pictures, such as sunsets. Having cataloged some 530 sunsets, WebSEEK gives the user a random selection of 20 sunsets to view first. The user then picks which of the random selections comes closest to what he or she is looking for and instructs the computer to search the other 510 sunset images for those that match the selected image most closely in terms of color distribution or the amount of red, green, and blue. This may not sound like a profound breakthrough, but a demonstration is remarkably convincing.[1] And this is just the beginning.

Within a few years, much more powerful search tools will be available that search not only on low-level features such as color or texture but on higher-order features such as objects, patterns, and semantic meaning. Imagine an automated surveillance system employed in a bank utilizing an omnicamera to monitor all traffic in the lobby. Faces are instantly scanned against known criminals or for anyone wearing a mask (other examples of visual search tools search on skin color and can recognize nude bodies).[2] Anyone meeting the known profile instantly triggers a silent alarm notifying bank security personnel and the police. One such system is employed in a German bank as final step in controlling access to the vault.

In 1998 Professor Chang developed VideoQ, a software tool for searching the content of digital video. Consider the time and human capital that might have been saved if such technology had been used to find an archived video clip of President Clinton embracing former White House intern Monica Lewinsky (of course, this assumes a future scenario in which video news is in digital form, but this is happening quickly with the coming digitization of television in the United States).

For journalism, these tools will create a system for automatically indexing and storing video as well as a powerful means to retrieve images and video that fully exploits both the information contained in the index and the actual content of the images themselves, thus making possible efficient searches that go beyond the scope of the original keyword index. Even a single reporter working for a local television station or a freelance Internet journalist will be able to conduct searches of massive databases of images and video in a fraction of the time teams of researchers need today.

Video and sound production are also undergoing a new media-morphosis (to adapt a term coined by new media pioneer Roger Fidler).[3] First-generation digital postproduction technologies have been cumbersome, slow, expensive, and inefficient. As a result, many producers have opted to continue working with analog production tools, such as tape cutters. New digital tools for audio, image, and video editing are being developed to run not just on expensive dedicated newsroom systems such as Avid but on portable personal computers that a reporter can take into the field. I discuss these applications further later in the portion of this chapter devoted to the mobile journalist workstation.

Digital Tools for Handwriting and Audio

Two staples of raw, unprocessed news data are a reporter's handwritten notes and her or his audio recordings of interviews and ambient sound. For most of the 20th century, these raw unedited data have been cumbersome, awkward (not to mention illegible in many cases) and difficult to work with, especially for an editor or producer who may not have been on the scene when they were acquired. As a result, handwritten notes and audio recordings are frequently a cause of one of the basic bottlenecks in the news production process. Typically, a reporter after returning from the field or after completing an interview, needs to sit down for a considerably lengthy time to review the raw data s/he has collected, index it, perhaps by subject and data, time code the audio (as is the case with video) and then begin to structure a story. All this is a relatively inefficient and time-consuming process for the journalist, and can lead to errors when the reporter faces a looming deadline.

Recent developments in new media technology present potential solutions to the problem of processing raw data in both handwritten and audio/video format. Handwriting recognition has proven to be a difficult challenge for engineers in the digital age, and despite the successful handwriting recognition capabilities of Apple's Newton MP 2000 (with roughly 90 percent reliable handwriting recognition), there have been no commercially successful handwriting recognition tools to date. The MP 2000 was discontinued in 1998 because of looming competition from a host of other small and cheaper PDAs, such as the Palm Pilot (which has an effective handwriting recognition system based on a form of "graffiti," or adapted writing style, the user must learn).

A new device from the Cross Pen Computing Group offers the first viable solution to the vexing handwriting recognition problem endemic to journalism (and other fields).[4] Rather than requiring the user to write with a special pen on an electronic screen (as with the MP 2000), the CrossPad (dubbed the first portable digital notepad, or PDN) allows the user to write on a regular pad of paper using a regular pen or pencil. Light weight (2.2 pounds), inexpensive (less than $400), and wireless, the CrossPad sits underneath any 8.5-by-11-inch pad of paper and uses a radio frequency (RF) transmitter to scan in the handwriting sensed from each pen stroke. The handwriting is not converted into so-called machine-readable text, however; rather, it is left in analog format as written, with the device using IBM hand-writing recognition software to scan in digital format only user-selected passages and automatically add indexes, such as date, subject, and so forth. The notepad can store up to fifty pages of single-spaced text or one hundred pages of loose notes (typically more than sufficient for an average reporter's day's work), which can be ported electronically into any desktop computer. A tray on the side of the notepad can hold up to five additional storage cartridges, each capable of storing another fifty pages of text, thereby meeting the needs of even the most prolific reporter's notes.

With such a device, after completing an interview (or set of interviews) the reporter can return to her workspace, transfer her notes to a desktop computer (this can also be done via modem from a remote location to another reporter or a central newsroom), and then begin writing up the story from data that are already partially organized and can be easily converted to machine-readable format.

Similar advances are poised to transform the processing of digital audio recordings. An increasing number of newsrooms are equipping their reporters with digital audio recorders for use in conducting interviews in the field or via the telephone. In digital format, those audio (or video) recordings can automatically create a time code and be seamlessly edited in digital audio workstations, supplanting the need for physical tape cutters. Experience at Columbia University's Digital Audio Newsroom at the Graduate School of Journalism indicates that even beginning reporters can learn to use digital audio production technology more easily and quickly than traditional analog systems, thus reducing the learning curve and enabling the reporters to focus on the content of their stories.

Only recently, however, has there been any increase in the efficiency of the scanning, indexing, and sorting of the actual audio content, even in digital format. Recently released voice recognition tools will soon change this situation dramatically. Via Voice™ from IBM, Dragon Dictate's Naturally Speaking™, and Kurzweil's VoicePro™ are part of a new class of voice recognition tools with significant implications for journalists. Unlike past computer dictation technologies, these new software products process continuous speech (i.e., speech that does not require discrete pronunciation, or a brief pause between each word), have vocabularies of some thirty thousand words, run on standard PCs, and cost less than $200. Although these systems are designed primarily for dictation and to transmit voice commands to a computer, they may also be useful in creating instant transcripts of audio interviews stored in digital format. In controlled environments, the IBM system has been found to be effective. The biggest immediate challenge will be to acquire clean audio in the field, when many competing sounds may introduce noise into the digital audio. These technical challenges will likely be solved in the coming months.

The Mobile Journalist Workstation

Finally, consider the mobile news system being developed through a collaboration of Columbia University's Center for New Media and its Computer Graphics and User Interfaces Lab. Now in prototype stage, the mobile journalist workstation (MJW) involves a combination of off-the-shelf technologies and software developed by Columbia computer science professor Steven Feiner and students in Feiner's lab.[5] It utilizes a hybrid user interface combining five primary technologies: a wearable computer backpack, a handheld PDA with a high-resolution screen, a GPS receiver that can pinpoint the user's location within one centimeter, a high-speed, eleven-megabits-per-second wireless WavLAN (local area network) link to the Internet and the World Wide Web, and a head-mounted display equipped with a see-through visor and silver-halide reflective mirror, earphones, and head tracker that provides a precise measurement of the spatial and directional orientation of the head.

Invented by Steve Mann in 1980 (founder of the Humanistic Computing Lab at the University of Toronto and formerly of the MIT Media Lab), such wearable systems have been refined and advanced by Feiner and others to develop what is called augmented reality. Primarily used in manufacturing, augmented reality provides the user with additional information layered on a real-life scene or situation. For example, in aerospace manufacturing, engineers estimate that as much as 60 percent of the time is spent referring to blueprints rather than welding. Augmented reality systems now in testing enable a welder to see a transparent overlay of the blueprint on top of his work, enabling him to locate precisely the position of the next weld, and almost eliminating the time spent referring to the blueprint.

The current generation of the MJW under development at Columbia University incorporates a variety of image and sound acquisition devices, including tools for digital audio and video acquisition. Similar research is under way at Kansas State University and at the Massachusetts Institute of Technology (the computer science department's Oxygen Project is headed up by Michael Dertouzos), as well as in the television news industry, where tools for more efficiently capturing and transmitting multimedia news content are at a premium.

The acquisition devices for the MJW include both digital audio and video sensors (microphones and cameras). Perhaps the most significant devices are the new generation of so-called megapixel cameras, which capture more than a million picture elements, or pixels, in a single picture. Although these megapixel cameras are still not of the quality of 35 mm film, they are getting reasonably close and produce images more than suitable for online publication, where one or two million pixels in a standard image provide more resolution than many monitors can display and more detail than the human eye can sometimes process. Among the best megapixel cameras are the Kodak DC4800, the Sony CyberShot DSC-S70, the Olympus C-2020, and the Nikon Coolpix 990.[6] They offer the quality of more expensive digital cameras priced between $2,000 and $15,000 but offer fewer options, such as interchangeable lenses and an extensive color range. In general, these new cameras represent a quantum improvement in image quality and at a lower price (about $500-$1,000) than earlier generations of digital still cameras. Megapixel cameras replace an earlier generation of VGA cameras producing images with 640 by 480 pixels (the product of these numbers yields a pixel count of 307,200 and a wallet-sized color photograph). With megapixel cameras print size can be increased to 4 by 6 inches without producing jagged edges, or what is termed pixelation. Amateur photographers can produce 5-by-7-inch glossy color prints at home. Kodak claims its DC4800 produces high-quality 8-by-10 prints. As a result, an increasing array of news organizations are using these cameras, which offer photographers the ability to take pictures on deadline and still make the late edition of the paper or go directly to online publication because there is no processing time as with film-based cameras. Most megapixel cameras have a liquid crystal display (LCD) permitting the photographer to see the image instantly. Images can then be stored, sorted, and transmitted anywhere.

Professor Steve Mann has pioneered the use of wearable photographic and video technology.[7] Details on how Mann has used his wearable camera to capture and publish news photos not only online but in traditional print newspapers follow in this chapter. For small news operations and for freelance journalists, it is worth noting that there is no incremental cost for using a digital camera, as there is with film cameras that require continual purchase of film and associated film processing. Digital storage cards can be reused indefinitely. In addition, the new megapixel cameras are smaller and lighter than earlier versions, thus making them more portable and an effective part of the MJW. The cameras vary slightly in size, weight, and battery life; the typical camera is 4-by-4-by-2 inches and weighs ten to fifteen ounces. When connected to a personal computer with image-editing software and attached to a color ink-jet printer, megapixel cameras bring additional advantages over conventional film photography: inside a digital darkroom, it is an easy matter to crop, enhance, resize, rotate, or recolor (this requires a scanner and imaging software such as Adobe Photodeluxe[a]) an image (these processing features raise important ethical issues, which I examine in detail in chapter 5). A typical digital darkroom includes a scanner (although this is not necessary when working exclusively with digital cameras), imaging software such as Adobe Photodeluxe[a], and a standard PC. All of this can be incorporated into an MJW.

High-quality MPEG (digital) video cameras are also increasingly ubiquitous, powerful, and cheap. Models such as the Hitachi MPEG1A, for example, can record motion video (MPEG, which is a form of video compression), still images (JPEG, a form of compression for still digital images), and JPEG with audio (or still images with accompanying audio in digital format). Such a camera can typically record twenty minutes of full-motion MPEG-1 video and audio, three thousand still JPEG images, or one thousand JPEGs with ten-second audio clips. The files are compressed in real time and stored on a removable 260 mb PC card. The camera features 6x zoom capabilities (which can magnify an image by six) for long shots. The user views the shots using a color 1.8-inch LCD and can instantly delete or retake any video clip or picture. Files are automatically indexed with recording mode, date, and time and include a thumbnail image for easy scanning and retrieval. The contents can be transferred to a computer for processing and editing, presentations, and Internet or intranet news delivery. These acquisition devices are an essential element of MJW technology.

Steve Mann has field tested applications of wearable computing for journalism. On at least two occasions, Mann, the original cyborg (he wears his wearable computer system virtually twenty-four hours a day), has happened across news events before local news providers could get to the scene. Mann, a two-time recipient of the top photography award in Canada with a Ph.D. in engineering from MIT, captured images of the events via his head-worn

camera, immediately contacted a local news organization by cellular communications and alerted them to the breaking news events, and had his
images published after the paper downloaded the images Mann had transmitted from his wearcam via wireless transmission to a remote Web server.
In one case, the paper's editor requested that Mann stop taking pictures and
get his film to the paper at once. Mann informed him that there was no film
and that the pictures were already available via the Internet.

The three following journalism scenarios illustrate how a reporter
equipped with an MJW (or similar device) might produce a more contextualized news report.

Scenario One: Political Reporting

As the candidate for district attorney began his speech, Jackie Oregel, a
reporter for the New Media News (NMN), listens intently to the former prosecutor's claim that he had an unprecedented conviction rate for homicide
cases. Oregel thinks this claim impressive, as do most of the other reporters
present at the press conference. But is it true?

Using her handheld PDA—which she uses for note taking (it recognizes
her handwriting as a security measure, so no one else can tamper with her
notes, and automatically indexes her notes by subject, keywords, and date),
communications, and a variety of other applications—Oregel taps on the
Web browser button of the touch-sensitive screen. Linking to the Internet's
World Wide Web via a 56 kbps digital personal communications service
(PCS), her PDA immediately goes to the NMN intranet, which provides not
only instant access to the entire contents of the Web, including an archive
of all NMN stories published to date, but also to the news service's digital
archive of public records. These records include data on the homicide conviction rates for the state. Running a cross-tabulation of the former prosecutor's name against the rates for homicide convictions for the past twelve
months quickly confirms his claim. He does have an unprecedented conviction rate for homicide cases: it is the worst.

"Would you elaborate on your unprecedented homicide conviction rate?"
Oregel asks the candidate, obtaining a time-coded digital audio recording
of the candidate's comments and a simultaneous transcript created using
voice recognition software. After finishing her questioning, Oregel prepares
to file her report. As part of the NMN reporting team, the first step is to use

her PDA to communicate via email with her editor, producer, and the news-room Web master regarding the lead, length, and modality of her story.

The team requests three reports: a linear text report for the news service, an audio report using the digital audio she recorded on her PDA and edited in the field via her portable PC, and an interactive report for the service's Web site, incorporating not only a written report but also audio and photos of the candidate, which she took with her megapixel digital still camera, as well as raw data culled from the candidate's prosecution record. She uses her wireless PCS link to file her three reports using file transfer protocols (FTP) for the Internet.

Is this scenario science fiction or journalistic reality? Although no com-mercial news organization currently makes use of this complete technology system—every element described above exists in off-the-shelf commercially available software and hardware products—many news organizations are ex-panding their use of these technologies, and many pioneering reporters use some of these tools. The facts of the case are real and are based on the true-life experiences of Elliot Jaspin, a pioneering investigative reporter who once reported a story in which a former nun turned prosecutor ran for district attorney in Rhode Island (which Jaspin dubbed a reporter's theme park) and made exactly this claim at a press conference. Subsequent investigative work by Jaspin proved her performance to be the worst on record, but the inves-tigation required Jaspin to return to the newsroom of the Providence *Journal-Bulletin*, thus eliminating the possibility of questioning the prosecutor at the time she made the claim.

Scenario Two: Foreign Reporting

Entering Kisangani, a formerly wealthy trading post on the Congo River, a young freelance journalist uses her MJW to survey the scene quickly. Look-ing at the crumbling ruins of a once-grand building, her head-mounted display overlays the identity of the building: the Hotel Leopold. Tapping her finger on the touch-sensitive screen of the personal digital appliance that serves as the information interface to the MJW, additional background infor-mation about the hotel appears on the display: Humphrey Bogart stayed there during the 1950 filming of *The African Queen*. As the reporter journeys deeper into the heart of the old Belgian colonial city, her MJW provides instant access to rich databases of news and other information available via the World Wide Web and other online sources, including text, images, graphics, video, and audio, all presented as augmented reality, or information layered onto the real scene she is reporting from. She uses this information to put into context the original reporting she is doing today. She takes a photograph documenting the scene, with the exact longitude, latitude, altitude, and time encoded into the digital watermark certifying the authenticity of her photographic work and protecting its copyright. Later, from a remote encampment in northeastern Zaire, the intrepid reporter transmits a series of digital dispatches via her MJW's satellite phone to an eagerly awaiting global audience. Imagine having access to such technology when reporting a terrorist attack such as happened in August 1998 in Kenya or Tanzania.

Scenario Three: Convention Coverage

A third scenario brings the MJW closer to home. At the Democratic National Convention in Chicago during the 1996 U.S. presidential campaign Vice President Al Gore delivered on August 28 an emotional and moving speech in which he explained how his sister had died of cancer in all probability caused by her cigarette smoking. The next day, most major newspapers and television networks reported on the front page about Gore's eloquent and stirring speech. Even PBS's *McNeil/Lehrer NewsHour*, the most-respected news program on television, reported that "when he [Gore] spoke of his sister's fight with cancer, one delegate writes that the United Center was 'quiet as a church.' "

The Gore speech was not delivered until late in the evening on the twenty-eighth, and there was little time to check facts afterward because the reporters were all on deadline. Forced to report without any context, they could only report on the event itself, the emotionally stirring speech. The next day, however, research uncovered the fact that the Clinton-Gore campaign had accepted contributions from a number of tobacco companies and lobbyists and that the Gore family had even accepted tobacco subsidies from the federal government long after his sister's death. Stories that explained this connection ran the next day in major papers, but they were generally small items deep inside the papers, not the front-page reports of the day-one story.

What difference might an MJW have made to this story? In 1996 it would probably have made little difference, largely because the infrastructure for accessing public transactional records on the Internet was relatively primitive and undeveloped. Two years later the case was entirely different. By accessing the Federal Election Commission's Web site for campaign contributions, a search on August 25, 1998, showed that Gore's campaign committee had received some $68,000 in contributions between January and June 1998 from fourteen organizations, including both corporate contributors and political action committees (PAC) as diverse as the AT&T Corporate PAC and the Walt Disney Productions Employees PAC.[9] Bell Atlantic Corp.'s PAC was the single biggest contributor, with three contributions totaling $15,000. Although there are no tobacco companies on this list, how useful might such information be as a reference point during future campaign speeches by the vice president, who is known for his leadership on issues involving telecommunications deregulation? Each contributor is linked to additional details, including committee identification number, mailing address, treasurer's name, and committee type (e.g., party affiliation). This information might be useful for a reporter conducting further research or in need of a source at a relevant PAC.

This spectrum of digital news-gathering technologies presents the journalist of the twenty-first century with an exciting and perhaps intimidating digital toolkit. None of the tools discussed in this chapter comes with any guarantee of success, nor is it certain they will be used wisely or ethically. They do, however, offer the well-trained journalist in the field the capabilities to put stories in much better context, to check facts on the spot, and to work more efficiently and effectively when in remote or unfamiliar locations or when under the pressure of deadline. It is also certain that the tools will continue to evolve, becoming smaller, lighter, and more powerful. No doubt the sources journalists cover, especially those in wealthy corporate behemoths, will have access to these same technologies.

4 A Reporter's Field Guide to the Internet

Prologue: About the Internet

The Internet is a global network of computer networks using a common set of technical protocols known as TCP/IP (Transmission Control Protocol/Internet Protocols). Born of various industry initiatives but primarily a U.S. Defense Department project to maintain communications in the advent of a nuclear holocaust, the Internet is largely a product of the inventive minds of Vinton Cerf, now a vice president for MCI, and Robert E. Kahn, president of the Corporation for National Research Initiatives. Not controlled by any one person or organization, the Internet is a medium of multimedia content, interactive communications, electronic mail, and much more. Content is produced by millions of people, companies, governments, and others in more than 180 countries on all seven continents. The quality of that content varies widely, from the exceptional to the confused to the deliberately misleading. Most of it is available at no cost to the user, although there are exceptions. Most of the material discussed here is available to journalists at no cost. Although there are other online resources outside the Internet (e.g., parts of proprietary online services such as *America Online* are not available via the Internet), the majority of online content and services is on the Internet. This primer therefore focuses on the Internet (although AOL membership now exceeds twenty million, its growth rate is slowing; according to David Simons, managing director of Digital Video Investments, membership took 133 days to move from twelve million to thirteen million, compared to the 86-day jump from eleven to twelve million).[1] For an excellent and thorough history of the Internet see *Hobbes'* Internet Timeline (hosted by the Internet Society).[2] See also the www.cnm.columbia.edu "research" link to CNM research reports by Mischa Schwartz on the telecommunications network, John Carey on the "adolescence" of the Internet, and Paul Sagan on the "network economy."

About the World Wide Web

The World Wide Web (www) is a global electronic publishing medium accessible via the Internet. It contains more than five thousand news sites published by newspapers, television and radio broadcasters, and magazine publishers, as well as some news sites original to the online world. The Web is perhaps the most important and fastest-growing part of the Internet. A Web axiom is that if it exists in the real world, there are probably at least one hundred Web sites about it. The corollary is that if it doesn't exist, there are probably at least a thousand Web sites about it (i.e., the Web is a haven for rumors).

The Web is an interconnected set of computer servers on the Internet that conform to a set of network interface protocols created by Tim Berners-Lee, then of CERN, the European high-energy physics laboratory in Geneva, Switzerland,[3] and now of MIT. The Web began as an electronic library for physicists and grew rapidly into a global publishing medium. Any individual or organization with Internet access can create what is called a home page, a document, or a site on the Web, as long as it uses the programming protocols established at CERN and since updated at least a half dozen times. The www protocols include assigning the home page a Uniform Resource Locator (URL) based on its TCP/IP Internet address and using what is known as hypertext transport protocol (http) that enables the standardized transfer of email and other text, audio, and video files. The creation of a URL involves selecting a domain name, which is the unique term that identifies a site, such as Columbia, IBM, or White House; domain names are registered for two years with any of more than two dozen accredited registration organizations, called registrars, at a cost of at least $200 (registration was free until 1996; ICANN, the Internet Corporation for Assigned Names and Numbers, is the nonprofit oversight body that accredits the registrars; see www.icann.org). The suffix after the domain name may be .com (for commercial), .edu (for education), .org (for not-for-profit organization), .gov (for governmental), .mil for military, or .net for Internet administration). For example, the URL for Columbia University is http://www.columbia.edu.

In addition, each Web document tagged with Hypertext Markup Language, or HTML, allows automatic routing from one electronic document to another, whether elsewhere in the same Web document or anywhere else in the entire World Wide Web. A user achieves this simply by clicking the mouse on highlighted text.

Assessing Quality of Online Information

Because so much information on the Internet is of high quality, it can be a very good source of journalistic information on important stories, sources, and leads. But because so much Internet content is of dubious or unknown origin, sometimes worthless or intentionally misleading, it is essential that all journalists critically evaluate the information they obtain online. It is also important to verify online information from off-line sources and never to rely exclusively on online information for a story, just as one should avoid relying on a single source for any story (e.g., many of the best news organizations generally will not publish a story until they have confirmed it with a second source). It is useful to develop a list of trusted sites that are produced by known organizations or people and contain reliable, quality content.

Dan Middleberg, CEO of Middleberg and Associates, and Columbia journalism professor Steven Sander Ross have collaborated on research on the evolving state of online journalism since the mid-1990s. The valuable Middleberg/Ross "Media in Cyberspace" study of how journalists increasingly use the Internet is published annually online. Here are some of the most important findings of the sixth edition of the study (released on March 2, 2000) for newspaper reporters:

- Virtually all print journalists (newspaper and magazines) now use online tools for researching and reporting. Fully 99 percent of respondents say they or their staffs in some way use online services at least occasionally. Three-quarters of the respondents say they or their staffs go online every day. Only 1 percent say they or their staffs never use online technology.

- When reporting a breaking story after hours, journalists try for the source first, almost every time, but indicate they next turn to company Web sites for information. During nonbusiness hours or when live sources are not available, Web sites thus play a significant role in delivering information to the media.
- Journalists cite as most useful Web sites containing financial information, followed by those with photos and press releases. Journalists expect complex sites to have a search engine.
- Most respondents indicate they are using the Web for gathering images and other materials that had to be physically carried to the newsroom just a few years ago.[4]

Middleberg and Ross also published in 1999 their first study of broadcast media in cyberspace.[5] The study shows that broadcast journalists who have a news-oriented Web site (only a small portion: about one in five) use online resources more often than do print journalists (compared to earlier cyberspace studies), especially for reporting breaking news and crises.

Another relevant online resource on how to evaluate and use online resources was developed by staff members of the newsroom at the *Columbia Missourian*, the student newspaper at the University of Missouri, home to the world's first journalism school.[6] Four rules established at the site are:

1. Verify with a source before publishing any information obtained online.
2. Attribute information obtained from a Web site (e.g., if information is obtained from the EPA Web site, write "EPA figures show").
3. Check the URL extension to assess the likely point of view of the publisher of the information. Don't assume that data are reliable because the source is the government (they may be trying to hide something); look for suspicious patterns or anomalies.
4. Check when the page was last updated and make sure the information is current.

Tools: Browsers, Search Engines, and More

A wide variety of powerful digital tools are available to journalists today. Among the basic building blocks on the Web are browsers, the graphical user tools for accessing Web content. In 1995 there were many browsers to choose from, but *Netscape* (*Navigator, Communicator*) soon became the dominate browser, controlling an estimated 70 percent of the market in 1998 (Microsoft's *Internet Explorer* controlled approximately 25 percent). With the release of *Windows* '98, however, and the incorporation of *Explorer* into the operating system, *Explorer* became the dominant browser in the late 1990s. Today, however, the antitrust case against Microsoft has opened up another window of opportunity for *Netscape*, and that browser may make a comeback in the early years of the twenty-first century. In addition, *Linux*, the alternative operating system and browser favored by many on college campuses, may make inroads into *Explorer*'s dominance.

Search engines are tools for searching for content on the Web. They typically use spiders (intelligent agents) to scour the Web for content or accept site registrations and compile their databases accordingly. Tips on how search engines work and how best to use them are available online.[7] Another effective resource containing online tutorials on how to use search engines and many other computer-related subjects (e.g., tutorials on designing Web pages, writing Java script, etc.) has been developed by business professor Bob Jensen of Trinity University.[8]

Search engines include directory-based tools, such as *Yahoo!*[9] The 1998 Middleberg/Ross cyberspace study shows that "Yahoo, which uses Alta Vista as a Web catalog and search system, and Alta Vista itself have become dominant as entry points for journalists on the Web. Combined, they get about half the search activity by journalists."

The directory approach employed by *Yahoo!* gives targeted results but may miss some things. Other search engines are text-based, such as *Web-Crawler*. One of the oldest search engines, it offers personalized channels of content (e.g., categories of news selected by the user). *Alta Vista* uses the full text of Web pages and offers advanced search capabilities, including instantaneous translation of Web sites into and from multiple languages, such as English, Spanish, French, and Portuguese. *InfoSeek* is similar to *Alta Vista*. *Lycos* is a popular search engine that also offers other Internet services, such as Web guides and the like. *HotBot* was created by *Wired* and is easy to use with customizable results and presentation. *Excite* offers concept-based searching and extensive company profiles useful in business and financial reporting. *Northern Light* is one of the newer text search engines and combines a comprehensive database of Web content and a special collection of twenty-nine hundred journals, books, magazines, and more, as well as video search tools, such as *WebSEEK* and *VideoQ*.[10]

Various computerized content analytic (CA) tools have been developed in journalism research. Two of the leading researchers in this regard are Mark Miller, University of Tennessee, and Roderick Hart, University of Texas. Miller's CA tools are available online, as are a variety of other CA tools. Such tools are useful to journalists interested in examining patterns of news coverage, such as the frequency of occurrence of certain key terms or people's names, or in identifying trends in the textual portions of public records. Some also provide similar capabilities in the audio and video realms.

Online headline aggregators are also of enormous use to journalists. In an age of frequent news and information overload, tools such as newshub.com and newslinx.com provide a valued service. Updated every fifteen minutes, these free services use a combination of intelligent agents (see chapter 11 for a detailed discussion of agent technology and its implications for journalism) and human editors to aggregate in near real time news headlines on every news subject, from health to sports, as well as general breaking news.

Yahoo! and many of the other major search engines have become significant portals into Web content and services and have evolved new forms of content access and presentation that go far beyond simple content searches. For example, *Yahoo!* offers *MyYahoo!*, which includes customizable news, chat, travel services, and much more.

Searching on deadline is a fundamental skill needed by all journalists. Since journalists are usually on deadline, it is important to conduct searches strategically in order to reduce wasted and irrelevant hits and quickly zero in on the desired information. Some strategic considerations include selecting search terms carefully, using advanced search tools that allow Boolean searching, and employing search engine combined searches called metasearch engines. Examples of these include www.metafind.com and www.metacrawler.com, although they don't offer as effective advanced or refined features on concept searches.

A new class of search tools emerging in 2000 may have profoundly important implications for journalists and news consumers alike. One experimental application being developed by Internet technologist Konata Stin-son, enables "associative" information discovery. *iNo* (*Internet Navigator and Organizer*) dynamically analyzes the content and structure of Internet re-sources to make contextual information salient. *iNo* is not a search tool as much as it is a discovery tool: it enables journalists, news consumers, and others to uncover information and relationships they may not know to look for. This speaks directly to the essence of journalism, which is to discover the unexpected but highly relevant. In contrast to traditional search tools, which narrow investigation, associative discovery tools broaden it to create a more contextualized analysis.

A related search technology is called *Google*. One of the most interesting search engines available, it was developed by Sergey Brin and Larry Page during their doctoral studies at Stanford University in 1998. Using link pat-terns and Web structure to identify sites relevant to keyword search terms, *Google* often turns up sites not found by the more traditional search engines. Many traditional search engines not only are organized by human editors, but their results are shaped by the amount of advertising dollars spent by different Web sites. In other words, if you enter a keyword search, the first site returned is likely to be the one whose owner/operator paid the highest advertising dollar to the search engine you used. *Google* doesn't work that way. The process is entirely coded by computer, and the sites returned are ranked according to their link patterns. Plus *Google* does not rank hit priority based on commercial funding. Those linked to most often are rated more authoritative and are returned first.

For example, an August 16, 1999, search for Walt Disney biographies returned one site when run on *Yahoo!*: "Walt Disney Records—Download sound clips, artist biographies, and song lists, as well as soundclips and pic-tures from read-alongs and sing-alongs." The same search run on *Google* returned 1,684 sites, including:

Books on The Walt Disney Company on Amazon.com
. . . how to enjoy them **WaltDisneyBiographies**—different looks . . .

. . . THE **WALTDISNEY** COMPANY Here are the books on the
    machine known as . . .
www.billcotter.com/tvbook/company.htm Cached (13k)

Walt Disney biographies on Amazon.com

. . . **WALTDISNEYBIOGRAPHIES** Come learn about the man behind it . . .

. . . the man behind it all—**WaltDisney**. The books here range from . . .

www.billcotter.com/tvbook/bios.htm Cached (11k)

Walt Disney: An Intimate History of the Man and His Magic

. . . Cédérom **WaltDisney**: An Intimate History of the Man and His Magic . . .

. . . Après plusieurs **biographies** non autorisées, **Disney** a maintenant . . .

www.entertainium.com/francais/divers/walt.html Cached (4k)

Disney books about Walt himself

. . . **Disney** reference books **Disney** books about **Walt** himself . . .

. . . in Russian. Bessy, Maurice: **Walt Disney** published by Seghers; . . .

www.pizarro.net/didier/_private/walt.htm Cached (14k)

SRVUSD School Accountability Report Card: Walt Disney School

. . . **WALT DISNEY** SCHOOL SCHOOL ACCOUNTABILITY REPORT CARD 3250 Pine . . .

. . . Established: 1974 Enrollment: 505 **WaltDisney** School serves the . . .

www.srvusd.k12.ca.us/sar9798/disney-rep.html Cached (32k)

A Walt Disney (Walter Elias Disney) Biography: Terraformers™ Tombtown™

. . . **Disney** was born in Chicago, Illinois, on December 5, 1901. **Walt** . . .

. . . parents were Elias and Flora **Disney**. **Walt** had three brothers, and . . .

www.tombtown.com/bios/disney.htm Cached (9k)

Autograph Reference Library—Walt Disney

. . . **WALT DISNEY** Below is an authentic **Walt Disney** . . .

. . . and signatures attributed to **Walt Disney** were actually done by . . .

www.autographics.com/ken/WaltDisney.html Cached (6k)

Walt Disney—Biography at Generation Terrorists

> . . . **Walt Disney** (1901–1966) Movie animator, producer, showman;
>   born . . .
> . . . drawing on his studio's productions; **Disney** World, in Orlando,
>   Fla., did . . .
> www.generationterrorists.com/bio/disney.html Cached (4k)

A related search tool also useful to journalists is *alltheweb.com*. It uses an approach similar to *Google* and is especially effective at finding news sources.

Email

Finding electronic mail (email) addresses is a straightforward process on the Internet. The typical structure of an email address is username or initials (such as jp35), an "at" sign (@), and a domain name (e.g., Columbia). This might include an additional two- or three-character abbreviation indicating a subdomain, such as .jrn.columbia, for journalism at Columbia. The address concludes with a suffix indicating the type of organization (.edu for education, .gov for government, .com for commercial, .org for nonprofit organization, etc.): jp35@columbia.edu. International addresses include a country code, such as .it for Italy or .jp for Japan.

Using email to interview a news source is an increasingly viable option, especially for international sources. Email can also be useful in obtaining a specific piece of information on deadline by allowing a journalist to send out a specific question to several known and reliable sources (anywhere in the country or the world). Because email uses asynchronous communication (i.e., there is no live, two-way exchange) one can send a request and frequently get a response within thirty minutes to an hour. Email also allows one to keep in touch with sources and to check facts easily and quickly by sending technical details to a source for verification as needed or wanted. Email can also help journalists stay in touch with their readers. One can include an email address (or one designed for readers to use) and then correspond as appropriate.

People Finders

Finding people, leads, and stories is a fundamental news-gathering skill. A variety of tools are available for locating email addresses, people, and possible news sources. Many are available at the search engine sites.

Here are some useful tips for finding people:

1. Take advantage of directories, e.g., http://www.switchboard.com/ or http://www.yahoo.com/search/people.
2. To find people, use search engines, such as http://www.four11.com.
3. To search for a phone number using an address or vice versa, try reverse phone and address directories. One such directory is http://www.databaseamerica.com/html/gpfind.htm; to use this directory, enter a phone number and get an address. Or search for neighbors who may live near the person you wish to locate. A useful service is http:www.555-1212.com/look_up.cfm; to use it, enter the street address, city, and state (two-letter abbreviation), and click on "find" (it uses the Four11 database).
4. Try using *Bigfoot.com* to acquire contact information, such as email address, as well as other personal information, such as gender, marital status, name of spouse and children, address, current and previous employers, and type of computer.

Mailing lists, newsgroups, and more.   A variety of other online resources are also useful for finding leads, story ideas, sources, and more. Surprisingly, the Middleberg/Ross cyberspace study reports that "LISTSERVS, email, the Web and Usenet Newsgroups together were named by 9 percent of respondents as their primary source of story ideas—together about the same as newswires." More than one hundred thousand electronic mailing lists, among them Listserv, provide detailed discussions of a wide range of topics. Those of particular interest to journalists include the Computer-Assisted Reporting and Research (CARR-L) journalism mailing list; subscribe via email to listserv@ulkyvm.louisville.edu. The Investigative Reporters and Editors (IRE) housed at the University of Missouri School of Journalism also maintains a popular mailing list; subscribe to IRE-L via email at listproc@lists.missouri.edu.

There are also numerous specialized mailing lists, covering areas such as children and families, the environment, higher education, international reporting, police and courts, religion, and science writing.[12]

Subscribing to, participating in, creating, and unjoining a mailing list can be somewhat complicated, although usually it is as simple as sending email. One good source of protocols, as well as a searchable directory of more than seventeen thousand of the more than one hundred thousand electronic mailing lists worldwide is maintained by L-Soft International.[13] Majordomo instructions (for managing lists) are available online courtesy of David Barr at Ohio State University.[14]

Although mailing lists and bulletin boards (BBS) can furnish story ideas, leads, sources, and more, they can also mislead, and one should never rely exclusively on information obtained from such as source for a published story. This is the mistake journalist Pierre Salinger made when he reported an Internet rumor suggesting that the U.S. military had itself downed TWA flight 800.

Usenet newsgroups and bulletin boards are also useful sources for finding stories and potential sources. Newsgroup categories include everything from computers, to sciences, news, and "alternative," which is a catchall category. A variety of Web-based search tools are available for finding a desired newsgroup; one such is *tile.net*, which also provides a searchable database of mailing lists.[15]

Intelligent agents—software robots that act autonomously on behalf of another entity (typically a human, but sometimes another software robot)— are also becoming increasingly common on the Web as tools for sifting through the millions of pages of Web content, conducting specific assigned tasks (such as booking flight reservations), making online purchases, or searching through newsgroups (see chapter 11 for a full discussion). Many of these agents are now being used in online journalism products, for tasks as varied as the automatic handling of subscriptions to online news products and services to sorting through thousands of Usenet newsgroups and thousands of news stories from hundreds of online news sources every day and compiling easily digested summaries. See http://www.newspage.com for an example.

Online source lists.   Online source lists are the digital equivalent of an online Rolodex. One particularly useful ready-made one is http://www.profnet.com/ped.html. Started at the State University of New York at Stony Brook, *Profnet* offers access to thousands of experts at more than two thousand participating institutions, mostly universities, although many corporations, not-for-profits, public relations firms, government agencies, and think tanks are also included. Journalists use *Profnet* by visiting the site and posting a request for a source on a particular subject. *Profnet* works best for enterprise stories, not spot news. Stories are kept confidential, and sources are verified. Reporter requests are sent out three times a day, at 10:30 A.M., 1:30 P.M., and 4 P.M. Eastern Standard Time. A reporter can also submit a request via email at profnet@profnet.com or via the phone at 1-800-PROF-NET.

The National Press Club provides a database of sources, searchable by category, including hundreds of categories from abortion to workplace.[16] Searches can be conducted using keywords or actual organization or contact names. A search on the environment turned up twenty-nine organizations, from Allied Signal Flourine Products to Zero Population Growth, most of which were linked to Web sites. The database also provided organizational descriptions and contact names, addresses, and phone numbers.

Place Finders

Finding places in the real world is a frequent challenge for journalists. Online technology provides a new set of tools for locating places, people, and properties. Visit some of the following sites to obtain directions, maps, and more:

http://www.Zip2.com
http://www.citysearch.com
http://maps.yahoo.com/
http://www.mapblast.com

Public Records

Obtaining public records is also increasingly straightforward. One important online portal to public records is the Federal Online Freedom of Information Act (FOIA) form (courtesy of the Reporters Committee for Freedom of the Press).[17] The FOIA form can get access to any information collected by the government, although agencies have the right to censor information deemed a threat to national security. Making the same request to multiple agencies may produce the desired information, since different agencies may deem different information a threat.

On a state level, the State Level Online Form (for each of the fifty states with open records laws) is available online courtesy of the Student Press Law Center.[18]

U.S. population statistics are also available online at the Department of the Census Web site. The news section of the Census site contains press releases linked to raw data and is especially useful for story ideas. Reporters use the search tool to find details by state, county, and city. Census state data centers are also available online.[19]

Legal citations (*Lexis/Nexis*), as well as news stories, are also available via the Web, but at a substantial cost.[20]

Also available online are reliable Internet statistics, including data on usage in the United States and around the world, published by Nua Ltd (*nua* means "new" in Gaelic), an Internet consultancy and developer with offices in Ireland and New York. Data are kept current. On September 15, 1999, I obtained the following data from an August 1999 report from Nielsen Media Research and CommerceNet: 94.03 million U.S. adults, aged sixteen and over, use the Internet, effectively representing 45 percent of the total U.S. population.[21] The most useful section of the site, headed "Internet Surveys," provides many pages of data on Internet use around the world.

Another site tracks the volume of Internet traffic.[22] The email portion of this site estimated (for the United States only) that in 1999 there were 150 million messages per day. The site also includes a chart graphing the increases in both messages and users from 1994, with projections to 2001.

Foreign country population statistics, maps, and so forth, are available online at http://www.odci.gov/cia/publications/factbook/index.html.

The U.S. Government Printing Office (GPO) provides extensive data online as well.[23] The GPO site includes day-of-publication digital copies of the federal budget; the *Federal Register*, the official daily publication for rules, proposed rules, and notices of federal agencies and organizations; and executive orders and other presidential documents. These are directly accessible online.[24]

The Inspector General's (IG) office also provides extensive data online from its audits of sixty federal agencies, "as well as their peers in state and local government, education, non-profit organizations, and the private sector."[25] The IG also provides detailed information on the Y2K (year 2000) computing problem, also known as the millennium bug.

Largely available only through a trip to Washington, D.C., until the mid-1990s, the Library of Congress (LC) is another important reporting resource available online.[25] The vast repositories of the LC contain the largest single-institution collection of human knowledge in the world.

Thomas, named after Thomas Jefferson, is a comprehensive and official source of legislative information on the U.S. Congress. It includes floor activities, bills, the *Congressional Record*, committee information, historical information, and documents, such as the *Federalist Papers*. It is available through the Library of Congress Web site.[26]

Another important reporting resource is the General Accounting Office (GAO), the investigative arm of Congress. "Charged with examining matters relating to the receipt and disbursement of public funds, GAO performs audits and evaluations of Government programs and activities."[27]

Environmental databases are also available online. One is offered by the Right to Know Network, created in 1989 as a result of the Emergency Planning and Community Right to Know Act (EPCRA), which mandated public access to the Toxic Release Inventory. It is operated by two nonprofit organizations—OMB Watch and the Unison Institute—and funded by various government agencies and foundations.[28]

A comprehensive inventory of online sources of public records is available online, courtesy of Steve Ross, at the Columbia University Graduate School of Journalism Web site.[29] Among the other types of databases available online are federal government sites, political and congressional representatives sites, sites on federal and state campaign finances, public opinion polls, business directories, nonprofits, the Securities and Exchange Commission, workplace health and safety, health and medical data, searchable full-text medical articles, health organizations and drug information, the Mayo Clinic online, federal and state appellate courts, Supreme Court legal references and directories, grand juries, and state and local governments, including mayoral, gubernatorial, and congressional records.[30]

Particularly notable is the comprehensive database of campaign finance information (state and federal) made available courtesy of the Investigative Reporters and Editors (IRE).[31] The Federal Election Commission also publishes online reports disclosing who contributes how much to the president, senators, and representatives or makes "soft money" contributions (money exempt from limits), as well as much more.[32] Available either free or for a small fee are reports from 1990 to the present. The site is extremely well designed and easy to use. Options available include an imaging system, which allows one to view actual financial disclosure reports for House and presidential campaigns (unfortunately, campaigns for the Senate file their disclosure statements with the secretary of the Senate, not with the FEC, so they are not included in the imaging system), electronic filings, and a query system that allows one to search the disclosure database for contributions to presidential, Senate, and House campaigns, parties, and PACs beginning with the 1997/98 election cycle. The resources at this site are now the central means available for accessing such public records for all federal campaigns. The query system is especially powerful and simple to use. It allows the user to conduct individual searches for contributions from individuals, committee searches for contributions made by a specific committee, and candidate searches for contributions received by an individual candidate. For instance, using the individual search, I entered Trump, Donald, and instantly learned that he gave $10,000 in soft money to the Democratic Senatorial Campaign Committee on April 24, 1998, as well as $1,000 on February 19, 1997, to incumbent Republican senator (Pennsylvania) Arlen Specter. In 1999 *Politics.com* launched a new search feature based on FEC data for the 2000 presidential campaign that permits users to enter any zip code and find out which citizens in the area covered by that zip code made donations, for how much, when, and to which candidates.

Jack Dolan of the National Institute for Computer Assisted Reporting provided this description of another online resource in 1999:

The Campaign Finance Information Center now has downloadable data from 10 states: Florida, Idaho, Illinois, Indiana, Kansas, Kentucky, Michigan, Minnesota, Ohio, and Wisconsin.

We have links to online search engines (or download sites) hosted by state boards of election or newspaper consortiums in 15 states: Arizona, Hawaii, Florida, Idaho, Indiana, Kansas, Louisiana, New Jersey, New York, North Carolina, Oklahoma, Texas, Utah, Virginia, and Washington.

In addition, Tracker editor Ann Kim just built a registry of campaign finance reporters. If you aren't on the list, and want to be, send an email with your name, affiliation, address, phone and email to ann@nicar.org.

Also, CFIC Staffer Aaron Rothenburger has just begun to make easy to read .html tables to guide you through the labyrinth of states' varying campaign contribution limits. We have these for: Indiana, Kansas,

Michigan, Ohio, Washington and Wisconsin. (More are on the way) Idaho and Kentucky already have usable tables on the Web, we have links to those.[33]

(personal email from jack@nicar.org, October 15, 1999)

Also worth noting is the nonprofit Center for Responsive Politics' Web site on the Federal Election Commission.[34] And a comprehensive set of links to a variety of public records is provided by the Columbia University libraries.[35]

Finally, of particular use to journalists working online or covering regulatory matters in communication or telecommunications is the Web site of the Federal Communications Commission.[36] The FCC has aggressively utilized the Web to reinvent itself as a virtual commission, and it publishes all its proceedings, rules, and much more online, including the full text of the Telecommunications Act of 1996.

General Reference Materials

A broad spectrum of general reference materials is also available online. Among the most useful for journalists is University of California professor Jim Martindale's online "reference desk."[37] Since 1994 Martindale collected hundreds of links to information on a wide variety of subjects from bioscience to the Y2K problem. The site is organized in directory fashion, with major sections on health sciences, interactive multimedia and the environment, and disasters and safety, as well as a general reference section. The site includes more than just text-based information (with translation capability for English, French, Russian, and Swedish), including maps, interactive tutorials, and translations into sign language and Braille. The site has links to 261 countries, territories, and principalities now online, ranging from Abkhazia to Zimbabwe (where you can find the *Zimbabwe Independent Online*, among other things), more than three dozen major international organizations from the Association of Caribbean States to the World Trade Organization, and live real-time video and interactive maps of automobile traffic congestion in some three dozen major cities such as Athens (with live traffic patterns updated every fifteen minutes), New York City (an interactive map for the tristate region and more), Rio de Janeiro (including real-time video), and Singapore (with cameras installed by the Television Corporation of Singapore that present views of two dozen locations around the island updated every fifteen minutes, including the view from the Marriott Hotel in the popular shopping district at the junction of Orchard and Scotts Roads). Although these images may seem a bit Orwellian, they may prove useful to news organizations covering breaking news events around the world.

Another useful resource for journalists is Bartlett's familiar quotations, which came online recently.[38] I selected the following quotation from Isaac Newton because it reminds me of new media and journalism: "I do not know what I may appear to the world; but to myself I seem to have been only like a boy playing on the seashore, and diverting myself in now and then finding a smoother pebble or a prettier shell than ordinary, whilst the great ocean of truth lay all undiscovered before me."

Roget's Thesaurus is another useful reference online. Similarly, the *Wordsmyth English Dictionary-Thesaurus* is available online. The ARTFL (American and French Research on the Treasury of the French Language) Project publishes online the 1913 edition of *Webster's Revised Unabridged Dictionary*. The Merriam Webster dictionary is also online. The March 2000 online publication of the *Oxford English Dictionary* (OED) marks the debut of another useful resource for journalists.[39] Published in complete form since 1928, the twenty-three-volume OED is the premier source of information for wordsmiths. The online edition offers a number of important advantages to journalists, especially when on deadline, including the ability to conduct keyword searches of all twenty-three volumes, search on meanings in order to locate specific words, find quotations from a specific year or from a particular author or work, and gain unique online access to one thousand new and revised words every quarter. Of course, the OED online is not available for free; an individual license to use the site costs $550 a year, while a network license costs $795 a year.

New media developments are online as well.[40]

Professional Development

The Internet is a useful resource for professional development and continuing education for journalists. Among those resources are mailing lists, bulletin boards, and Web sites on broadcast journalism (subscribe to *BRDCST-L* at listserv@unlvm.unl.edu, or visit the Radio Television

News Directors Association site at www.rtnda.org), copy editing (join *COPYEDITING-L* at llistproc@cornell.edu, or visit the American Copy Editors Society site at www.copydesk.org), design (visit the Society of Newspaper Designers' site at www.snd.org), and journalism education (subscribe to *JOURNET-L* at listserv@american.edu, or visit the Association for Education in Journalism and Mass Communication site at www.aejmc.sc.edu), journalism ethics (subscribe to *SPJ-ETHICS* at majordomo@dworkin.wustl.edu), and online publishing (contact Steve Outing at www.planetarynews.com/). An increasing number of journalism courses are being offered online, including "Exploring New Media Online," a summer course I taught in 1998.[41]

A variety of online journalism publications are worth occasional visits. Among those are the *Columbia Journalism Review*, whose Web site offers a searchable online database (called "paper finder") of more than eleven thousand U.S. and Canadian newspapers, including contact information, mailing address, phone numbers, email addresses, Web sites, and other information. *American Journalism Review* maintains a similar set of links and other online resources. *Editor & Publisher* also maintains a useful online presence.[42] The *Online Journalism Review* (www.orj.org) is an exclusively online journalism review published by the Annenberg School of Journalism at the University of Southern California.

One growing source of continuing education and content for journalism is the Freedom Forum's online publication *Free!* (http://freedomforum.org). Veteran news executive Adam Clayton Powell III, vice president of Technology for the Freedom Forum, regularly reports on developments in online journalism, freedom of expression, and new media technology. Frequent visits to the site are worthwhile. The Poynter Institute's Web site is also a useful resource.[43]

Rich Meislin, editor-in-chief of the News York Times Electronic Media Company, has also developed a useful guide to Internet resources, with a special section on resources for journalists. Meislin's "cybernavigator" is available at the *Times's* Web site.[44]

All the national minority journalism associations also maintain active online presences. Among those available online are the Asian American Journalism Association, National Association of Black Journalists, National Association of Hispanic Journalists, National Association of Minority Media Executives, National Lesbian and Gay Journalists Association, and Native American Journalists Association.[45]

Privacy and Other Intellectual Property Considerations

Databases and online services raise a host of thorny questions about privacy and intellectual property rights.[46] Among the most important issues from the point of view of journalism is where to draw the line between the public's right to know and the individual's right to privacy. In many cases, this is a balancing act that hinges on the importance of the story, whether public figures are involved, and whether there are reasonable alternatives to get the needed information without jeopardizing anyone's privacy.

Intellectual property rights involve not violating anyone's copyright, trademark, or other legally protected intellectual good, including a story, image, sound clip, or other content available on the Internet. As a rule, a journalist should rely exclusively on primary sources and original content that he or she creates for use in a story. If a reporter must use someone else's material, it should be done only with permission and proper credit. Under limited circumstances (such as fair use for a news story of importance to the public or for educational purposes) it is permissible to use a portion of a body of a copyrighted work (such as a quote or a thumbnail picture), but these are rare and represent something of a legal gray area, especially outside the United States, where "fair use" is a much less well established legal concept.

A growing number of companies and others are employing increasingly sophisticated techniques to uncover illegal uses (i.e., pirated or plagiarized copies) of their copyrighted or trademarked content on the Internet. For example, BMI, the not-for-profit organization representing more than two hundred thousand songwriters, composers, and music publishers, uses an intelligent agent (i.e., software robot) to scour the Internet twenty-four hours a day looking for pirated clips of copyrighted music.[47]

A Caveat

Spending a great deal of time typing can be hazardous to your health, especially if your workspace has less than ideal ergonomics (i.e., your workspace posture isn't correct). One of the most frequent problems that can result from spending a great deal of time typing without adequate breaks is repetitive stress injury (RSI). Many journalists suffer from this complaint. For details on RSI and how to prevent and treat it, see the Harvard RSI Action home page.[48]

The Internet is a valuable resource for reporting. It contains a wealth of information that may be helpful to journalists in identifying potential stories, leads, and sources. It provides instant access to vast databases that once were available only through on-site examination. Reporting for virtually every story can be enriched through online research. Online reporters should also look at how these databases can be integrated into their news reports, giving the audience access to primary source material as a supplement to a news report. Though not all readers will find value in this, many will at least occasionally want to dig deeper into the background of a story. In some cases, a user-friendly interface can be added to the story to permit the reader easy, customized analysis of the data, such as zip code entry to get data for a specific locality.

Most reporters regularly check certain sources (e.g., reporters covering crime regularly check police reports). These days, every reporter should also integrate the Internet and various online sources into her or his beat, developing a list of regularly checked online sources. No reporter covering terrorism should have been surprised when terrorists linked to Saudi multimillionaire Osama bin Laden attacked U.S. embassies in Kenya and Tanzania and the United States conducted retaliatory strikes in Afghanistan and Sudan. A regular check of important online information sources would have revealed the likelihood of these developments. Weeks before the bombings took place half a world away, for example, the Emergency Response and Research Institute of Chicago, Illinois, posted the following report:

> Exiled Saudi millionaire Osama bin Laden remains hidden somewhere in the mountains of Afghanistan. He is wealthy, elusive and an Islamic extremist who is plotting against the United States. . . . Osama bin Laden has set his sights on and has sworn to bring an end to U.S. influence in his native Saudi Arabia and the Islamic world. It is said he has the money to do it. . . . Bin Laden reportedly made his militant contacts during the Afghan war. He then set up terrorist training camps in Sudan and financed attacks against the moderate governments of Algeria, Egypt, his native Saudi Arabia and Yemen.[50]

Despite its news-gathering benefits, however, the Internet is not a panacea for reporters. Much of the content available online is of dubious origin, and some may be intentionally misleading. Reporters must explore the Internet with a very cautious and skeptical eye. Moreover, reporters should not use the Internet as a replacement for good, old-fashioned shoe-leather reporting. Rather, the Internet should be an additional tool in the modern journalist's news-gathering and reporting toolkit.

5   Journalism Ethics and New Media

A graphic artist darkens a photograph of a celebrity accused of a heinous crime so that his face appears more brooding on the cover of a national news magazine.[1] An editor places a banner ad at the top of her newspaper's Web site, although she would never place an ad on the front page of her newspaper. A producer runs a story featuring a high-resolution satellite image of a well-known princess on holiday at a private beach on the Caribbean. These are just samples of the many knotty ethical issues new media raise for journalism in the digital age.[2]

In this chapter, I examine four questions that frame the ethical issues facing journalists and the public in today's digital environment, including the extent to which they differ from the ethical issues of traditional journalism. First, what are or should be the ethical standards of digital news gathering? Second, what are the ethical rules of digital news production? Third, what are the ethical boundaries of online news content? And, fourth, what are the broad ethical issues confronting journalists in an increasingly interactive, global news system?

Ethics of Digital News Gathering

Consider the case of a journalist equipped with an omnidirectional video camera. She could use it to present dynamic events in a compelling immersive environment and to help put stories in better context. But an om-

nicamera means more than just better news gathering. It raises serious ethical concerns as well. For one thing, omnidirectional video can place
everyone at a scene under surveillance, whether the camera is pointed at
them or not. What rights do journalists have to include anyone at a scene/
location in a news report, whether they are part of the story or not? Will
they need, or should they get, permission from everyone? What happens to
the individual's right to privacy in an age of omnidirectional imaging?
Should an omnidirectional video camera be allowed in a courtroom? Arguably, yes, although no judge has yet ruled on the matter as of 2000. Is it
permissible to show the jurors? No, although with software, it is a simple
matter to block them from view.

These possible developments have the potential to erode the credibility
of the media/journalism even further. One hundred fifty years of photography have taught people to understand that they are being watched when a
camera lens is pointed at them. But a single-lens omnicamera shoots video
by pointing the lens at a parabolic mirror, which means one is being watched
even when the omnicamera is pointing away. Further, when watching conventional video, the viewer does not have control (or only has minimal
control if s/he has videotaped a program) over what s/he is watching. Because
omnivideo is digital, the viewer has full control over the video, including
the ability to pan, tilt, and zoom. This means the viewer may use the video
in ways the journalist never intended. What are the implications for responsible journalists and news organizations? Are there implications for legal
liability beyond the ethical questions?

Hidden cameras raise many of the same issues. Undercover and investigative reporting aided by a variety of new media applications may increasingly invade people's privacy. Consider the 1998 introduction of Sony's new
infrared camcorder, which when used during daylight conditions can actually see through people's clothing. How might paparazzi put this camera
to use? The use of remote sensing technology offers unobstructed views from
space of individuals at home in their backyards. If a news organization uses
a high-powered satellite imaging camera to photograph from hundreds of
miles above someone relaxing on a private beach, even a public figure, does
that individual have a right to expect privacy? What are the ethical boundaries of news gathering from outer space? The advent of low-cost unmanned
(or -womanned) air vehicles (UAVS) equipped with remotely controlled still
or motion video cameras makes this a practical option for even the lowest-
budget news operation. In fact, one group of freelance journalists commis-

sioned a UAV to run an aerial photoreconnaissance mission over Kosovo during the spring of 1999, but they were arrested by the military authorities before they were able to file any stories or images. Remote-controlled photo-capable UAVs are already being sold at a retail price of just $119 through Hammacher Schlemmer, the retail catalog merchandiser.

As public records and documents have become increasingly electronic and as journalists have used the Freedom of Information Act and electronic FOIA requests to access those digital records, prickly ethical issues arise. Many of these documents and records were available exclusively in paper form or only on nine-track magnetic tape, making access expensive, awkward, or difficult. Now, many records are available on the World Wide Web. Witness the recent controversial case of the Social Security Department's launch of a Web site that permitted anyone anywhere in the world to access their (or others') financial life histories if they had access to the Web and a name, social security number, and mother's maiden name. A boon to those seeking information about their financial records, it was an electronic nightmare to those concerned about personal privacy. Some states have published drivers' records on the Web, only to shut down those services, as California did after a stalker used its database to track down a movie starlet whose address he had obtained at no cost and without requiring anyone's permission (he murdered her).

Journalists have traditionally been among the heaviest users of such public records (in the civilian sector, only private detectives and bill collectors have used them more). They have fought valiantly to protect and expand access to such records, arguing that freedom of expression, as guaranteed under the First Amendment to the U.S. Constitution, has little meaning if access to information is not guaranteed. Consider the case of Terry Anderson, the former AP correspondent held hostage for seven years in Beirut. After returning to the United States, Anderson pursued a fellowship at the Freedom Forum Media Studies Center, where his project was to write a memoir, *Den of Lions*, about his captivity in the Middle East. In doing his research, Anderson encountered endless roadblocks raised by the federal government to stymie his attempts to obtain documents about his own case. Ultimately, he received much of the sought-after material only when President Bill Clinton personally intervened and instructed the federal departments to return complete files to Anderson. In similar fashion, in 1999 APBnews sought access to the financial records of federal judges, a request routinely granted to print media such as newspapers, which often request the records of a single judge, under the Freedom of Information Act. When APBnews made its request for the records of all sixteen hundred federal judges, they were denied access. The argument was that releasing such information on the Internet would threaten the safety of the judges and their families. APBnews argued in its legal challenge to this decision that its FOIA request was just as protected by law as that of a newspaper. The records themselves do not provide information that identifies family members, and, if they did, this information could be deleted before posting the records online. The public has a right to know if a judge has a financial conflict of interest in a case, and only these records would reveal the truth. In 2000 APBnews won this case, and it may help define freedom of speech in the digital world and the ethical limits of a responsible online press.

Clearly, journalists and the public need access to public records and records of governmental transactions in order to check on government activities and uncover potential abuse (see the Transactional Records Access Clearinghouse—TRAC—program at Syracuse University).[3] This is often called the watchdog function of the press, the reason the press is often described as the fourth estate or the fourth branch of government. Yet in a digital age the nature of information and what can be done with it changes dramatically. How should journalists use such information as drivers' records, federal election commission filings, and census data online? Should journalists have privileged access to such information in order to prevent cases like that of the California stalker? If so, how do we decide who is a journalist? Would this require some form of licensing?

On the other hand, consider a system whose testing began in 1999 on a heavily trafficked section of Interstate 15 in San Diego, California. Using a combination of technologies, CalTrans (the California Department of Transportation) began testing a system wherein cars use advanced sensors to drive themselves at high speed in congested traffic. It is expected that such systems will reduce traffic accidents by as much as 80 percent, ease congestion, and increase average speeds by as much as 100 percent. This may be hype, but the technology is real.

Now add augmented reality to the mix. Imagine yourself in such a car equipped with thousands of sensor chips and communications devices. As you head down the highway, your silver-halide reflective windshield displays information about the cars around you culled from public records. You discover that the car in front of you is registered to a driver whose license has been suspended twelve times for driving while intoxicated. Using voice command, you instruct your car to change lanes. The car in front of you now registers on your license plate sensor as stolen, and an alert instantly goes into the California highway patrol. You instruct your car to take the next exit. You need a break. As you pull over and glance at the "E-Z Pass" automatic electronic highway toll payment device attached to your car's windshield, you begin to ponder, "What do the other drivers know about me? What's happening to my privacy?"

Digital News Production

Digital news production can raise a variety of ethical concerns. A 1995 study by the Radio and Television News Directors Foundation (RTNDF) indicates that news directors and reporters share a strong concern (27 percent of news directors and 34 percent of reporters) that image manipulation is a potential problem with digital newsroom technology. Other concerns include the use of unconfirmed electronic data, information overload, and violation of copyright and privacy laws.

The availability of late-received digital video raises what is perhaps the biggest concern in the era of the digital newsroom: the veracity of video received from an increasingly diverse array of digital sources. When news footage arrived in the newsroom in canisters of 16 or 35 mm film, it was relatively easy to confirm the accuracy of the content received: the film negative established the authenticity of the images. Even in the days of exclusively analog video a producer could be reasonably confident that images had not been manipulated since being recorded on tape. In the age of desktop video, however, any image, still or moving, can be manipulated as easily as words on a computer screen.

Another question concerns what happens when virtually anyone can easily edit video in a digital environment and quality controls begin to erode. In the old-fashioned analog television newsroom, it took an entire team of reporters, editors, and union technicians to gather, edit, and put on the air a single piece of video. Many pairs of eyes routinely viewed every video clip that made it on to the air. In the digital video newsroom, the number of eyes and concomitant amount of experience reviewing any given video is greatly reduced, not just for technical reasons but for reasons of cost cutting. Not only will this reduce the chances of honest mistakes being identified and corrected, it will make it much easier for downright fakery to occur.

The most notorious example of digital image manipulation happened several years ago when editors at the *National Geographic Magazine* used a digital darkroom to improve the aspect ratio of the three great pyramids in the Valley of the Kings in Egypt. Today, digital technologies make it possible to change the aspect ratio or any other dimension of even moving images and to do so seamlessly so that no viewer can tell the images have been manipulated.

Digital image manipulation comes in three basic forms: addition, subtraction, and modification (e.g., enhancement, merger). Digital addition refers to putting something into a picture that wasn't originally there, such as a crowd at a football stadium. Digital subtraction refers to removing something from a picture, such as deleting someone or something, such as a cable supporting an actor who appears to be flying. Digital manipulation means transforming an image, such as making it lighter or darker (as on the infamous *Time* cover photo of O. J. Simpson to which I alluded at the beginning of the chapter), blending two objects into one, or distorting one face into another (referred to as a morph in the movie industry).

As a result of the advent of digital image processing and potentially manipulation in the television newsroom, the traditional value of verifying any news content through multiple reliable sources is more critical than ever. The importance of maintaining the veracity of news content is underscored by the findings of a recent public opinion survey conducted by the Times Mirror Center for Press and the Public. The study shows that media credibility is at an all-time low (the first media credibility study was conducted in 1973). In the age of the digital newsroom and the information superhighway, news organizations will need to be vigilant in their pursuit of reliable news video, digital or not.

Digital technologies have magnified the traditional ethical issues surrounding news production. Although it has always been possible for darkroom technicians to manipulate images, digital technologies make such manipulation easier than ever and much harder to detect. Aside from alterations such as those described above, it is now possible to use such technology to create completely synthetic moving pictures, or video, as well as sound. It is relatively easy and inexpensive to use what are called nonlinear digital video editors, such as the Avid Media Composer—the number one system in television newsrooms in the United States—to create completely realistic video sequences of events that never took place. Don E. Tomlinson, an associate professor of journalism at Texas A&M University, contends,

"Soon, then, the capability will be such that the recorded, digitized, sampled voice of, say, the President of the United States, could be made to sound perfectly as if he had said something he in fact had not said. All it would require, once a representative sample of his voice's binary codes have been fed into the computer, is their rearrangement."[4] Such manipulation of digital video once required expensive technology that only a large and likely responsible news organization such as a television network could afford, which acted as something of a check on digital abuses. In 2000, however, inexpensive desktop tools provide similar capability, opening the field to nearly anyone.

Although this has not yet occurred in a U.S. newsroom—at least no one in a U.S. newsroom has publicly admitted to creating and airing a completely synthetic news video—the possibility became all too real during the 1996 senatorial campaign in Virginia. In that campaign, Senator John W. Warner (R-Virginia) hired an advertising consultant named Greg Stevens of Alexandria, Virginia, to create and air on television a negative political advertisement against his opponent. The ad Stevens created depicted Senator Warner's Republican rival, Mark R. Warner, shaking hands at a political rally with former governor L. Douglas Wilder while President Clinton smiled between them. Although the event looked real, the handshake never occurred. Stevens had digitally manufactured a completely undetectable synthetic video by electronically placing Mark Warner's head on the body of Senator Charles S. Robb, a Virginia Democrat.

This event raised important legal and ethical issues for journalism. Although the ethical issues of image and sound manipulation may not be new (image manipulation has occurred even in chemical darkrooms), the dramatic impact of digital technology has magnified the problem. It is now possible for even those with limited training and resources to create completely synthetic still or moving images and transmit them via the Internet to a global audience, perhaps on the eve of an important election, possibly exerting a dramatic impact on the outcome of a close vote.

Bringing this issue closer to home, the broadcast networks in 1999 began embracing new digital imaging technologies, such as those provided by Princeton Video Image, or PVI. This company offers broadcasters a variety of digital imaging tools for creating virtual signage, virtual game enhancements, and virtual product placements. Networks such as CBS, ABC, Fox, and ESPN have begun using these technologies extensively to place virtual logos in programs such as CBS's *The Early Show* or to place a yellow line on the football field during National Football League games to indicate the so-called first down marker. Although these tools are highly effective in a commercial sense, their use has come under some heavy criticism when used in news programming as being an unethical manipulation of reality. When *CBS News with Dan Rather* superimposed a CBS logo in Times Square on New Year's Eve 1999, a number of critics cried "foul," especially competitor NBC, whose physical signage in Times Square was obliterated by the CBS virtual sign.

Radio broadcasters have also employed the new digital tools. One particularly interesting technology is called time compression or, in the industry vernacular, simply Cash, for the money it makes. This technology enables radio broadcasters to speed up recorded or even live programs ever so slightly—unnoticeably to the listener—by compressing pauses and thereby have room to insert eight additional thirty-second commercials into each program hour. Again, this is highly desirable commercially but has been criticized as inappropriate ethically. One New York station, WABC, used Cash time compression in the Rush Limbaugh show—without first telling Limbaugh—and when he heard about it he was so upset he complained during a broadcast. About fifty radio stations around the United States have used Cash.

To date, no industrywide standards define the level of image or sound alteration that is acceptable within the boundaries of ethical journalism. On one end of the spectrum, there is universal agreement that it is permissible to crop pictures or edit actualities (i.e., voice recordings), although not to change a speaker's meaning. On the other end of the spectrum, all journalists agree that creating completely synthetic news events is unethical. It is the great gray area in between where there is no consensus. Is it permissible to lighten a picture or enhance color quality to make the sky look bluer or make a face more visible? Is it okay to show two people facing each other, although they may never have met, as long as a disclaimer below the image states that it has been altered?

In some fields, such as advertising, digital image manipulation is the de facto standard, yet the public might still be surprised by the lengths to which it is done. Should the public learn how widespread digital image manipulation is, confidence in all the media, journalism included, will likely fall, unless journalism as a whole adopts a universal code of digital ethics.

Consider the digital image manipulation that occurs at one well-known women's lingerie company. Nearly everyone probably suspects that editors in digital darkrooms use electronic airbrushes and other techniques to enhance the beauty of the models. But probably few would suspect that a simple digital darkroom technique is used to stretch models about 5 percent in height. The amount of stretching is not detectable by the human eye, but it is enough to make the models look slightly taller and thinner and their legs that much longer and, arguably, lovelier.

Online Content Concerns

The rise of the Internet and the World Wide Web have not only brought journalism online but have delivered a host of complex ethical conundrums as well. As news organizations have poured resources into building and maintaining dynamic and compelling sites on the Web, they have increasingly sought the means to make their Web-based efforts commercially viable. Because Web culture expects content to be free, few news organizations have offered subscription services (those that have tend to be specialized, such as the *Wall Street Journal Interactive Edition*), opting instead for advertising-supported free Web sites. As the online advertising industry has grown, clickable banner ads have become an industry standard. As such, most advertisers want their ads positioned as effectively as possible online, preferably at the top of the screen where virtually anyone visiting the site, however briefly, will see them. Although few newspapers or news magazines would run a banner ad on their cover, many do not hesitate to run such banner ads at the top of the opening screen of their news Web site. Many news organizations that have launched online efforts now operate and staff their Web operations separately from their traditional newsrooms. A 1999 *Editor & Publisher* survey showed that 65 percent of those surveyed maintain separate new media staffs and that 84 percent of those with a separate new media staff use it to create banner ads for their advertisers.[5]

Is this ethical? Is it appropriate to permit advertisers to sponsor selected editorial content, even when such sponsorship might be impermissible in the printed product, where even the slightest perceived conflict of interest between editorial integrity and independence is not tolerated? What will happen to the sacred separation of editorial and business in news organizations in an online world where advertising and editorial are closely intertwined? Will editorial credibility erode even further?

Consider the case of newspaper sites that feature book reviews linked to online booksellers, such as *Amazon.com* or *bn.com* (Barnes and Noble). These newspapers receive a commission when a reader buys a book the news site has reviewed. Very few news sites reveal this to the reader, or, if they do publish this information, it is often buried deep in the site. Is this nondisclosure ethical?

A fascinating spin on advertiser influence on online editorial content involves the Intel Corporation's online "Intel Inside" campaign. In 1998 Intel offered a commission to Web sites that featured its "Intel Inside" logo, with a clickable link back to the Intel Web site. In a scenario only possible online, Intel asked Web sites to slow down their Web sites intentionally by adding three-dimensional graphics and animations and including a message saying that if one upgraded to an Intel Pentium II processor, the site would run faster. In return, the sites receive an even larger commission from Intel.

This very clever campaign takes full advantage of the unique capabilities of the online media, but what ethical issues does it raise? For online content providers, especially news providers, it raises difficult questions about the blurring boundary between advertising and editorial content online. Although it may not have been unethical to make the requested change to one's site, because it does not actually change editorial content, are visitors misled if the site does not disclose the fact that it has been changed to accommodate a request from an advertiser?

What, if any, ethical questions does this raise for the publisher? Addressing this issue is the American Society of Magazine Editors, which issued its guidelines for the treatment of editorial and advertising content in new media, based on the premise that

> the dynamic technology of electronic pages and hypertext links create high potential for reader confusion. Permitting such confusion betrays reader trust and undermines the credibility not only of the offending online publication or editorial product, but also of the publisher itself. Therefore, it is the responsibility of each online publication to make clear to its users which online content is editorial and which is advertising and to prevent any juxtaposition that gives the impression that editorial material was created for—or influenced by—advertisers.[6]

In this regard, ASME lays out a set of new media advertising and editorial guidelines that direct editors, publishers, and advertisers to

- display clearly the name and logo of the organization that controls the content of the site;
- distinguish clearly between editorial and advertising content on all pages;
- label as advertising all special advertising sections, "advertorials," and the like;
- never allow editors to create content for advertising; and,
- put no links to advertising in the table of contents, directory of contents or in any listing of editorial content of an online publication.

These and three other ASME directives underscore the central importance of full disclosure and maintaining editorial control in the online arena.

The Audience and Society

New media present the promise of democracy fulfilled. As the journalist-philosopher A. J. Liebling once observed, "Freedom of the press is guaranteed only to those who own one."[7] Today's Internet and World Wide Web make it possible for nearly everyone to own an electronic press.

But many traditional news organizations that own a press have a commitment to act responsibly; they view their work as part of a public trust. Those who operate a licensed broadcast operation have a legal obligation to serve in the public interest. Do those same rules of responsibility apply to the public at large when everyone can be a journalist, a publisher, or a "Webcaster"? I believe that they do. Not everyone agrees, however. Consider the case of Matt Drudge, the creator and publisher of the online *Drudge Report*, which on January 17, 1998, broke the story of the affair between President Bill Clinton and former White House intern Monica Lewinsky.[8] Although the reporting was done by journalists at *Newsweek*, the respected news magazine was not ready to publish the story until it had done additional fact checking. Drudge, however, felt the rumor was enough to go on. The rest is history.

It is incumbent upon schools and departments of journalism to play an active role in educating the public to act responsibly in creating electronic content and in assuming a leadership role in shaping public behaviors on the Net. If we do in fact live in what former *NBC News* president Lawrence Grossman calls "the Electronic Republic," then it is vital to the health of our democracy that all citizens exercise and enjoy their full First Amendment rights vigorously, yes, but also responsibly and ethically.[9]

Objectivity, Fairness, and Accuracy

The issue of who is a journalist in the digital age also raises what is perhaps the most vexing ethical question facing journalism today. American journalism has held tightly to the notion that three standards are central to a responsible press: (1) objectivity, defined by Columbia University emeritus journalism professor Melvin Mencher in his popular text *Basic Media Writing* as avoiding bias and sensationalism or presenting impartial information, a notion based on the work of Walter Lippmann, noted philosopher of journalism;[10] (2) fairness, that is, providing balanced coverage reflecting all sides of an issue; and (3) accuracy, that is, getting the facts right and representing a story completely. These three standards define how an ethical press, online or off, should operate in its pursuit of the truth.

Increasingly, many argue that objectivity, fairness, and accuracy are not only problematic but may in fact be fostering irresponsibility by limiting the accountability of the reporter to the truthfulness of what s/he reports.[11] In other words, the journalist can hide behind the cloak of objectivity, fairness, and accuracy, without addressing the more fundamental issue of whether what s/he has reported is actually true. In other words, a story may be impartial, but that doesn't make it true.

The rise of online journalism transforms this issue. As new sources of news emerge and as the public turns to an ever-widening array of news sources, the practices and standards of those diverse sources is increasingly uncertain. Perhaps by moving outside the ideology of objectivity, these alternative news sources may help to put the facts into a more complete context and perspective. Perhaps society collectively will then be able to triangulate on the truth in a way that traditional journalism cannot, because of its objectivity ideology.

Contributing to the problem of truthfulness in reporting is journalism's most sacred of holy cows, the deadline. For more than a century, members of the press have been obsessed with the notion that a reporter must make his or her deadline. In other words, a story turned in past deadline is virtually worthless. Why is this? There are several reasons, including the belief that by not making a deadline, a journalist is not acting professionally or not working hard enough. Another important reason is the belief that missing a deadline, especially on breaking news, means that a competitor will likely get the story first. In a fiercely competitive field, this is unacceptable. In the 1800s, before the advent of transatlantic cable and the wireless and their adoption by news organizations, newspapers even used to send reporters in rowboats to meet ships coming into New York Harbor to get the news from Europe as fast as possible.

But perhaps the most important reason, and the reason that drives the others, involves the technological requirements of the analog world. Specifically, newspapers require reporters to make certain closing times in order to make their print runs and be on the delivery truck or in the newsstands in time for the morning rush hour. As a result of this technical requirement, newspapers and other news media (which traditionally view newspapers as being at the top of the journalism value chain), have developed an obsession with making their deadlines. The requirements of analog television, especially with timed broadcasts, reinforce this orientation. But at what cost?

Frequently, deadline pressures have serious negative consequences for the truthfulness of the news. Journalists under intense deadline pressure can make errors, sometimes serious ones (ranging from a misspelled name to a major factual error), have little time for fact checking, and can even get a story fundamentally wrong—all for the sake of making a deadline. Sources may not be reached for comment because of the need to make a deadline. News organizations less obsessed with deadlines might very well be better at getting a story right, although they might sometimes sacrifice getting the story first. But, ultimately, which is more important?

All this is extremely relevant to new media. Although some critics contend that new media, because of the instantaneous quality of the online world, suffer the ill effects of speed even more than their traditional analog counterparts, the reality is somewhat more complex. Online news organizations, especially those that are original to the Internet, in reality have no particular deadline, or, rather, they face a continuous deadline: their deadlines are totally self-imposed. Of course, when news is breaking, the pressure is now even more intense to get the story before any of a thousand (or more) competitors. But on just about any story after day one, online news providers can take as much time as they feel necessary to get the story right before posting it online. Because they don't need to make a 4 P.M. closing time, reporters working online can continue to work on a story as long as it takes to get it right, say, to reach a final source in order to confirm an important fact. Or they can post the story they were able to confirm at 4 P.M., continue reporting it (i.e., gathering information), and then post a revised story whenever they have it ready. This is impossible in the world of analog print media or even in television or radio, where news is broadcast according to a predetermined schedule.

By freeing journalists from the artificial, technologically induced deadline delirium of twentieth-century journalism, the digital age may usher in an era of journalism dominated less by the clock and more by the need to get the facts—and the story—right. This is an ethical standard that rises above the rest.

A Conflict of Interest

A major ethical concern for news organizations is the real or perceived potential conflicts of interest reporters or news organizations might have that would prevent them from covering a news story fairly or objectively. A major potential conflict of interest faces many online news providers involved in covering the world's increasingly electronic financial markets. What rules should govern reporters' personal investment portfolios? In contrast to the analog media and investment worlds, the digital age has brought real-time stock quotes, data, and online trading capabilities to virtually everyone with a computer and a modem. Day traders, as they are called, as well as computer-automated trading programs, make split-second decisions based on narrow decision rules and newly acquired information that they think may give them a slight, short-lived market advantage. Stock is bought and sold on little more than rumors that can circle the globe in seconds via online financial news services, message boards, or email. Moreover, investment decisions of all kinds can now hinge on an Internet rumor.

Consider the 1999 case of the *dot com* magazine rumor. Two college students created a fictitious Internet magazine they dubbed *dot com*, which in Internet vernacular refers to a commercial online venture. Armed with nothing more than a name and a rumor, the two posted an online request for funding and within a day had received serious offers from investors totaling more than $3 million. It was not until news media pointed out the hoax that the hungry (and no doubt embarrassed) investors learned of their error and withdrew their offer (although in today's Internet IPO frenzy a name like *dot com* might very well be worth more than $3 million to some; some popular domain names have sold for more in 2000).

To avoid any potential problem with its reporters attempting to influence stock prices for their personal gain, one leading financial news service prohibits its editorial staff to hold positions on individual stocks. This restriction is among the most stringent in financial journalism. "Editorial staffers are permitted to own mutual funds," *TheStreet.com* guidelines state. "However, if a staffer writes about a mutual fund in which he or she holds shares, appropriate disclosure is made." The reasons for prohibiting a reporter from owning stock (except in their own news company) primarily include concerns about insider trading and profiting from promoting the stocks in their own portfolios via their news reports. Insider trading is against the law (see the Securities and Exchange Commission Web site for more details, www.sec.gov) and is defined essentially as having access to information to which the general public would be denied and then trading stocks based on that information. Reporters who cover the financial markets frequently have information unavailable to the general public because they have access to sources inside companies and others who might intentionally or accidentally disclose some fact (e.g., an impending acquisition), perhaps in the hopes of seeing a report about it in the next day's column that might cause the price of the stock to rise. Based on such insider information, a reporter might buy or sell a stock, making a profit the general public could not make. Reporters might also use their own columns to report on the value of a stock they own (or even promote it, perhaps by interviewing a guest who recommends buying the stock), thus seeing their own portfolio improve.

Of course, there's a flip side to every coin. In this case, reporters have historically been underpaid, especially those working for traditional media such as newspapers. Online reporters tend to make higher salaries, and with stock options and a bull market reporters have an opportunity to increase their personal wealth substantially. Although this does not necessarily make for better journalists (it might even make them worse, although many great journalists have been very well paid; consider network anchors such as ABC's Peter Jennings, NBC's Tom Brokaw, and CBS's Dan Rather, each of whom makes a salary of at least seven figures), it might keep talented journalists working for great news organizations rather than jumping ship to dot com operations where the financial returns are much greater. Prohibiting reporters from owning stock might be just enough to make some talented reporters leave for greener pastures. Besides, maintaining a disclosure policy in which each reporter's stock portfolio is fully revealed may be sufficient to permit audience members to understand where conflicts of interest may lie. After all, is a reporter with conservative or liberal political leanings any less qualified to cover a political campaign than a journalist with more moderate views? Isn't it enough to know what that reporter's political sensibilities are and use that knowledge to put her or his political reporting in context?

Part III

Restructuring the Newsroom and the News Industry

Part III examines the organizational or structural implications of new media. The traditional newsroom is organized along the lines almost of a military unit, with a strong publisher, editor, or news director overseeing a relatively rigid hierarchical organization. Decisions follow a strong chain of command. Online newsrooms tend to be increasingly decentralized and flexible, especially those that are original to the Internet, and they reflect a more experimental and adaptable entrepreneurial culture. Staffs are much more likely to include legions of freelance contributors. Although this gives the online newsroom an adaptable design, it also makes it more difficult to instill and maintain a strong newsroom culture of traditional news values. The boundary between advertising and editorial sometimes blurs.

The entire news industry is also evolving. Competition attacks from many corners, and news providers are not just the traditional newspapers, magazines, and broadcasters. Rather, the World Wide Web furnishes a low-cost global forum for anyone with a message, especially corporate, not-for-profit, and government enterprises, whose voices formerly filtered through a news media gatekeeper. Among the most powerful are the portals *Yahoo!*, *AOL*, and others who publish syndicated news content from Reuters, the Associated Press, and a host of other organizations. Breaking news has become a commodity, and the news consumer can't tell the difference between one provider and another. But what happens to the value added by traditional journalism? What is the future of investigative reporting in a commodified news environment?

Chapter 6 examines the management implications of the virtual news-room, and chapter 7 discusses the challenge of digital television and video journalism.

6   Newsroom for a New Age:
Managing the Virtual Newsroom

Many of the newspapers worldwide that have launched news Web sites have created separate newsrooms for their online products.[1] The advantages of maintaining a separate new media staff include creating a mechanism to generate original news reporting for online publication. In some cases, newspapers that have not set up a separate new media staff have put incredible demands on their reporters, who must now report for both the newspaper and online. People are putting in sixteen- to twenty-hour days and getting burned out.

In the case of the *Wall Street Journal Interactive Edition*, one of the most successful online news efforts to date (at least as measured by the number of paid subscribers: more than three hundred thousand as of February 2000), success has been achieved at least in part by integrating the online and print staff. The forty editors, reporters, and artists are "smack in the middle of the national newsroom," notes Rich Jaroslovsky, managing editor of the *Wall Street Journal Interactive Edition*.[2] They sit back-to-back with the print team.[3] "My geographic position is one that I cherish," Jaroslovsky observed during the "Online News Summit" held in New York City in September 1997.

It is important to get print reporters more involved in the online arena, even if they don't actually report for the online product. Until recently, a surprisingly high number of print and electronic (i.e., broadcast) reporters working even for large news organizations still did not have Internet access from their office workstations. The annual Middleberg/Ross "Media in Cyberspace" study showed that in 1997 almost half of reporters did not have

Internet access from their office workstation, although this situation was much improved from 1995, when only about a third had such access. Nearly one in ten (9 percent) had absolutely no individual Internet access in 1997, although by 1998 nearly all reporters had obtained at least some level of Internet access. In 1999 virtually all had Internet access from their desktops (lagging behind is wireless, mobile Internet access to support news gathering from the field).[4] The slow integration of Internet access in the newsroom was partly the result of a belief that the Internet is not a terribly important tool for the modern journalist. This view is dying, but there remains another reason for the slow integration of Internet technologies into the newsroom: the presence of computer systems that were custom-built for the newsroom with specialized text-editing software that many newsroom managers find too expensive to replace. Some journalists are even nostalgic for the good old days of "XyWrite—the 'GOD of word processors,' as one posting to alt.folklore.computers recently put it," observed Amy Virshup in *Salon* magazine in 1998.[5]

As I discussed in the previous chapter, the biggest problem that arises with maintaining a separate new media staff is that in many cases the line between editorial and advertising is blurring. Robin Goldwyn Blumenthal has written a provocative article on this.[6] She notes that the *New York Times on the Web*, for example, places logos for advertisers such as Maxwell House or Delta Airlines next to the *Times*'s own logo, a practice not seen in the printed product. Goldwyn adds that the *Wall Street Journal Interactive Edition* once partnered with Microsoft to offer users of Microsoft's *Internet Explorer* Web browser free subscriptions to the *Interactive Edition*. Such practices, she contends, raise both a real or potential conflict of interest and threaten the credibility of the news. Moreover, some new media staff don't have strong journalistic credentials (instead, they're experts in HTML, Java, or C + +), and they don't always follow the same standards and practices of journalists found in the newspaper newsroom (i.e., they don't always use multiple sources, they don't rigorously fact check, etc.).

Wall Street Journal Interactive Edition managing editor Jaroslovsky takes umbrage at the allegation that his company's allowing Microsoft to purchase short-term bulk subscriptions to the *Interactive Journal* for users of its browser was somehow a conflict of interest. "The notion that we would sell out our tradition of journalistic integrity and excellence for a three-month marketing deal is just silly," he counters. "Hotel chains move a lot of copies of *USA Today*; is that a conflict of interest?" he asks. "I strongly suspect that objections had less to do with some sort of perceived conflict of interest than it did with many people's hatred of Microsoft; had the same deal been made with Netscape, there would have been nary a peep."

At the *Interactive Journal*, Jaroslovsky explains, the same principles that hold in the print realm apply online, even if the issues are not precisely the same. "The business side has no say over the content of the edition; they have no idea of the contents of any article before publication; it is not permissible to present advertising in such a manner that it can be mistaken for news." It is worth noting that Jaroslovsky was a reporter and editor on the print paper for nineteen years before joining the *Interactive Journal*, and his specific mandate when he was hired to serve as managing editor of the *Interactive Journal* was "to adapt and apply *WSJ* standards and values to this new medium" (interview by author, March 19, 1998).

Rob Fixmer, the creator and former editor of *Cybertimes* (part of the *New York Times on the Web*), explains that his primary objective during his tenure as *Cybertimes* editor (he's now on the business technology desk of the *Times*) was to create original quality content for the Web. "That's a very expensive proposition," Fixmer explains, reporting in 1997 that "if done to the same standards that we maintain for the printed product. Each original story we run in the *Cybertimes* costs us at least $1,000."[7]

When questions or new issues arise as to what is acceptable in the online arena, they come to the news side. Jaroslovsky notes, "If I see a problem — and occasionally I do — I say so. In every case where I've raised such an objection my objection has ended the discussion." One example comes from the area of online publications, which typically link book titles directly to a "buy this book!" page on *Amazon.com*. Jaroslovsky acknowledges that one of the most enticing capabilities of the online medium is the potential to marry information to transactions. "But I think the practice is journalistically unacceptable in this context; it crosses the line, leaving readers confused about whether they are looking at editorial or advertising matter" (interview by author, March 19, 1998).

Building on the notion of integrating the online operation with the main newsroom is the Tribune Co., which announced in March 2000 its plans to acquire the Times Mirror Co., ending 119 years of ownership of the *Los Angeles Times* by the Otis and Chandler families.[8] The Tribune Co. has been turning its newspaper reporters into what it calls "multimedia journalists" and merging its Chicago media properties into one combined newsgathering source. The combined newsroom model will likely be extended to all its media properties nationwide, which in the wake of the $6.45 billion merger will include twenty-two television stations, four radio stations, a range of Internet properties, the *Chicago Tribune*, and now three more of the nation's best-known newspapers, the *Los Angeles Times*, the *Baltimore Sun*, and *Newsday* in New York.

Other newspapers, such as the *New York Times*, have built online properties and have encouraged their reporters to contribute in other media, including cable and network television. The process is breaking down the walls dividing television, newspapers, radio, and the Internet, as well as saving money and potentially increasing quality by creating a newsroom where communication is improved. The downside is that diversity may be decreased, as fewer reporters for any one media company may cover individual stories.

Collaboration

Regardless of how the online operation is structured, new media present an unprecedented opportunity for creating collaborative approaches to reporting. The advent of much-improved wireless communications, such as personal communications services (both broadband and narrowband PCS); improved news-gathering tools, such as high-resolution digital cameras (e.g., the Sony PC-7) or experimental imaging sensors such as Columbia University's omnidirectional camera; and powerful lightweight portable handheld personal computers (including devices such as the ill-fated Newton MessagePad 2000, the popular Palm Pilot from 3COM, or the Visor) combine to give reporters in the field as many computing and communications capabilities as their central newsroom counterparts. Powerful handheld personal computers (HPCs) and lightweight ultrathin notebooks such as the Sony Vaio offer perhaps the broadest and most powerful range of mobile computing and communications services for journalists. Featuring fast microprocessors and multiple communications ports (which can be used for additional memory cards or for wireless communications), these devices put full computational and communications capabilities (in 2000 bandwidth is usually limited to approximately 9.6 kbps, adequate only for text and asynchronous communications, but will soon increase dramatically) into the hands of the reporter in the field. Broadband personal communications services (BPCS) that will be developing over the next twelve to eighteen months will offer the potential to upgrade these services to include full motion video and audio transmission. One interesting commercial development in Europe may point the way to the future of mobile journalism. A derivative of research at Columbia University, the Urban Jungle Pack (UJP) is the first commercially available wearable computer for journalists. The system involves a belt-worn computer, head-mounted camera, and see-through head-worn display for acquiring and processing news information. The UJP was tested Berlin in July 1999 by a consortium of European television producers, including German telephone giant Deutsche Telekom; Avid Technology, a pioneer in digital video editing; ORB (Ostdeutscher Rundfunk Brandenburg), part of the Association of Public Broadcasting Corporations in the Federal Republic of Germany (ARD); Radio Telefís Eírann (RTE), the national broadcaster of Ireland; and Planet 24, a programming producer for Britain's Channel 4.

In standard mode, the UJP streams low-resolution thumbnail images from the reporter to the newsroom. Each frame is tagged electronically with GPS locational data and other descriptive data and is scalable to higher resolution, up to 640 by 480 pixels. The UJP is designed around a portable Linux-driven computer, the so-called open source computer code vying with Microsoft Windows as the operating system of the future in the personal computer marketplace. "The first news story covered using the new device was an annual street festival in Berlin, where the UJP was as much the news as the festival, attracting attention from newspapers including *Die Welt*, the *Berlin News* and Germany's mass-circulation news magazine *Der Spiegel*," reported Adam Powell in July 1999.[9]

Although this is the first nearly complete package available commercially, a variety of other important related tools offer partial capabilities. Among them is the Palm Pilot, an immensely popular handheld computer. Described most often in the press as an electronic organizer/calendar/address book, the Palm is really much more than that, including many other functions, depending largely on what applications the user installs, most of which are available free from the Internet. Among the applications most useful to journalists and news consumers is Avantgo's Palm-based news digest, which permits the user to access full text news reports from dozens of premier news organizations, such as the *New York Times*, CNET, and *Salon*. Also useful is the desktop synchronization feature, which permits the user to synchronize the Palm with his or her desktop computer simply by touching a single button. The system automatically synchronizes the entire contents of the

Palm and all related desktop applications, including Microsoft Outlook, which supports email, an address book, a scheduler/calendar, and an online mapping application from Expedia. In its most advanced form, the Palm VII also has a wireless link to the Internet, permitting it to go online at any time, sending and receiving email and browsing the Web. Here is what one reporter said about the value of the Palm VII to journalists everywhere. "I don't recall the exact moment I became addicted to my Palm VII handheld computer. It might have been Day One when, sitting in the backseat of a New York City cab trapped in rush-hour traffic, I downloaded our escape route from the MapQuest site in 10 seconds flat."[10]

The Virtual Newsroom

The introduction of a commercial device for mobile news reporting demonstrates the viability of what the Freedom Forum Media Studies Center has called the "virtual newsroom." A virtual newsroom exists without any physical boundaries. Through electronic mail, remote electronic access to databases, and the ability to transmit multimedia content via the existing public telecommunications infrastructure, journalists are able to work entirely from the field without ever needing to enter a central newsroom location and to exchange messages, stories, and picture files with editors anchored firmly in cyberspace. In the virtual newsroom, news directors can completely rethink the structure of how their newsrooms are organized. Rather than being constrained by the limits and requirements of analog technology, management can organize the digital newsroom in whatever fashion facilitates the production and distribution of quality multimedia news content. An editor or producer can sit in front of any networked computer workstation and view or manipulate any content on any other workstation in that network, regardless of where in the world those computers are physically located (although security is a critically important concern).

Virtual newsrooms of the future will reduce or even eliminate the fixed overhead costs of maintaining a television production center. Management and accounting systems are available to monitor and evaluate usage and communications patterns on the network. For better or worse, management can assess who is doing what, how often, and how efficiently. Based on such assessments, management can implement revised work or communication patterns to enhance efficiency even further. Such systems can even be automated via artificial intelligence applications to evaluate systematically everything from writing style to patterns of video editing and the use of graphics. Virtual newsrooms can even extend beyond the limits of the news organization to embrace the news audience. With inexpensive digital video cameras, audience members can transmit video content over the public telecommunications network for possible consideration by newsroom editors.

Unlike newsrooms of the past, virtual newsrooms allow reporters in the field to have the same level of access to information, people, and processing power that central newsrooms have traditionally enjoyed. The importance of this development is that it enables breaking news stories to be managed from the field. The best journalism is based on good, shoe-leather reporting, and today it is possible to support such reporting with state-of-the-art technology for news gathering, computing, and communications. As in telemedicine, where an attending physician can use advanced telecommunications to bring in a remotely located medical specialist to consult on a patient's diagnosis or treatment, journalists will soon be able to consult in real time with other journalists, content experts, or sources potentially located anywhere else. This could greatly increase the accuracy of reporting, especially when on deadline, by facilitating fact checking and improving access to reliable information.

Reorganizing the Digital Newsroom

The world's first all-digital newsroom was KHNL-TV of Honolulu, Hawaii, launched on April 17, 1995, as a joint development with Avid Technology. Alex McGehee, executive producer for KHNL-TV, says the Avid system enables the newsroom to "get out of the linear age." The technology will offer time saving and increased versatility," McGehee explains. "If you are editing in a linear fashion, and you want to make a change, you have to redo all your edits. With nonlinear editing, it's just a matter of cut and paste" (interview by author, October 12, 1995).

Nonlinear editing means you can do things in a number of sequences: "You can throw down pictures in a storyboard, add an audio track, rearrange those pictures. This is a liberating feeling for the staff. It allows us to cut various packages of a story for different uses." Notably, the Avid system uses workstations called news cutters rather than digital edit bays. The cutters are tied together by a common server. This enables any news producer to have full access to all news content on the server.

A 1995 study by the Radio and Television News Directors Foundation (RTNDF), called the "News of the Future Project," confirms that a majority of news directors and other television newsroom personnel recognize at least some of the potential benefits of the digital newsroom.[11] More than half (59 percent) of television news directors believe that the new technology can help improve efficiency both on and off air. Only a fifth (17 percent), however, expect digital technology to improve accuracy.

Digital tools make it increasingly practical to work close to deadline, opening up growing possibilities for deadline operations in video journalism. Moreover, in the analog world, the rules imposed by the broadcasting unions heavily constrain the production of television news. Every operation, from changing a tape to making an edit, is performed by a union member under strict rules. These rules simply don't apply in the digital age. In a digital newsroom, any journalist can perform any editorial or production operation on video. Any reporter can produce video and edit in the field or the newsroom, whether on deadline or not. The tools are also increasingly easy to use and soon will be as straightforward to use as a word processor is for editing text. Of course, the consequences for unionized labor in the television newsroom are significant.

Converging computing and telecommunications technologies are rapidly rewriting the traditional assumptions of newsroom organization and structure. Mobile communications, portable computing, and digital news gathering signal the end of the television newsroom, or even station, as we have known it for the past half century. The virtual newsroom, station, or network will be a twenty-first century digital reality. Consider how I am writing this chapter. I'm sitting on an airplane flying from New York to San Francisco and typing on a detachable keyboard linked through a serial port into a Newton MessagePad 2000. The MP2000, an ill-fated entrant into the PDA marketplace, nevertheless represents a fundamental shift in computing, much as the personal computer signaled a transformation in the traditional model of mainframe computing. The MP2000 had the following notable features: a 160-megahertz processor (making it a fast portable computer in 1998), five megabits of RAM (enabling it to run a variety of applications, such as a word processor or a spreadsheet), a World Wide Web browser, email and fax capability, thirty minutes of digital audio recording capability, and a full-size detachable keyboard. Notably, all the communications capabilities were supported through wireless technology, meaning a reporter could file a report without connecting to a phone line. Connected to a GPS receiver and using off-the-shelf geographic mapping software, the MP2000 could act as a universal locator for a field reporter in even the most remote corner of North America, as well as many other parts of the world. Future generations of similar PDAs or handheld PCs will offer digital imaging and video editing and transmission capabilities, all for a price less than $1,000. Of course, not all journalists would want to be monitored wherever they go, but in an age of endangered journalists (see the latest report of the Committee to Protect Journalists), such technology may be a necessary life-saving device. New devices, including so-called proxy servers, are making it even easier to access content on the Web via PDAs, by reconfiguring Web content in smaller packets and easily downloaded graphics files that don't overtax either bandwidth or the limited memory or processor speed of PDAs.

New management models emphasizing communication with members of a highly decentralized, distributed newsroom are a clear imperative of research on mobile journalism technologies. The unsettled newsroom management issues including figuring out how to

- transition to a twenty-four-hour news cycle (this is especially a challenge for new media efforts that emerged from print parent organizations);
- maintain efficient and reliable communication when technological advances have made high-speed and ubiquitous communication the de facto standard; and
- produce effective news packages that utilize the full palette of new media software tools but don't overburden the news consumer with endless plug-ins, downloads, software glitches, and hardware upgrades.

Regardless of technological advances, however, emphasis needs to be maintained on core journalistic values, including:

- getting the story right (accuracy, fact checking);
- maintaining specificity and detail;
- having protocols for making corrections (using hyperlinks) and links to other Web sites;

- using multiple, known, and identified sources (i.e., source authentication and attribution);
- avoiding conflicts of interest;
- effectively using Web/online technologies but not abusing them; and
- integrating software development/programming models into collaborative digital storytelling for an increasingly interactive and nonlocal audience.

Introducing New Technology

Despite the potential benefits of the digital newsroom, there is no guarantee that simply introducing new technology will enhance newsroom performance and news content. Although digital technology has brought us to "the edge of a new era in television news, we're not there yet," cautions Candy Altman, news director for WCVB-TV, the ABC affiliate in Boston. "There is still no single standard for the digital newsroom." As a result, although stations had begun planning fully digital operations in the late 1990s, most were moving cautiously. "No one wants to be stuck with the 8-track cassette of the 1990s." On the other hand, "There is no question it will happen," Altman adds, "in the next three to five years" (interview by author, October 12, 1995).

New technology can produce many unexpected consequences. A study conducted for the Media Studies Center in 1988 by newsroom veteran Adam Clayton Powell III, now vice president of technology studies and programs for the Freedom Forum Media Studies Center, revealed that the introduction of videotape in television newsrooms in the 1970s did more than simply provide an easier way to edit moving images. Despite their claims to the contrary, news directors confronted by the evidence in Powell's study admitted that replacing film with video seemed directly linked to new styles, patterns, and pacing of video edits, what the late Bud Benjamin of *CBS News* referred to as NTV, or the conversion of news into an MTV (Music Television) format.[12]

Maintaining News Integrity

What the unexpected consequences of the digital newsroom will be is anyone's guess. But there are sure to be some. The critical concern is to maintain editorial control and quality while introducing the new system. The technology does not in itself necessarily produce any benefits. Crucial to the process of introducing digital technology into the newsroom is staff training. At KHNL-TV, "all staff went through training courses to introduce a non-linear way of thinking," says executive producer McGehee about the technologies his station introduced in the early 1990s. "We are at the very beginning phase of digital technologies for storage, access and processing of television news," notes new media pioneer Paul Sagan, a cofounder of Akamai Technologies and creator of Time Warner's twenty-four-hour local cable news channel, New York One News. Digital technology "blurs the line between technician and journalist. The journalist will also be a technician. Newsroom managers need to think of ways to embrace this shift without losing their commitment to quality news products."[13]

The Role of Leadership in Technological Change

Introducing technology in the newsroom is never an easy task. It is expensive and risky, and many personnel may not readily accept the new way of doing things because of fear of the unknown and a potentially steep learning curve, even if the new technology is ultimately easier and more efficient and produces a better news product. There are at least three principles one should follow in introducing new technology in the newsroom: (1) include newsroom staff in the process of identifying the appropriate technology; (2) provide extensive training on the new technology before expecting staff to use it, especially on deadline; and (3) provide sufficient technical support.

Despite the best-laid plans, however, sometimes the difference between technological success and failure can come down to one person's leadership. In the case of the television newsroom, the new medium of the 1940s and 1950s, that one person at *CBS News* was Fred W. Friendly, an icon of twentieth-century broadcast journalism. Journalist Les Brown wrote of Friendly that he was "one of the larger-than-life figures in broadcasting who proceeded from a career as a news producer and partner of the famed Edward R. Murrow, to the executive echelons of CBS as president of *CBS News* and then on to become a pervasive influence in U.S. public television."[14] Friendly was the ethical compass and leader not for just *CBS News* but for the entire news industry.

Although known more for its program quality than for technical innovativeness (p. 234), *CBS News* became the first news organization of any type, print or broadcast, to introduce a computer into its news coverage. Under Friendly's leadership, CBS News had a computer running in its studio during the 1952 election-night coverage. The Boston (Mass.) Computer Museum has an exhibit based on Friendly's innovation and features a kinescope of him in gray suit, crewcut, and black horn-rim glasses, tending the machine. "On election night, November 4, CBS News borrowed a UNIVAC to make a scientific prediction of the outcome of the race for the presidency between Dwight D. Eisenhower and Adlai Stevenson," notes the museum's computer timeline. "The opinion polls predicted a landslide in favor Stevenson, but the UNIVAC's analysis of early returns showed a clear victory for Eisenhower."[15] Columbia journalism professor and long-time Friendly associate Steven Sander Ross recalls, "Fred told me the computer got them a bit overconfident. They called California too soon, pulled it back, but California went the way they originally called it anyway. Keep in mind that a digital watch today has more computing power than this thing [the UNIVAC computer] had in 1952." Ultimately, CBS News got it right: they called Eisenhower's victory.

Friendly kept a close eye on technological developments. And although he was a champion of the effective and appropriate use of technology in the newsroom, he knew it wasn't always reliable. "Inanimate objects are out to screw you!" he was known to say. Among his other technical achievements in the newsroom, Friendly was the first to do a transatlantic television hookup, as well as the first to do a transcontinental hookup live. "If the Omnicamera had been invented fifteen years ago [1985], Fred would have been the FIRST user, and would have been smart enough to IMMEDIATELY figure out where to put it to invent a new way to tell a story," Ross speculates. "He also would have poured money into it, to improve the resolution" (interview by author, February 15, 2000).

Who is the Fred Friendly of the twenty-first century newsroom? It's hard to say, and very likely there will never be another producer just like the award-winning Friendly. Yet there is a producer at CBS News today who is pioneering digital technology in the newsroom and doing so by insisting on maintaining the highest levels of journalistic integrity. His name is Dan Dubno, technologist and award-winning producer for CBS News Special Events. Special events are those news events that require the network to break into its normally scheduled programming, such as the disappearance and death of John F. Kennedy Jr. in 1999 or the shootings in Columbine, Colorado, that same year. Dubno is responsible for coordinating coverage of major national and international news stories, including elections, military conflicts, and natural disasters. He has pioneered the network's use of powerful graphic technologies, satellite imagery, visualization tools, and other innovative technologies for news coverage. During the 1996 presidential elections, Dubno produced *CBS News*'s critically acclaimed virtual reality election results with Harry Smith. The next time you watch *CBS Evening News with Dan Rather,* and you see a special report that opens with a 3-D fly-through of a remote region that places the story in geographic context, most likely it was Dan Dubno who produced that coverage.

Preparing the next generation of journalists is a vital step in the process of creating newsrooms for a new age. At Columbia's Graduate School of Journalism, the approach to training tomorrow's journalists builds on the school's tradition of emphasizing the basics of good reporting and writing but adds a new media wrinkle as well.

The more than two hundred students in the journalism master's program are now required to take a course in the basics of new media production and design. Students select from one of six concentrations. Those in the new media concentration take advanced specialized courses in new media journalism. These courses are designed to develop not only a set of skills needed to produce high-quality journalism in a new media environment but also to help students understand some of the critical issues facing journalists today and in the future, such as balancing the need to uphold the highest standards of journalism in an online environment against the need to create a profitable news business in an emerging new medium of communication and commerce. Students also explore the implications of experimental new media technologies for journalism, including how such technologies are used, the nature of news content, and the evolving structure of news organizations. Throughout their year of study, they learn the fundamentals of good traditional journalism but also how to report in an online, networked world where deadlines are nonstop, stories are interactive and multimedia, and newsrooms are increasingly decentralized.

The principle of integrating new media education into the journalism curriculum was best articulated more than a decade ago by Pulitzer-prize-winning investigative reporter Bill Dedman, who spearheaded the *Atlanta-Journal Constitution*'s computer-assisted coverage of racially discriminatory lending practices at Atlanta-area banks, a practice known as redlining. During his fellowship at the Freedom Forum Media Studies Center, Dedman observed how journalists today don't need to consult a resident telephone expert every time they want to make a phone call; neither should they need to consult an expert on computer-assisted reporting every time they want to run an analysis of public records. At Columbia University's Graduate School of Journalism, the same principle holds true for new media. Every graduate is taught the basics of going online, browsing the Web, sifting and sorting through public records, and even producing and publishing an interactive, multimedia report on the Internet.

7   Digital Television and Video News: A Crisis of Opportunity

The Chinese character for *crisis* is a combination of two characters, one meaning "danger," the other meaning "opportunity." Television news is clearly entering a period of such crisis as it confronts the prospect of full-scale digitization: the transformation of analog audio and video into digital form.[1]

Traditional audio and video technologies captured light and sound wave patterns directly on film, magnetic tape, or plastic disk (i.e., the phonographic recording). Digital technologies, such as magnetic or optical disk, sample from those continuous wave patterns and represent each observation in a numeric, computer form of binary digits, 1's and 0's representing "on" and "off," or the presence or absence of a sound or lightwave. Once in digital form, all content, whether text, audio, video, or data, can be seamlessly manipulated by computer. And therein lies its revolutionary aspect. As was made evident in the exhibition hall of the 1998 National Association of Broadcasters (NAB) Convention in Las Vegas, the digital way heralds profound changes in how we gather and report news and information. Key to this future is the all-digital newsroom, now made entirely possible by the appearance of enabling technologies from such companies as Sony, Oracle, and Avid.

A digital newsroom is one in which every component processes information in digital, computerized form. All text, data, graphics, audio, and video are digital. There is no analog content or technology. From telephone to television, everything is computerized. In a digital newsroom, analog or digital video news feeds from tape; satellite or other sources are transferred into digital format. Editors and producers then process that content in nonlinear fashion, cutting, pasting, or manipulating motion video and audio as easily as text in a word processor.

Digital technology makes it easy to experiment with different video sequences and to move back and forth among original video segments to refine the product. Everything from camera movements to anchor scripts for the teleprompter is encoded in the digital newscast. Once completed, the digital newscast is converted back to analog format for broadcast or cablecast or kept in digital format for distribution or storage on a video server or database that viewers access via the Internet or another video on demand service.

One of the most dramatic advances is the ability to create a virtual studio. Systems by Sony, Microsoft, and others offer newsroom management the opportunity to create any newsroom set with the click of a mouse button. Using a live anchor set against a blue matte background, virtual studio software permits a producer to place that anchor anywhere in the world superimposed against a live or recorded video backdrop. Demonstrations at a recent NAB convention featured one anchor magically transported for a "live" report from Paris, France.

The virtual studio permits the incorporation of three-dimensional animation as well. For example, the anchor reporting on springtime in Paris might have a colorful butterfly circling his head, all courtesy of virtual studio software engineering and all completely lifelike to the viewer.

"You can't be sure of anything you see on television anymore," observes Sy Decoy, a senior programmer for the San Diego Data Processing Corporation (interview by author, October 15, 1995). Decoy is himself an accomplished creator of artificial realities, having developed the virtual reality tour of the San Diego Convention Center that helped convince GOP strategists to bring their convention to San Diego in 1996.

Digital newsrooms promise several advantages over traditional analog newsrooms, including:

- increased efficiency;
- greater productivity;
- enhanced creativity;
- greater accuracy, coverage, and timeliness; and
- fully searchable digital archives or news libraries.

A Boost to Efficiency

Digital technology offers increased efficiency by enabling video editors to process video in a single computer environment. There is no need to insert tapes, rewind, or fast-forward. Video is scanned quickly and easily, with the capacity to view simultaneously different video clips in multiple windows on the computer monitor. Productivity can be enhanced through digital technology by enabling news producers to command the entire news operation from a single location. "Digital systems allow for integration and streamlining of responsibilities," notes WCVB-TV's Candy Altman. "I've seen it in radio, where everything's at one desk. It allows people to be more productive at a time when we're all being asked to do more with less" (interview by author, October 12, 1995).

Digital technology can increase creativity by enabling editors to incorporate multiple video sources into a single story, combining full-motion imagery, graphics, and animation from a single networked workstation. With the end of the cold war, digital technology and the Clinton administration's move toward declassifying much government information are also providing improved access to such traditionally secret content as remote-sensing imagery captured by satellite-based cameras some four hundred miles in orbit around the earth. *ABC News*, *CBS News*, and other news organizations have incorporated such digital images into a variety of news stories, ranging from the Persian Gulf war, to environmental stories examining natural disasters, deforestation, or urban sprawl, to archaeological reports on ancient frankincense routes in the Middle East.

The digital environment affords new potential for expanded use of handheld digital video cameras, which because of their lightweight, portable, and inexpensive nature enable television news producers to equip armies of single-person news crews with broadcast-quality video technology. Video can now be captured of virtually every news event. The first video of Kuwaiti oil well fires during the Persian Gulf war was captured on hi-8 cameras, high-resolution (more than four hundred lines of horizontal resolution) eight-millimeter tape video cameras with high-quality audio capture as well. Hi-8 cameras have even been mounted on robotic cameras to monitor traffic patterns and other street scenes and public events, providing twenty-four hour news coverage at little cost. The use of 360-degree cameras adds to the video surveillance capabilities of the media and others (bringing not only expanded news coverage but also new threats to privacy, as discussed in chapter 5). These cameras can also be equipped with motion detection sensors, high-resolution directional cameras, and other smart technology to automate the news process even further. For example, a robotic camera equipped with a motion detector could be placed in a high-crime area; when a person walks into view, the camera would automatically send an alert to a human monitor or begin recording the scene.

Among the most interesting new technologies for the digital newsroom is the flat-panel computer display. The flat panel, or tablet, typically utilizes liquid crystal display (LCD) technology, the same technology used in laptop computers. By 2005 we are likely to see the development of much improved low-cost flat panels, with the resolution of ink on paper, capable of delivering multimedia content, including text, data, audio, graphics, and full-motion video.

Tablet-sized flat panels eventually will be lightweight—less than a pound—and will cost about two to three hundred dollars (some even less). They will offer interactivity through touch-sensitive screens and cellular or wireless telecommunications links and will have ports to allow high-band-width connections to TV or telephone lines, thus enabling television news organizations to deliver multimedia newscasts directly to flat panel devices. In the forefront of experimentation is CNN, which is working on creating video news reports delivered directly to hand-held cellular phones. An even more recent development known as light-emitting diodes (LED), based on organic polymers, may make possible by 2010 the creation of high-resolution, low-power, and even lighter-weight flexible panels that can be rolled up like window shades.

Improvement in Quality

The accuracy of news reporting can be enhanced through digital technology in a number of ways, including the ability to confirm any information from multiple sources easily and quickly. Perhaps most important, digital technology enables journalists to find the best set of methods to communicate each story. Whether through video, graphics, animation, or audio, digital technology gives every journalist easy access to a full palette of communications tools for each news story.

Digital technology can also enhance the quality of the television news product by enabling news organizations to expand their geographic news coverage areas. Marty Haag, vice president for broadcast news at A. H. Belo Corporation in Dallas, Texas, observed in 1996 that fiber optics and other digital technologies make it possible to bring in feeds from many more places than ever before. "You can actually feed from someone's house," he adds, "The idea of a bureau goes out the window." Haag explains that especially in large markets such as Los Angeles or New York City "news managers are constantly making decisions about what areas they are able to cover, and more area is not covered than covered. That may change in the era of digital technology. The one man band might be employed more creatively in some outlying areas, which would provide greater coverage of a more diverse area" (interview by author, October 15, 1995).

Timeliness is improved by facilitating the use of video of late-breaking news. Digital video feeds can be processed in near real time, making it possible to incorporate video moments before air time. For example, a producer can view a news feed received in digital format and simply by clicking on an electronic icon have that video (or any portion of it) fed directly into the on-air newscast, without even having to rewind a tape. This would completely eliminate any technical reason for a station to be unable to cut away in an instant from an unexpected turn of events during live coverage, such as the televised suicide on a Los Angeles freeway in 1998.

Another benefit of the digital newsroom is the ability to create a digital video news archive or library. Once digitized, video is easily stored in magnetic—or, preferably, optical—format for long-term storage and easy and fast retrieval. Storage of full-motion video, however, requires large-capacity storage systems (a typical one-minute news story requires more than 10 megabits of storage). Write Once Read Many (WORM) storage systems now have significant capacity to record video in digital format, with modular (expandable) terabit (one trillion) storage systems becoming common.

Problems in Digital Video

The digitization of video raises at least four significant challenges, or requirements, in the television newsroom. First, there is the immediate challenge of encoding and retrieving video and audio content. Typically, video or audio content must be encoded with text descriptors of the scene or sequence in order to facilitate rapid retrieval of selected material at a later date. This requires an archivist to view all video content and write the descriptions, a labor-intensive process that adds significantly to the time and cost of archiving digital video news content. As I discussed in chapter 3, advances in digital video image processing will eliminate much of the need for human indexing of content and will automate much of the indexing and retrieval of video content, thus reducing cost, improving efficiency, and accuracy when on deadline (in 1999 Virage introduced a system for automatically indexing video, and it is in use at a variety of media organizations, including CNN.com, pbs.org and abcnews.com). Moreover, the indexing will be even more extensive, as computerized cameras will automatically encode each video frame not only with a digital watermark (for later identification and copyright protection) but also with locational information provided by technologies such as the Global Positioning System (GPS). By reducing the cost of gathering news, says Paul Sagan, former senior vice president at Time, Inc., NewMedia, television news organizations can create news products for smaller audiences. They can even provide news products for "affinity groups," or audiences defined not by geography but by their common areas of interest.

A second concern is that storing digital information is complicated by the possible electronic decay or technology obsolescence of digital storage media. Magnetic storage media, such as the common magnetic floppy diskette, have an expected life span of less than ten years but can experience obsolescence in just five. Optical media have an expected lifespan of fifty years but may also become obsolete much more quickly. Solutions to this perplexing problem are not immediately apparent. As a result, accessing records, whether video, audio, or text, in years to come may be increasingly problematic. Unlike the analog days, when records were stored on paper and on other analog media and have lasted intact till 2000 (making it possible, for example, for filmmaker Ken Burns to make the acclaimed PBS documentary The Civil War), future historians, journalists, and others may find their access to historical records blocked by the rapid obsolescence of once-powerful digital storage media.

Third, although digitization removes many of the technical and organizational (i.e., union) barriers to the editing of video, it also raises potentially significant negative implications for television news, as individual reporters come increasingly under pressure to act as one-person news and production crews for cost-cutting reasons. At KGO-TV, the ABC-owned station in San Francisco, the digital newsroom was completed in 1999, at a cost of roughly $22 million. According to Jim Topping, the ABC News senior vice president who oversaw the implementation of the digital system (he is also former general manager of the station), the transition to digital was both a threat and an opportunity. The opportunity is especially great for stations in major markets, which have the staff size, experience, and other resources to implement a digital system fully and successfully. The danger is greatest in smaller markets, Topping says, where inexperienced reporters will be asked to serve as one-person crews, sometimes on major stories that occur in relatively remote, small markets. Topping is rightly concerned about what will happen when unseasoned one-person news crews in small markets are sent out to cover important stories and don't have a camera operator to look them in the eye during an on-camera stand-up and say, "I didn't understand a word of what you just said."[2]

A final issue in the digital newsroom is cost and its consequences for news quality. A video server powerful enough for today's average television station costs at least $1 million, and depending on the size of the station involved and the amount of new equipment required (e.g., cameras), the total cost of a digital newsroom may run anywhere from $10 million to more than $20 million. At KGO-TV, the $22 million digital station included $9 million for a digital video server and $12 to $14 million for the remainder of the needed digital technology. Part of the cost of the technology is being recouped through improved efficiencies of production, but much is gained through reduced staffing. In the control room, for example, a staff of sixteen was reduced to six, saving perhaps more than $1 million a year in salaries and benefits. And because union rules don't apply to digital technology, more costs can be saved by having journalists fully produce their own videos. Further, digital editing systems reduce the time needed to edit news video by eliminating the rewind and fast-forward steps in analog tape; this time saving adds up to real dollars in today's television operations.

Digital technology poses an interesting dilemma for today's television news. Although it is now possible to create an all-digital newsroom, doing so means letting go of a comfortable analog past in favor of an uncertain digital future. For the journalist, the digital newsroom promises help in creating more accurate, complete, and timely news stories. For most television viewers, however, who will likely remain passive for the most part, at least in the short term, digital television may not make a dramatic difference, except perhaps for enhanced graphics and animation and an incrementally greater amount and choice of news.

Digital television should mean much to those viewers engaged in more active viewing via their home or office computer linked to the Internet and

the World Wide Web: they should see a significant rise in their news consumption and interaction with leading news providers. The development of
Virtual Reality Modeling Language and other object-oriented multimedia
authoring tools promises to open a new generation of three-dimensional,
dynamic graphics on the World Wide Web.

In the not-too-distant future, creative news producers may exploit this
opportunity virtually to transport the viewer into the news location itself.
Elizabeth Osder, former content editor for the New York Times Electronic
Media Company and currently vice president for ixL Media and Entertainment, predicts that immersive news reporting will become an important part
of the digital journalist's toolkit by about 2005.[3] Virtual, or immersive, news
may be the ultimate in news reporting. Imagine not just showing viewers
the latest developments in a hostage crisis in Bosnia but actually taking them
into the room where the hostages are being held. Viewers might even be
able to use their remote controls to move around a three-dimensional space
created from real video footage.

The implications of such virtual news experiences are profound. Will
viewers be traumatized by powerful virtual news events? Or will they just be
better informed? Will journalists use these tools to create a better, serious
form of news, or will they simply produce more sensational coverage? We
are only beginning to debate the great ethical and social issues that are sure
to arise from the travail of technological transition. The character of our
new journalistic enterprise will be shaped by how we cope with the digital
challenge and the standards we set for it: whether we see it primarily as a
danger to the status quo or as a crisis of opportunity to be embraced fully.

Part IV

Redefining Relationships

Part IV of the book posits that new media are transforming the relationships that exist among news organizations, journalists, and their many publics, including audiences, advertisers, competitors, regulators, and news sources. Traditional news providers typically have served well-defined geographic communities. Local newspapers and local broadcasters served their local city, town, suburb, or regional market. National news providers served primarily a single country or extended region.

Today's online news operations may continue to serve local communities, but those that hope for eventual financial viability are retooling to serve much larger and geographically diverse communities of interest that may include local citizenry but also larger numbers who live well beyond the local or even national boundary. This shift brings with it profound implications not just for commerce and culture but for democracy, which in the United States has traditionally been based on geographic boundaries, with a corresponding news media system among whose primary responsibilities was the creation of a well-informed electorate.

Chapter 8 examines the redefinition of the news audiences, and chapter 9 outlines the emerging business models for online journalism.

8   Audiences Redefined, Boundaries Removed, Relationships Reinvented

The most important relationship any news organization has is with its audience. It is the economic foundation of the commercial press. Because of the advertising and subscription-based business model of most commercial media, audience size determines the profitability of the news. Yet even more importantly it is the public the press serves in a democracy. Through its role in helping build an informed citizenry, the press functions as the so-called fourth estate, or fourth branch of government. It is thereby uniquely provided constitutional protection in the First Amendment.

But despite its importance, the relationship between the audience and the news media has steadily deteriorated for nearly three decades, as studies have repeatedly confirmed. Furthermore, newspaper readership has been declining since the end of World War II, and younger audiences are showing decreasing interest and trust in television news. Recent events from the late 1990s have fueled even further erosion of the news media–audience relationship. Consider the retraction of a sensational story that CNN and *Time* collaborated to produce that alleged U.S. military use of nerve gas against its own soldiers during the Vietnam War. And what about the much-criticized media coverage of the Clinton-Lewinsky affair, the *Boston Globe* reporter who was fired for fabricating sources and quotes, and the controversial case of another *Globe* journalist, star columnist Mike Barnicle, who appropriated without attribution jokes from comedian George Carlin. In response, one guest editorial in the *New York Times* observed, "Trust is the glue that holds newsrooms together and ultimately binds readers to a specific newspaper and to newspapers in general."[1] (Barnicle eventually resigned his post at the *Globe* after further questions about the veracity of his reporting arose.)

Are New Media Part of the Problem?

What is the effect of new media on the audience-journalism relationship? Some have suggested (perhaps rightly) that new media, and online journalism in particular, are part of the problem. Andrew Schneider, two-time Pulitzer prize winner and assistant managing editor for Scripps Howard News Service in Washington, D.C., observes that computers can be a useful investigative tool but can also contribute to mistakes, especially when on deadline.[2] The rising importance of real-time journalism has also contributed to inaccuracy in online reporting, with some claiming that speed is the enemy of accuracy. Witness the case of the alleged secret service agent witness to the Clinton-Lewinsky affair whose presence was first reported and then retracted the same day by the *Dallas Morning News* on its Web site. Even more dramatically, though having less to do with timeliness and more with the culture of Internet journalism, the Mercury Center published a provocative report titled "Dark Alliance" about an alleged connection between the CIA and the crack epidemic in Los Angeles. The series was retracted after months of attention and debate, with editor Jerry Ceppos admitting the series failed to meet the journalistic standards of the *San Jose (Calif.) Mercury* newspaper, the site's parent news organization.

Three Reasons the Answer Is No

This view, however, is limited and short-sighted for at least three reasons. First, online journalism is in its infancy and as it matures will provide increasingly compelling news content. Journalists will become more comfortable with reporting online, and online news operations will develop the necessary culture and newsroom policies to manage in a real-time, twenty-four-hour news environment. News services such as the Associated Press, Reuters, and the BBC, not to mention twenty-four-hour cable news providers and twenty-four-hour radio news broadcasters have generally maintained quality news judgment and decision making despite a real-time news cycle. These news providers, once called wire services, are also steadily shedding their roles as "wholesale" news providers (traditionally providing news to retail news providers for the general public, such as newspapers, television news operations, and news magazines) and into the realm of "retail" news, providing news directly to the public. Reuters has become perhaps the leading retail news provider in the world, with its news now available ubiquitously on the Internet on portal sites such as *Yahoo!*

There is no reason to believe online news providers won't prove equally successful in managing a real-time news environment. This does not mean that online journalists don't need to maintain a vigilant eye for the truth. If anything, they face an even greater mandate for accuracy and fairness than their print and broadcast counterparts. One study of source attribution suggests that online news stories can significantly increase their credibility (or perceived believability) by including more quotations, or statements that are attributed to a known source, defined as either a person or an institution. In an experiment, Shyam Sundar found that readers of online news stories rated those stories containing quotations significantly higher in credibility than those same stories without quotations. There is no evidence that news stories in print would not also benefit from the use of greater source attribution, or quotations from identified sources. As Sundar points out, "Getting quotes and attributing them to credible sources are essential aspects of journalistic practice, regardless of the medium of news delivery. While the print media publish the quotes as far as possible within direct quotation marks and sometimes with photographs of the quoted sources, the electronic media make elaborate arrangements to record sources for broadcasting. Sometimes, television crews travel hundreds of miles just to get a one-line quote from a source on camera."[3] Sundar also notes, however, that the culture of the Internet may override the need for source attribution. Some of his most recent research suggests that consumers may rate unattributed news obtained online just as highly as news attributed to an identifiable source.[4] This finding may challenge conventional notions of source attribution in online journalism.

Because online journalism and the Internet are in their relative infancy, however, many news consumers are still unsure of the credibility of online sources. Only with time will these consumers become accustomed to certain reliable online brand names. This is no different from the world of print or broadcast media. "There's *The New York Times* and the *National Enquirer*," notes Jai Singh, editor of CNET (http://www.cnet.com), as reported by Paul Sagan in the *Columbia Journalism Review*. "It's the same on the Net."[5]

Second, most online news providers typically hear almost instantaneously via email from readers who find even the smallest of errors in their reporting. This intimate audience relationship places a premium on accuracy. Or consider the case of an online news operation such as *TheStreet.com*, an online news product covering the financial markets. As editor Dave Kansas points out, "The SEC [Securities and Exchange Commission] watches us very carefully," understandably, given its interest in issues related to online trading. Not only does *TheStreet* have the SEC paying close attention to what it publishes, but because the site exists only online, its credibility hangs by a thin thread. Even the slightest slip can mean a substantial loss in audience and revenue (*TheStreet* is a subscription-only service, with more than eighteen thousand paid subscribers in 1999 and growing at a rate of more than one hundred per day).

One notable example of the transformation of the news media audience online comes from the online financial site called *Raging Bull* (www.ragingbull.com). *Raging Bull* features online market news but also has active online subscriber message boards and other interactive news sections. In 1999 online day traders were drawn to an announcement on a *Yahoo!* message board that reported the impending acquisition of the North Carolina Internet firm PairGain Technology (http://www.pairgain.com/index.html). The *Yahoo!* posting linked to an apparent Bloomberg Web page (Bloomberg is a leading financial news provider) reporting on the impending PairGain takeover. Based on this report, many day traders started buying PairGain stock, and within hours its value shot up some 30 percent. Before the final bell at the exchange, however, it was revealed that the PairGain takeover was nothing more than a rumor and the supposed Bloomberg page was a hoax. The stock tumbled back down to just below its initial price at the start of the day. Notably, while it took most mainstream news media hours to learn about the hoax, members of the *Raging Bull* site knew the PairGain takeover was a figment within minutes. A member of the site had conducted his own due diligence and quickly determined that both the *Yahoo!* posting and the Bloomberg site were false and posted a message to that effect on a *Raging Bull* message board. Few if any *Raging Bull* investors were taken in by the scam, which, it was later revealed, had been perpetrated by a net-savvy PairGain employee.

This example illustrates both the perils and the promises of the Internet. It is possible for anyone with Web access and some interactive design skill to create and publish a hoax; it is also relatively easy for such hoaxes to be sniffed out. And the sniffing need not be done by what we would traditionally call a journalist. In the case of the PairGain "takeover," *Raging Bull* members acted like a massive human parallel processor and quickly identified the hoax. It took traditional news media, even those online, much longer. Is this new audience-based publishing journalism? It certainly is if one considers journalism to be defined by the traditional measures of surveillance, skepticism, and speed. The question is, what becomes of sources in such public online journalism?

The online financial news arena faces other problems, as well. Sites such as *TheStreet, Motley Fool,* and *CBS Marketwatch* are in an intensely competitive field, where each financial news site is vying for an elusive audience of day traders, institutional investors, and market analysts. The pressure to gain and keep that audience is tremendous, and online financial sites may be tempted to introduce reporting practices that some find questionable, including providing stories updated every hour, even when no significant developments have occurred, just to keep people coming to their sites.

Third, and perhaps most importantly, online news can provide much greater context than traditional news providers, whether print or electronic. This context is provided in a number of ways, most notably through hyperlinks, or electronic links to other content or Web sites providing alternative views or additional details about a story, subject, or person. Research suggests that this additional context or perspective is of increasing importance to the audience, especially younger audiences. A 1998 Pew Center study shows that news appetites among younger audiences, the so-called Generation X, are evolving because of or with the development of new media. This research shows that 77 percent of those eighteen to twenty-nine say they value the diversity of perspectives they get from online news sources; the percentage declines steadily for older audiences (70 percent of those thirty to forty-nine, 64 percent of those fifty to sixty-four, and 52 percent of those sixty-five and older say they value this diversity).[6] Adding to this, a 1998 Gallup poll shows that news reported on the Internet is viewed as "fair and impartial" by the largest percentage of adults in the United States, 53 percent, a number higher than for any other medium.[7] Fifty-one percent of Americans say local television news is fair and impartial, 47 percent say so about national cable TV news, 46 percent say so about radio news, 43 percent say so about national network TV news, and just 40 percent say so about local newspapers and 39 percent about national newspapers.

Shifting Sands

Newspapers and most other news media have traditionally served communities bounded by geographic (i.e., local, with some national), political, or cultural borders. The Internet is transforming this traditional bounded media model. More than five thousand news sites created by traditional news providers are available to anyone anywhere in the world with a computer and Internet access.

For journalists, this increasingly means a relinquishing of control. The traditional journalist is accustomed to serving in the role of omnipotent storyteller, and rarely in the past have audience members had an opportunity to read many different reports on the same event. This role is best characterized by former CBS network news anchor Walter Cronkite's familiar closing, "And that's the way it is." But since the advent of the multichannel universe and the rise of the Internet, it has become as easy for a New Yorker to read the *New Zealand Herald*'s account of President Clinton's grand jury testimony in the Lewinsky case as it is to read that of the *New York Times*. No longer need audience members accept any single point of view as the full story or the complete truth.

Authenticating the News

A final troubling dimension of the digital age is the demise of the trusted adage, "seeing is believing." Not only has this never really been true (the next time you look at a five-dollar bill, consider the fact that while you may recognize the face of Abraham Lincoln, it is the body of Southern statesman John Calhoun upon which his head rests),[8] but digital imaging technologies make it possible to create completely synthetic and real-looking motion video of events that never took place. Although most members of the U.S. public may not fully appreciate this fact (as may not most journalists), virtually anything can be made to look real on a computer, and without expensive equipment.

One important potential solution to this problem is offered through digital watermarking, a branch of so-called encryption technology that is typically used to lock electronic content so that only authorized people can access or see it. A digital watermark being developed by Columbia University professor Shih-Fu Chang may provide by 2005 an indelible electronic signature that will not only offer copyright protection but authenticate the source of video. After encoding with the watermark, any tampering with an image would immediately destroy the video. Conversely, a viewer could easily check the watermark or signature of a video news report to determine its source and authenticity. Such authentication might be even more important in a digital newsroom where video and other news reports are being filed by an increasingly diverse crew of freelance correspondents whose credentials may not always be fully known.

Why New Media Are Important to Journalism and Society

These new media applications to journalism will produce not just better, more contextualized reporting but ultimately a more well-informed viewer and citizenry. Perhaps better journalism can help to slow, if not stop, the downward slide in media credibility over the past quarter century. In the end, democracy may be well served by the effective and ethical application of new media tools to journalism. But, as I have observed more than once, simply making the tools available does not ensure their appropriate use. Just as the technology to provide live reports from helicopters has produced sensational coverage of a live suicide on a Los Angeles highway, new media tools may be used unwisely. It is incumbent on both the industry and journalism education to take aggressive leadership roles in practicing and teaching the standards and procedures for the appropriate use of new media tools for journalism in the new millennium.

New Media, Journalism, and Democracy

In founding the Graduate School of Journalism at Columbia University nearly a century ago, publisher Joseph Pulitzer observed, "Our republic and its press shall rise and fall together."[9] Print or electronic, the press still carries the responsibility to serve as the fourth estate, or fourth branch of government; to serve in the role of watchdog on government, big business, and other sources of power in society; and to provide the information and analysis that society needs to constitute an informed electorate. This is the basis for the unique protection afforded the press in the First Amendment to the U.S. Constitution.

How are new media reshaping the role of the press in the republic, and how is the republic responding to that new role? The remainder of this chapter focuses on these two questions.

New media are exerting a profound, though perhaps subtle, effect on the role of the press in the democratic process. This effect will become substantially more pronounced by 2010, as the Internet, World Wide Web, and other interactive new media technologies (e.g., digital television, broadband wireless communications) become much more widely and inexpensively accessible to the public.

This new media effect has three basic characteristics. First, civic journalism is rapidly growing via the online media and will become a vital part of the electronic republic of the twenty-first century. Second, public electronic access to information relevant to the democratic process is expanding at an astounding rate, as is citizen access to government services via the Internet. Third, and perhaps most importantly, citizens are increasingly able to obtain via the Internet information directly from political and governmental sources. Conversely, political candidates as well as those with a political cause are able to communicate directly via the Internet with members of the public, without the traditional filter of the press.

Civic journalism is a much-debated subject both in journalism education and in the journalism industry. It refers essentially to a form of journalism in which the press participates actively in the public life of the geographic, political, and cultural communities it serves. Many advocates of civic journalism argue that this is the essential nature of all good journalism, to help improve the communities in which we live. Critics contend that by participating in those communities, journalists and journalistic organizations are co-opted and thereby lose their ability report fairly. In the digital age, however, which side of the fence you sit on may not really matter. Civic journalism is simply an increasing part of the new media landscape.

Championing civic journalism is the Pew Center for Civic Journalism, whose mission is to serve as "an incubator for civic journalism experiments that enable news organizations to create and refine better ways of reporting the news to re-engage people in public life."[10] By providing funding for civic journalism projects, hosting conferences, and instituting the James K. Batten Award for Excellence in Civic Journalism, the Pew Center is facilitating the growth of the civic journalism movement.

One civic journalism enterprise supported by the Pew Center that involved new media was conducted in partnership with the *Record* (Hackensack, N.J.), a respected newspaper whose efforts in civic journalism have drawn much attention. In what is now called the North Jersey Community, the "Quality of Life" project was designed "to stimulate public discussion about the choices citizens face as the region strives to maintain its best characteristics."[11] As part of the paper's strategic plan to achieve this goal, Glenn Ritt, former editor and now vice president for news and information at the *Record*, has helped shaped the *Record Online* into an innovative and important online news publication. With original online news reporting, breaking news coverage, and extensive online graphics and animation, the site offers online readers a thorough and comprehensive news resource. Perhaps its most distinctive enterprise, though, involves Ritt's efforts to promote civic journalism online through the North Jersey Community. With online forums, electronic mail, and links on a variety of subjects, including education, politics, and the region's economy, the community has helped to involve the public actively in issues critical to the future of the region. In many ways, the North Jersey Community is building stronger relationships between the newspaper and its many publics. Ritt explains that the community is enabling area groups to self-publish online. Through the parent company of the *Record*, Macromedia, the North Jersey Community licenses any of eighteen "content channels" (ranging from the Bergen On Line, which provides information about human services in Bergen County, to the United Way and developed using community-building software created by KOZ) to local groups of all types in order for them to create their own online content, organize their members and activities, and communicate electronically in an economical and efficient manner. Since the site's May 1998 launch, hundreds of organizations have signed on, ranging from houses of worship to public schools to governmental groups, to publish content online and thereby make information widely accessible on a timely basis to their members and to the public at large.

There are a number of benefits of this online civic journalism, both to the public in northern New Jersey and to the parent news organization. Among them are increased public access to information (e.g., twenty-four-hour access), a more cohesive set of community organizations (many now have increased contact with other community organizations because of their online activity), and a community moving coherently in the same direction (i.e., toward a more well-informed and better served public). Indirectly, the *Record* receives many benefits as well, including an excellent set of ongoing connections at a wide spectrum of community groups, a comprehensive set of up-to-date community links from its Web site, and assurance that its role as the primary information provider in northern New Jersey is solidified against potential competitors such as Microsoft, with its well-financed online city services.[12]

Ritt said that it is "ironic that I had to leave the newsroom to make this happen, but it was necessary in order to avoid any potential conflicts." The newsroom can't collaborate with the sources it covers, he explains. But it can still benefit from Ritt's online operation. Ritt notes that newsroom productivity directly benefits from the North Jersey Community by improving the flow of communication between the *Record* and the various organizations involved in the North Jersey Community. One reporter with seventeen years' experience admitted to Ritt, "I had no idea there was an office for children in this department [one involved in the North Jersey Community]." She expected her new sources in that office to be valuable in future reporting. The bilateral information flow in the North Jersey Community also extends its newsroom benefits beyond the *Record* and the *Record Online*: the parent company also operates twenty-five weekly newspapers covering communities throughout northern New Jersey. Each of these can access and use information that flows through the online community. Ritt is not just committed to fostering a successful online operation in New Jersey. "My drive is to help revolutionize reporting for the 21st century," he concludes (interview by author, October 12, 1999).

New media are also giving rise to a wide spectrum of opportunities for the public to connect to government directly and to access public information and governmental services. Many resources are available to the public via the Internet (see Rich Meislin's compilation at the *New York Times on the Web*). Among them are:

- The White House;
- The House of Representatives, including *HillSource*, a Web site maintained by the House Republican Conference; *Freedom Works* (from Dick Armey, House Majority Leader); and the U.S. House Democratic leadership page (Richard Gephardt, Democratic leader);
- The Senate;
- The federal judiciary page;
- federal government agencies, including the Federal Election Commission (www.fec.gov) and the U.S. Department of the Census (www.census.gov);

- all major political parties and many so-called third parties;
- various political groups, lobbying groups, and associations;
- general political reference material, including the particularly useful *Project Vote Smart*, which offers current information tracking the performance of more than thirteen thousand candidates and elected officials;[13] and
- news sites covering the political world, including *AllPolitics* (from CNN and the *Times*), *The Netizen* (*Hotwired*'s political source), and *Cloakroom.com* (from the *National Journal*).

Federal, state, and local government services are now increasingly available online, although the extent of online services varies widely at the state and local levels. Among the most developed government service available online is the Internal Revenue Service, which now permits citizens to file their income tax returns electronically and to have their refunds directly deposited in their bank accounts. States with the most advanced online services include California and Minnesota, states with a traditional strength in the new technology industry. Services available online in California range from filing for a business license online to attending the California Virtual University. The Southern California Executive Leadership Forum, a consortium of leaders from the public and private sector, instituted a series of two-day symposiums designed to facilitate the effective harnessing of telecomputing technologies for the improved delivery of government services at all levels of government. A government-sponsored briefing in Los Angeles focused on the use of telecomputing technologies in a variety of public sector areas, including electronic city halls and electronic town meetings.

These increasingly diverse and powerful online government services are slowly beginning to transform the relationship between the government and its citizenry. Increasingly frustrated by entrenched governmental bureaucracy and alienated by the impenetrability of many government agencies, many citizens find it more and more attractive to interact online with government at all levels.

Paralleling this shift toward online government in the United States is a rising level of political mobilization occurring online around the world. Imagine what might have happened two hundred years ago if the organizers of the great Irish uprising of 1798 had had access to the Internet. Near the medieval village of Mullinahone, Irish peasants planned to attack the Norman castle and its occupants at the lighting of a signal fire. But the British lord had an informer among the Irish who alerted him to the plan. The night before the attack was scheduled, the British lord lit the signal fire, leading the unsuspecting revolutionaries straight into an awaiting trap. Having defeated the uprising, the lord had its leaders hanged in the town square to discourage any further revolt. In 1998, by contrast, students half a world away in Indonesia employed the Internet and cellular communications to organize a revolt against their ruler, President Suharto. Facing riots and protests effectively organized through new media technology, Suharto resigned his presidency. Despite considerable differences in the circumstances of 1998 and 1798, there can be little doubt that the new media tools available today helped the students in Jakarta in their more successful efforts at political change.

What are the implications for journalism? In the old paradigm of broadcast journalism, a few central publishers broadcast their message to a mass public. In today's digital media system, access to publishing is no longer limited to a handful of news organizations. Instead, the members of the public—the audience—are active participants in the communication process. Journalistic organizations that hope to remain relevant in this new, interactive media environment need to adapt their definition of journalism to embrace such participation. Journalism must be transformed from a largely one-way discourse to a two-way dialogue responsive to the views and vision of the public. In this way, not only will journalism survive, but democracy will be better served.

Anarchy on Usenet

Writing for Wired, the journal of record for the digital age, Steve Silberman recalled how poet Allen Ginsberg once called the prodigious, sprawling life's work of poet Walt Whitman "a mountain too vast to be seen." Silberman noted that for the thirty thousand people who post to Usenet newsgroups every day and the one million who read them, Usenet is no different. It is everything the Internet ever was intended to be: "a decentralized, chaotic global conversation stretching off beyond the digital horizon, distributed across hundreds of thousands of news servers."[14]

Usenet is a part of the Internet where interactivity and user participation are the core. It represents the essential nature of what Rondha Hauben calls "the netizen," or citizen of the Internet. Netizens may be the future of democracy in the twenty-first century. In Usenet newsgroups, netizens have discussed and debated issues ranging from the possible impeachment of President Clinton to the environmental cause of the Hudson River Clearwater festival.

To date in 2000 *Usenet* has predominantly exercised a form of self-governance and self-regulation that rarely transcends the virtual world. But with increasing frequency, connections are being made between the virtual and the real world. As the Internet embraces an ever-greater cross-section of the public, the opportunities for political and democratic impact are growing proportionately. This online activism may signal a turning point for democracy. Although representative democracy has served the United States well for most of its history, recent decades have seen a troubling decline in voter turnout and other measures of citizen participation in civic life. Alienation is on the rise, and today's Generation X may be the most politically apathetic yet.

Life on the Internet, especially among *Usenet* participants and other netizens, is remarkably different. Activism is rampant, and public discourse evokes the spirit of town meetings not seen since eighteenth-century Vermont. Although some might quickly respond that *Usenet* participants are not the average Internet user—and they are probably right—the spirit of *Usenet* is traveling beyond the network itself. The North Jersey Community, described earlier in this chapter, is not the only example of civic journalism from around the country. Silicon Valley (San Jose to San Francisco, California), Silicon Alley (south of Forty-first Street in Manhattan), and Salt Lake City, Utah, are just a few of the many and growing number of communities where the worlds of virtual and real-life political activism are increasingly intersecting, enabled both by the convergence of telecommunications and computing (what some call telecomputing) and by civic journalism. Although many may not be surprised to see Silicon Valley and Silicon Alley on this list, Salt Lake City may come as a surprise. It shouldn't: by 1998 it had become the U.S. city with the highest percentage of home personal computers, according to research from Scarborough Research of New York.[15]

The cities with the highest penetration of home PCs are:

1. Salt Lake City, Utah (64.6 percent);
2. San Francisco, including San Jose and Silicon Valley (63.8 percent);
3. Washington, D.C. (60.2 percent); and
4. Seattle-Tacoma, Wash. (59.5 percent).

The lowest-ranked cities among the top sixty markets are:

58. Wilkes Barre–Scranton, Pennsylvania (37.0 percent);
59. Louisville, Kentucky (36.3 percent); and
60. Charleston, West Virginia (35.2 percent).

These numbers indicate that personal computers are increasingly penetrating U.S. households, and not just in major cities known for high technology but in much of America. Moreover, as Internet access grows, the role of online communications and online political activism will enter society's mainstream. Consider the results of studies released since 1998 by Nielsen Media Research and *CommerceNet* and by the Office of Research, International Broadcasting Bureau, of the U.S. Information Agency.[16] A 2000 study by Nielsen Media Research and *CommerceNet* estimated that 143.96 million adult Americans used the Internet, or more than one-third of Americans over sixteen. This was an increase of more than 18 million people in nine months.

Combining the results of the Nielsen and *CommerceNet* studies with data reported by the USIA Office of Research, the findings indicate that, as of September 2000, there are an estimated 359.8 million users (age twelve or older) of the Internet worldwide. Table 8.1 provides a breakdown of these users. The greatest number of Internet users reside in the United States (143.96 million), but Internet usage, once heavily dominated by the United States (more than 90 percent of users were in the United States in 1995), is rapidly becoming a global phenomenon. As of September 2000, more than half (60 percent), or 215.84 million users, are outside the United States. Although most are in Western Europe (94.22 million) and Asia and the Pacific Rim (89.43 million), many millions more are distributed throughout the rest of the 237 nation-states or administrations around the world, particularly Latin America.

Moreover, Internet usage and broadcasting are rapidly spreading to all quarters of the earth, not just the so-called information societies. The USIA report indicates that all but 40 of the world's 237 national entities have some form of Internet connection, if only email and the ability to send and receive large text files via the Internet. (Most of the 40 countries on the nonconnected list are African or small Pacific Island or Caribbean states.) Table 8.2 lists the countries with five million or more Internet users in 2000.

TABLE 8.1 Worldwide Internet Users (in millions)

2000 Audience Ratings	
United States	143.96
Europe	94.22
Asia/Pacific	89.43
Latin America	13.40
Canada	13.28
Africa	3.11
Middle East	2.40
World Total	359.80

Source: Various, compiled by NUA *Internet Surveys, www.nua.ie*, February 2000; Nielsen Media Research and CommerceNet, August 1998.

Unlike newspapers, Internet usage is even more popular among younger people. A report from FIND/SVP indicates that by 1998 some 10 million children less than twelve years of age were online and that despite the relative cost of Internet use given children's limited disposable incomes (especially those in this age group) as well as the limited literacy skills of children less than six years of age, some 14 percent of people under 18 were online. The author's children, who at the time of this writing were aged four and five (both prekindergarten), have email addresses and regularly visit their favorite Web sites (under parental supervision, of course). The FIND/SVP report predicts that 45 million children will be online by 2002.[17] Moreover, for the first time in history, television usage dropped among children in 1997, and much of that drop is directly attributable to Internet and other new media consumption. It is particularly notable that among sixteen- to seventeen-year-olds, the teenage group most notoriously hard to reach by adult-designed media, nearly a third (32 percent) spent five or more hours per week online.

Women represent another group increasingly finding the Internet a welcome destination, in contrast to newspapers. Jupiter Communications reports that more than 46 million women were online in 1999, and *NetSmart*

TABLE 8.2 Countries with Five Million or More Internet Users (in millions)

United States	143.96
Japan	27.06
United Kingdom	19.47
China	16.90
Germany	15.90
South Korea	15.3
Canada	13.28
Italy	11.60
France	9.00
Australia	7.55
Brazil	6.79
Russia	6.60
Taiwan	6.40

Source: Various, compiled by Nua Internet Surveys, September 2000, www.nua.ie; Nielsen Media Research, Commercenet, August 1998.

expects women to make up more than half of all Internet users worldwide by 2002.[18] This is in contrast to a relatively recently held belief that the Internet is for males. Blacks and other minority groups are increasingly going online as well, disproving another belief, that the Internet is for well-to-do-whites only. E. David Ellington, founder of a leading black virtual community, NetNoir, forecasts any remaining racial inequalities online will soon disappear, and the rapid rise of his site and its movement toward profitability is testament to his expectation. The journal Science reports that more than 3.7 million blacks were online in the United States in 1997.[19] The Nielsen Media Research and CommerceNet study of Internet usage confirms these numbers, indicating that the largest increases in Internet usage are "among blacks and American Indians and among young adults and women over 50 in the nine months through June 1998."

Iceland is one of the most wired nations in the world in terms of per capita Internet access: fifty-two of every hundred people nationwide are connected. Other countries with high Internet penetration include the United States, Sweden, Norway, and Finland. U.S. Internet penetration has reached 52 percent, up from 27 percent in October 1998. Fifty percent is the level typically assigned special significance as needed to achieve a critical mass or mass market.[20]

The rising overall number of Internet users worldwide is part of a trend that dominated the 1990s without precedent in any other media technology ever invented. Although other media technologies have diffused rapidly in so-called information societies, the global diffusion of the Internet is exceptional. Table 8.3 lists the top countries ranked by per capita Internet usage. Overall, these data show that among the top ten countries, average Internet per capita usage is 433 out of every 1,000. The Internet Industry Almanac projects that the United States will have more than 207 million Internet users, or 29 percent of the estimated total 720 million worldwide Internet users by the end of the year 2005.[21]

A 1997 Internet connectivity survey by Professor Larry Landweber of the University of Wisconsin indicates that the national entities with no international network connectivity include:[22]

Afghanistan	Iraq
Bhutan	North Korea
Burundi	Libya
Cape Verde	Martinique
Comoros	Myanmar
Congo	Rwanda
Brazzaville	St. Kitts/Nevis
East Timor	Sao Tome
Equatorial Guinea	Somalia
Gabon	Syria
Guinea-Bissau	West Sahara

(Note, however, that the Congo and Somalia had both gained Internet service by 1999.) Despite these data, the USIA concludes that the "Internet can supplement international broadcasting." The USIA has traditionally broadcast to much of the world through the government's propa-

TABLE 8.3 Countries with More than Three Hundred Internet Users per
Thousand

United States	522
Iceland	521
Norway	496
Sweden	443
Canada	428
Singapore	419
Finland	416
Australia	394
Denmark	355
New Zealand	341
United Kingdom	327
South Korea	323

Note: These numbers include business, educational, and home Internet users.
Source: Internet Industry Almanac, March 20, 1998, www.nua.ie.

ganda broadcasting service known as the Voice of America. A review of the above list of nations with no Internet connectivity not only reveals a pattern of national poverty but a historic tradition of little support for freedom of expression, as in countries such as Afghanistan, North Korea, Myanmar, and Rwanda.

Of course, despite the encouraging numbers for global Internet usage, overall penetration of the Internet is still quite low in an absolute sense. Of the world's estimated population of 6 billion, less than 50 percent have ever made a phone call, and even if the estimate of 359 million Internet users is correct, that still leaves nearly 5.64 billion people without access: more than 94 percent of the world's population. Although some estimates show Internet penetration reaching as much as 20 percent by 2010, we still have a long way to go to achieve global universal access.

These sobering numbers should be considered in the context of other emerging media, however. Digital television is rapidly developing as well, and by 2010 most of the world's television systems will have been converted to the digital format, bringing a variety of new services to complement the Internet. Combined, the Internet, DTV, and other emerging media will bring a richer information environment for news and information to an increasing proportion of the world's population.

Why Internet Access Matters to Journalism and Democracy

There is a simple reason why these patterns of Internet distribution matter to journalism; as media scholar Robert W. McChesney writes: "Democracy requires that there be an effective system of political communication, broadly construed, that informs and engages the citizenry, drawing people meaningfully into the polity. This becomes especially important as societies grow larger and more complex."[23] As the Internet becomes a vital part of the system of political communication, of which journalism is a cornerstone, it is necessary that the public have universal access to it. If the public cannot participate in the system of political communication, then it cannot be effective.

A Knowledge Gap

Of course, access alone is not enough to guarantee a more informed public. Research has repeatedly shown that providing more information doesn't necessarily lead to uniform increases in the public's knowledge levels. Researchers Clarice Olien, George Donohue, and Philip Tichenor have demonstrated through a program of research spanning more than two decades that the result of pouring more information into the public communication environment is a widely held knowledge gap: those who start out with more information (the information rich) frequently gain knowledge more rapidly than those who start out with less information (the information poor).[24] This widening knowledge gap occurs for a number of reasons, including the fact that the information rich have greater access to better information technology (e.g., in the case of the Internet, even if we were to provide all citizens with access to the Internet, the information rich would likely have faster access through multiple access devices or portals at home and at work or school), more well-developed knowledge skills (e.g., they may know more about using computers and telecommunications or have received greater training/experience), and access to information more well tailored to their interests, prior knowledge, or concerns.

Is the knowledge gap reason enough to resist the development and growth of online journalism? Definitely not. Although some segments of society are likely to benefit more rapidly than others, all groups will eventually gain. Moreover, even the classical media are subject to the same knowledge-gap effect. In fact, Tichenor, Donohue, and Olien have specifically studied the effects of the classical media—newspapers, magazines, books, television, and radio—on public knowledge of a variety of issues and topics. Their research has shown the knowledge gap to widen just as much for print as electronic media, whether classical or new. If anything, new media present a possible reversal of the knowledge gap by eliminating the barriers to entry into the journalism marketplace. In the past, most minority groups were excluded from the publishing arena because of the high cost of starting a publication or broadcast outlet. In the age of the Internet, resource-limited minority groups, whether African-American, Asian-American, Latino, Native American, gay, or other, can publish news products serving a geographically unbounded audience with little more than hard work. Anyone can go to a cybercafé, library, or other public venue; for a few dollars or even nothing—on *Geocities* or a host of other free virtual communities—get a Web site; and begin publishing "the truth" to anyone anywhere in the world who is willing to listen, watch, or read.

Circumventing Media Gatekeepers

An increasing number of political candidates and other individuals and organizations with political objectives, whether acting as part of a major party or from a fringe group, are using the Internet increasingly effectively to reach the public, without the filter of a traditional news media gatekeeper. During the 1992 presidential campaign, a variety of candidates used video news releases, videocassettes, and early Internet technology to deliver messages directly to voters and other decision makers.[25] The 1996 campaign witnessed even more of this, and by 2000 it has become a phenomenon spreading beyond the federal level to the state and even local level. In New York, for example, Democratic challenger Peter Vallone brought his campaign for governor to the Internet through a well-designed Web site.[26] Vallone provided a campaign update, county updates, interactive features (including an online voter survey), and an online voter registration application request form. Although his site was one of the better produced, Vallone's was not the only candidate Web site that enabled voters to access and interact easily with campaign information, without the intervention of traditional news media. Republican governor George Pataki also has a well-produced site paid for by public funds.[27] Of course, the Web is also home to many anti-candidate Web sites that are not produced by traditional news gatekeepers. *Reality Check: A Look Inside the Pataki Administration* is just one of those sites.[28]

One of the most important reasons candidates have extended their campaigns to the Web, however, goes far beyond information dissemination and volunteerism. Many candidates are using the Web to generate campaign contributions. Arizona senator (R) John McCain, challenger for the Republican presidential nomination in 2000, captured headlines in the early part of the 2000 primary season when he raised an estimated $2 million via the Web within hours of his surprising victory over Texas governor George W. Bush in the New Hampshire primary.

Government and Public Response to the Rise of the Internet

Ironically, although not perhaps surprisingly, the response of the government and of the public in general to the rise of the Internet has been somewhat ambivalent. Though born of a U.S. Defense Department initiative and having exceeded probably everyone but Vinton Cerf's wildest dreams, the Internet is seen as a mixed blessing. Although it can give a voice to almost anyone however disenfranchised (e.g., a landmark article on the promise of online communities was coauthored by communications scholar Everett Rogers and a homeless man from Santa Monica), the Internet is viewed as dangerous by many who fear its uncontrollable nature. Public libraries around the country have installed filtering software in an effort to block access to so-called pornographic sites. Governments around the world have taken similar steps to ensure that their citizenry does not access objectionable material.

Freedom of the online press is endangered online by many government agencies both in the United States and around the world. Although the Internet makes freedom much more technically and economically feasible, government's fear of the unknown and uncontrollable has pushed it to impose restrictions. In many cases, the restrictions are meant to protect well-merited interests. A case in Scotland involves what in the vernacular of the World Wide Web is called "the right to link." Most sites provide "clickable hyperlinks" to other sites. These links are often done with the permission of those being linked to and may involve payment of a fee. But many are done without anyone's permission or even knowledge. In 1996 the *Shetland News*, an electronic newspaper published exclusively on the Web since November 1995, linked to the site of the *Shetland Times*, a newspaper founded in 1872, with a printed circulation of eleven thousand, as well as an online distribution via the Web.[29] The *Shetland Times* objected to the link and sued the *News* to terminate its unwelcome connection. Arguing that the undesired hyperlink represented a copyright infringement, the *Times* won its case on appeal to Scotland's supreme civil court, the Court of Sessions. A visit in February 2000 to the Shetland *News*'s Web site reveals links to a variety of Shetland media, including Radio Shetland and the BBC, but not to the Shetland *Times*. Whether and how this case may set international legal precedent is yet to be seen.

Traditional notions of copyright and other intellectual property rights are threatened by the rise of digital online media, where making copies is as easy as highlighting text and pressing the "enter" key. Naturally, those who have invested in creating content or other intellectual properties want to protect those investments. This is an especially justified concern when one examines the data on piracy of intellectual property around the world. The Software Piracy Association reports that although global business software sales reached $17.2 billion in 1997, the amount of business software piracy was an estimated $11.2 billion for the same year.[30] This number does not include the amount of piracy of entertainment and educational software piracy, which may double the estimate. The following list itemizes some of the countries designated by the SPA as piracy trouble spots in May 1998, ranking them according to the level of the problem as perceived by the organization:

China	Section 306 Monitoring
Bulgaria	Priority Foreign Countries
Argentina, Greece, India, Indonesia, Macau, Russia	Priority Watch List
Brazil, Hong Kong, Ireland, Israel, Korea, Malaysia, Pakistan, Philippines, Poland, Singapore, Spain, Thailand, Turkey, Vietnam	Watch List
Mexico, Taiwan	Special Mention

Another technological aspect of the nature of online content piracy is the development of MP3 (MPEG–audio layer 3), originally the digital platform for much pirated music content on the Internet and now an Internet standard for not only pirated but also legal audio content. As a result of the demand for bootleg or shared copies of digital music on the Internet (some via Napster — http://www.napster.com — an alternative enterprise specializing in Internet-based music sharing, using the MP3 format, that is especially popular among college students), various MP3 players are now available.[31] Although there were once large libraries of digital music at *MP3.com*, the online MP3 music field has been drastically reduced to mainly fringe recordings by fringe musical groups that have not found another publisher and the various artists who have signed on legally with *MP3.com*, as other music publishers have sought out and destroyed illegal online copies and distribution of their copyrighted music. (Note that MP3 is the digital music format, and *MP3.com* is a commercial service specializing in the sale and distribution of MP3-formatted music.) Napster (and other similar services, such as Gnutella [http://gnutella.wego.com]) still, however, makes available vast collections of digital music in MP3 format. The outcome of a lawsuit against Napster had not yet been resolved as of this writing, in September 2000.

In response to the serious problem of intellectual property piracy worldwide, on August 4, 1998, the U.S. House of Representatives passed by voice vote the Digital Millennium Copyright Act, formerly known as the WIPO (World Intellectual Property Organization) Copyright Treaties Implementation Act. The act, which is likely to be passed into law in the United States before the end of 2000, will bring U.S. copyright law in line with various international copyright treaties and open the door for ratification of the international copyright treaty.

"Information Wants to Be Free"

Nevertheless, vigorous legal protection of intellectual property laws comes with its own social and cultural cost. The Internet is a medium whose early culture held the belief that information wants to be free. Many individuals and groups have clung tenaciously and rightly to that belief. The Electronic Frontier Foundation (www.eff.org) has taken a leadership role in promoting the free flow of information online yet balancing that interest against the serious problems that may arise when information flows freely, such as protecting children against unwanted exposure to potentially offensive material.

The World Piracy Initiative has gone so far as to advocate computer hacking and other forms of online political activism, with links to late breaking news on computer security and access to information, online term papers for sale, and "deviant" pornography.[32] One link of potential value for journalists interested in a good story is to Paladin Press, whose moniker is "the most dangerous press in America." With controversial publications on weaponry, combat shooting, and espionage, the site evokes memories of the ill-fated 1970s attempt by the *Progressive* magazine to publish the "secrets" of the hydrogen bomb, until a federal judge (appointed by President Richard M. Nixon) issued a prior restraint order blocking publication of the magazine, which had obtained all its "secrets" from the public library. How might the fate of this case have differed in the age of the Internet? The *Dallas Morning News* allegedly ran its story about the convicted Oklahoma City bomber Timothy McVeigh's confession at its Web site not only for its newsworthiness but to circumvent a federal judge's potential prior restraint order against publication of the confession (which may have been illegally obtained from stolen materials) in the newspaper the next morning.

9   Business Models for Online Journalism

Since the early days of online publishing, making a profit from content sites has proven elusive (with the exception of adult-oriented sites). Even without the costs of distribution, e-zines, online newspapers, and online broadcasters have struggled to find the road to profitability. Gradually, that's beginning to change.[1] Claiming profitability or at least being at the break-even point by 1998 were a diverse range of sites including not just niche sites but mainstream news providers, such as the *timesunion.com* (an online spin-off from the *Albany, N.Y., Times Union* newspaper), *Channel 4000* (the first television station site to register a profit), and the *Motley Fool* (an Internet-original site covering the financial markets), whose CFO Gary Hill responds to the question "Has your site made a profit?" by saying in true *Fool* form, "We have and haven't and have."[2]

Of course, some of the profitability that is beginning to emerge is a result of creative accounting. In some cases, for example, reporters are occasionally borrowed from a parent news operation, and although they may be paid for their online reports, some related costs are not included, such as the complete overhead related to keeping those employees on staff. A radio station may not charge its online operation for overhead but only for the cost of a Web master and sales representative. As Peter M. Zollman points out, "What are profits, anyway? Are they return on investment (ROI)? Are they return on equity (ROE)? Or does 'profitable' mean just 'more money came in than went out'?"[3] The Tribune Company views its online enterprises as an investment and does not expect a near-term profit. Meanwhile, Thomson

Newspaper Corp. (Stamford, Conn.) expects all its operations, online and off, to be profitable. Jonathan Sheer, vice president for electronic products, states, "Our whole orientation is to make money. Every site we have within Thomson is, with rare exception, generating a profit on its Internet activity" (interview by author, October 12, 1999). Thomson had a $2 million profit from its online ventures in 1998.

Perhaps more important, many news sites that are not profitable, and even some that had become profitable by 2000, are deferring short-term profits in return for greater long-term profits in the future. Such is the case at *TheStreet.com*, where editor Dave Kansas indicates that although his site is committed to profitability, it has invested much of its revenue to build its online franchise (interview by author, September 6, 1999). Despite this, the site expects to become profitable before the end of 2000. *timesunion.com* is one profitable site that could have been even more profitable in 2000 but is investing heavily for greater expected profits as the Internet matures as a medium of mass communication. Dave White, advertising director for the newspaper and the site, says that his company's online operation believes that greater profits will come from investing in making an even better product journalistically. Just as with the newspaper parent, quality content brings more "eyeballs," and this attracts more advertising dollars. The site is making a substantial investment of resources in 1999 and 2000, such as hiring more editorial and advertising staff, which may raise costs in the short run but will increase revenues down the road. Reflecting the overall quality of the site, *timesunion.com* received the 1999 Newspaper Association of America Digital Edge Award for the best online newspaper in its circulation class, between 75,000 and 150,000.[4]

Profitable Sites

An increasing number and range of sites are turning the corner to long-term financial viability in 2000, including the *Fort Worth Star-Telegram*; the *Hartford Courant*; HomeArts (a Hearst new media offering; Hearst is also the parent organization that owns the *Albany Times Union* and its profitable online operation); *Internet Broadcasting System*, which delivers WCCO's online *Channel 4000*, among others; and KLAS-TV8's Las Vegas Online operation, which brings the television station's newscasts live over the Internet via

RealPlayer, as well as original Internet informational content, such as a Las Vegas business guide, a relocation guide, and information on alternative culture in Las Vegas (this last is very well done, in fact, with a wide variety information available, including local alternative media, local music, and Las Vegas related "weirdness").[5] This transition to profitability reflects a number of developments, including the continuing evolution of the Internet as a medium of mass audience (drawing more advertising dollars), the increasing availability of low-cost bandwidth (enabling more multimedia and interactivity), and the maturation of online news products that are more fully adapted to the unique characteristics and capabilities of the online environment.

Perhaps the most well-known site to turn the corner to profitability by 2000 is *CNN.com* (the online edition of CNN).[6] Mark Bernstein, vice president and general manager of *CNN.com*, reports the site has shown periods of profitability in the past and was in the black in 1999. Quality original content is one of the hallmarks of the site and has been instrumental in drawing traffic and advertisers. *CNN.com* produced more than forty-five special sections in 1997, 1998, and 1999. Many of these sections expanded on content produced for television, and many featured unique interactive elements possible only online. *CNN.com* has even introduced a new staff position—interactive producer—charged with developing interactive components to complement original online content. Examples include interactive maps and an interactive "Quick Vote" template that can be used in a variety of stories where content producers want to engage readers more fully. For example, on August 3, 1998, the site featured a "Quick Vote" on whether Puerto Rico should remain a U.S. commonwealth, become a U.S. state, or declare independence. A related story examined how Puerto Rican lawmakers are considering legislation on the island's future. The site is also now available in multiple languages, including Portuguese, Spanish, and Swedish.

One of the most interesting public affairs news sites to return a profit is the *National Journal's Cloakroom.com*. As a members-only site, *Cloakroom* uses a rich blend of multimedia and interactive tools to cover the political scene and campaigns in the United States. Publisher Dan Solomon says the site is "one of the best-kept secrets in new media" (interview by author, May 18, 1999). Founded in 1997, the site had begun making a profit by 1999 and continues to do so through a combination of revenues from subscriptions and advertising. *Cloakroom's* "Ad Spotlight" illustrates the site's content strategy. Offering an online guide to political and issue advertisements from throughout the United States, "Ad Spotlight" combines reporting and analysis with digital video of recent political ads (via RealPlayer video and audio), enabling members to view the ads themselves, read accompanying news reports and analysis, and make up their own minds as to the state of the campaign in a context much richer than traditional media can provide.

A third example of the growing profitability of online sites is *NetNoir Online*, the leading black interactive online community.[7] E. David Ellington, *NetNoir*'s cofounder, president, and CEO, has built the site to near profitability in 2000 through a combination of e-commerce, advertising supported free channels, including black-oriented news, and a members-only Club NetNoir.

One of the most closely watched sites, the *Wall Street Journal Interactive Edition*, is not profitable just yet but expects to hit black ink by 2000.[8] Tom Baker, general manager of the *Interactive Edition*, says that subscriptions are the cornerstone of the site's revenue, with more than 300,000 paying subscribers, but the site generates an equal amount of revenue from advertising. Other revenue sources, such as transactional streams, are inconsequential at this point. The site features more than fifty journalists on the news side and produces an extensive amount of original content.

The July 19, 1999, issue of Media Industry News's *New Media Report* noted that *Consumer Reports Online* now rivals the *WSJ Online* in paid subscribers, with 310,000, and is gaining 1,000 per day. This suggests that having unique, valuable content is something people are willing to pay for online. *New Media Report* also notes that the most popular online newspaper content is local news (72 percent of those surveyed by EDITOR & PUBLISHER); weather (40 percent), national news (39 percent), and classifieds (38 percent) are a distant second, third, and fourth.

These sites represent the beginning of a trend that is likely soon to extend well beyond the borders of U.S.-based online news operations. As connectivity and low-cost bandwidth grow around the world, advertisers, subscribers, and less-developed transactional models will support quality online news content. Sites that establish a tradition of publishing quality original news content based on the unique capabilities of the online environment (e.g., combining text, interactivity, digital audio, and video delivered in increasingly high quality) will see an increasingly profitable road ahead. Research suggests this may be fast coming. The 1998 edition of the Middleberg/Ross

"Media in Cyberspace" study revealed several notable trends in online content. Some of the most relevant follow:

- Original content being published online has seen significant growth. In 1996 only 7 percent of newspapers with Web sites said 50 percent or more of their sites' content was original and not appearing in their print versions. Today, more than 20 percent of newspapers with Web sites said original content made up at least 50 percent of their online offering.
- For magazines, 48 percent said their Web sites are at least 50 percent original, up from 17 percent in 1996.
- The trend for online scoops continues. This year more than one-third of publications' Web sites scoop their corresponding print products, at least sometimes.
- The growth of online publishing is tremendous. More than half of responding journalists indicate they use the Web to distribute news. Fifty-five percent say their publication, or portions of it, were online by 1998. That is double the 25 percent reported in 1995. Only 9 percent of respondents say their publications have no plans to go online.[9]

The 1999 Middleberg/Ross study of broadcast media in cyberspace adds these findings regarding the state of online news content at local television stations:

- A quarter of local broadcast stations have Web sites, but less than 15 percent publish news online.
- Of those with news, 85 percent of the content is produced from within the local market of the station with the rest provided by a parent company, typically a network.
- Site visitors to local television news–oriented sites numbered an average 50,000 a week, three times the number of visitors received in 1998. Network-level sites such as *CNN.com* and *MSNBC.com* get millions of visitors a day.[10]

As a whole, these results indicate that most online news providers are committed to publishing original news content online. This is a critical part of the foundation for an online news business.

Online Classifieds

One of the greatest challenges and opportunities for the online news enterprises spawned by newspapers is to create an effective online classified advertising business. If they don't, new competitors will, and by 1999 many had begun to do so. Among those competitors are Microsoft's *CarPoint.com*, *rent.net*, and *classifieds.yahoo.com*, all of which feature national online classified advertising services that are far more efficient than traditional paper-based classified advertising. *CarPoint* offers online shoppers research, prices, reviews, and more on new and used cars of all makes and models and is fully customizable. *Rent.net* is a national rental and relocation service, and *classifieds.yahoo.com* offers classifieds on just about everything, from autos to groceries, computers to dating, tickets to employment. As portal sites such as *Yahoo!* and *MSN* draw increasing traffic, local and national news providers, who historically have owed much of their value to classified advertisers to their own audience traffic, are quickly losing all competitive edge. And since classifieds traditionally provide newspapers with a major profit center (roughly 40 percent of newspaper revenues and 50 percent of newspaper profits come from classifieds), newspapers have a great incentive to become competitive in the classified arena. Unfortunately, few newspaper Web sites have developed a significant online classified service. *Cars.com* is one venture linking some sixty-two newspapers in an online classified venture to sell cars in competition with *CarPoint*. Unfortunately, the site is not yet a major portal for Internet traffic. Real estate is another major area of online commerce. Established online brands include Microsoft's, "whose recently launched HomeAdvisor seeks to be a one-stop source for everything related to home sales," reports Dylan Tweney (personal email, April 1999). "HomeAdvisor is a remarkably well-designed, well-organized site, and it provides a wealth of information for prospective buyers, including financing information, local home sale information, and general guides for getting started and understanding the language of real estate."[11] Properties for *HomeAdvisor* are culled from the Multiple Listing Service (MLS), the exclusive property database used by all real estate agents that provides information on all the houses for sale in a particular area, including a description of each property, its location, asking price, and pictures.

A new Internet startup real estate venture is called the *Owners' Network* (formerly, *Abele Owners' Network*).[12] Although it doesn't feature the MLS database, it offers one major advantage over traditional realtor services, including HomeAdvisor: no 6 percent realtor's commission. Of course, "for sale by owner" properties also share that advantage. But what they don't share is the considerable traffic of qualified buyers *Owners'* can draw to a real estate advertisement. In 1999 *Owners'* contained some 200,000 property listings, all of which were available at no charge to anyone with Internet access. Moreover, a seller can get a listing without pictures for free and pay just $65 to $115 for packages that include online pictures and "for sale" yard signs.

An interesting spin-off from online classifieds is the online auction. A variety of newspapers, such as the *Hartford (Conn.) Courant* and the *Los Angeles Times,* are attempting to launch online auctions where everything from airline tickets to Beanie Babies is being sold to the highest bidder. As Martha L. Stone points out, the "competition is fierce in this nascent segment of the online industry."[13] One leading competitor, *eBay.com* of San Jose, California, had auctioned more than 30 million items and was auctioning 2.585 million items in 1,687 categories at 2 P.M. EST, August 17, 1999. The site draws more than 1.5 *billion* page views each month. Few newspapers can match this traffic (as of August 1999).

Perhaps most important to the long-run financial viability of online news sites is the development of not only subscription and advertising revenues but also electronic commerce and content syndication opportunities. Whether in the form of online sales (of merchandise and services) or Web-enabled sales (e.g., where a Web promotion leads to an off-line sale), e-commerce is a rapidly growing part of the online business model. Many sites are also using a growing network of e-commerce partners to develop revenue streams. For online news providers, these partners may be either other news providers or other companies seeking greater traffic to their own sites.

One newspaper site that has made significant progress in developing on-line revenue streams, including online classifieds, is the *timesunion.com* (Albany, N.Y.). The site was the first newspaper-based site to publish its region's MLS for real estate sales and was among the first to offer auto dealers' classifieds online, notes Dave White, advertising director for the site (interview by author, May 15, 1998). Importantly, the site links its online and print classifieds, so that virtually every print classified sale brings additional dollars to the site. When the site launched its classified services, the newspaper's classified rates went up some 10 to 15 percent because of the additional audience delivered online. The site is also looking to extend its online franchise by partnering with *Zip2* to deliver online Yellow pages.[14] White sees e-commerce as another important future revenue source for the online operation, although it is not significant yet. For now, the site brings in modest revenues from selling access to its online archives.

An important dimension of online advertising that had found a niche by 1999 is the online banner ad. Banner ads (an advertising graphic, typically a GIF file format, linked to an associated advertiser's product site, measured in pixels; major portal site *Lycos* defines the size as 468 pixels—a pixel is a picture element—wide by 60 pixels high and limits file sizes to 7.5 kilobits) are frequently placed in prominent positions on news sites. In August 1998, however, Internet usability analyst Jakob Nielsen, formerly of Sun Micro-systems, concluded that banner ads are not working and are likely to disappear in the not-too-distant future.[15] Nielsen says advertisers are increasingly disappointed with the results they get from banner ad campaigns and will likely migrate their online campaigns to the realm of micropayments: pay-per-view content, an increasingly important area of e-commerce, where viewers will pay a very small fee for the content they access. This is especially likely to prove important in areas of high-value content, such as financial and sports reporting, where timeliness considerations place an urgency on access.

Not all are convinced of the potential of micropayments. One is commentator Dylan Tweney, who writes, "Micropayments are awkward and annoying. Besides, there's very little content that consumers are willing to pay for, apart from financial data and dirty pictures. Ads will become more ubiquitous on Web sites. They'll take up more space, and start appearing in new locations—such as alongside and in between paragraphs of content, where they'll impinge on readers' consciousness to a greater degree" (personal email, April 1999).

Glossary of Online Advertising

A brief but useful glossary of online advertising terms is provided by Dr. Ralph F. Wilson of *Web Marketing Today*:[16]

Banner ad   An ad graphic, usually a GIF image,
                             measured in pixels.

Click	When a visitor clicks his or her mouse on a banner ad, the visitor is automatically transported to the advertiser's Web page.
Click rate	The percentage of visitors who click on a banner ad.
Click throughs	The number of people who click on a banner ad and get to the advertiser's Web site.
CPM	The cost per thousand impressions or page views.
Hits	A fuzzy term meaning number of files downloaded.
Page impressions or page views	The number of visitors who view a page or a banner ad on that page.
Raw hits	The number of files downloaded, using a combination of graphic images and HTML pages. To be accurate one must subtract the images, which may account for five out of six raw hits.

Why Profitability Matters to Journalism

The news business has traditionally been one of the most profitable in the United States. It is one reason so many leading news organizations and journalists have been able to stand firmly behind their principles of free speech. Without a healthy bottom line, it is much harder to commit extensive resources to serious investigative reporting and quality content, whether online or off. It is similarly difficult to withstand the pressure of advertising boycotts and other tactics media sponsors use to object to the intense spotlight of critical reporting. In many ways, the key to the future of online journalism rests at least as much on the development of a successful business model as it does on the growth of quality online news content.

In that context, it is also important to recognize that profitability for most online news operations may be many years off, even for sites that satisfy all the criteria and standards of excellence for journalism, either online or off. There are several reasons for this. First, despite the wide growth of the Internet, a majority of people in the United States still lack Internet access at home (as reported in chapter 8, in 2000 only 52 percent of U.S. citizens had access to the Internet). Second, the business model for online publishing is still taking shape, as are the rules for publishing online content, and it is unrealistic to expect most online news ventures to have struck upon a workable profit model at this stage. Finally, and perhaps most important, it is critical to recognize that not only are online news ventures new businesses selling new products but the entire medium of the Internet is less than a decade old (as a medium of public communication). Compare this to the case of *USA Today*, a newspaper introduced in 1984. *USA Today* was a new entrant in a medium three hundred years old. The basic business model was already established. Yet it took *USA Today* ten years to become profitable. Today, however, it is not only one of the Gannett Company's most profitable newspapers (out of eighty some in all) but one of the most profitable newspapers in the world (with annual double-digit profit margins). It is also increasingly respected for the integrity and quality of its news content, and this was not always the case (remember "McNuggets," the unflattering term used to allude to the brief news items common to early editions of the paper). Had newspaper mogul Al Neuharth (the founder of *USA Today* and then chairman of the Gannett Company; more recently chairman of the Freedom Forum) not stood behind his creation, pumping millions each year into the new paper, *USA Today* would never have matured into the quality, profitable newspaper (and news site) that it is today. Against this backdrop, how can anyone realistically expect online newspapers to return a profit in less than a decade?

Part V

Implications for the Future:
The Telecommunications Act,
Intelligent Agents, and Journalism
Practice and Education

This section of the book speculates on the future of journalism and journalism education in the context of emerging technology. It suggests that the changes in journalism are only beginning and that regulatory changes and emerging artificial intelligence tools will exert subtle but profound influences on the nature of journalism in the twenty-first century. Leadership must come from both the industry and the academy if the fourth estate, journalism, is to continue to serve democracy effectively.

Chapter 10 provides a detailed discussion of the long-term consequences of the Telecommunications Act of 1996 for the future of news, both in traditional and new media environments. Chapter 11 outlines the implications of intelligent agent technology for journalism in the twenty-first century. Chapter 12 examines the preparation of the next generation of journalists, and chapter 13 reviews the prospects for employment in online journalism. Finally, an afterword offers speculation on the evolving role of the journalist in an age of ubiquitous information provided by a wide-ranging set of news and content providers, many of whom may be seeking influence in the court of public opinion but may be largely indistinguishable to the public.

10 Long-Term Consequences of the Telecommunications Act of 1996: New Rules of the Game

> Congress shall make no law abridging freedom of speech or of the press.
> —First Amendment to the U.S. Constitution

Journalists in the United States have historically enjoyed an elevated professional status: theirs is perhaps the only job offered explicit legal protection in the Constitution of the United States. But this protection has primarily protected the speech of journalists who write for products printed on paper. Although the terms *speech* and *press* have been generally interpreted by judges and legal scholars to extend beyond the printed word, electronic media have always enjoyed a much lower level of legal protection and have been subject to direct content regulation by the congressionally mandated Federal Communications Commission (FCC).[1]

As the nation's system of communication has become more and more electronic, journalism is increasingly being subjected to real and potential legal restrictions, both by governmental agencies in the United States and around the world. As Lawrence K. Grossman, former president of *NBC News* and PBS, has observed, "Each new information technology has received less constitutional protection than its predecessors. It's as if the First Amendment has had to be reinvented for every new medium."[2] This chapter examines the evolution of the twenty-first-century legal framework to regulate electronic communications, including journalism, in the United States and around the world.

Federal Telecommunications Law

For more than half a century, the world of electronic communications in the United States was defined by a simple premise of the 1934 Communications Act: broadcasters were licensed to serve in the public interest, convenience, and necessity. Although the 1934 act articulated a variety of rules regarding broadcast station ownership, telephony, and other aspects of the communications industry, it was the emphasis on the public interest that drove much of the twentieth century's communications world.

Broadly speaking, public interest was defined in terms of providing universal service. Through their use of public airwaves and public rights-of-way for laying telephone lines, broadcasters and telephone companies had a federal mandate to provide service at a reasonable and fair cost to all Americans. For individual station owners, public interest translated into serving the needs of each broadcaster's community and providing a steady diet of public affairs programming (i.e., news). It was a requirement for license renewal.

How will this world change in the next decade and beyond in the wake of the first rewrite of an act written during the Depression? How will television programming change, especially news and public affairs? What will be the effect on competition in the broadcast and electronic news industry in general? How will consumer access to video and other online news and information change?

I propose that programming, competition, and consumer access will change dramatically, but not necessarily in the expected fashion. Never perfect, video programming will become more diverse and interactive. Viewers will gain some control over violent and sexual programming, but the promise of the so-called violence chip, or v-chip, will be more hype than reality, at least for the next decade. Perhaps more importantly, an increasing proportion of programming will come from the advertisers, public relations, and corporate sources who today produce video news releases and tomorrow will program "news" directly to viewers without the need to go through a traditional news programmer (such as a network news division) or television station. Most troubling, however, is the failure that is likely to occur in opening up public records to the public via the online media, especially the Internet and World Wide Web.

As expected, U.S. news companies will become more competitive in the international arena. More significantly, however, mergers, acquisitions, and

alliances across telecommunications, computer, and traditional media industries will propel the formation of an oligarchy in video news programming. Within a decade we will see a cartel of about half a dozen major
providers of video news programming dominate the U.S. and international
markets. The Cable News Network is a dominant player in this arena.

Consumer access to video and interactive news programming will increasingly come via full-service communication providers, such as the Walt
Disney Company, which not only produces popular children's programming
but also the number-one-rated network newscast for much of the 1990s, *ABC
Evening News with Peter Jennings*. Consumers will care (or at least know)
less about who provides the service (e.g., television broadcaster, cable service
provider, or telephone company) and more about the quality of the programming they receive. Unfortunately, consumers will see an increasing
portion of their disposable income go to paying for an increasingly expensive
communications bill each month (more than one hundred dollars a month
for the average home by 2000). This will drive a growing wedge between
the information haves and have-nots in the United States. This is a significant component of the threat increasingly expensive, corporate media pose
to democratic societies in the twenty-first century. Media scholar and critic
Robert W. McChesney brilliantly articulates this problem in his landmark
book *Rich Media, Poor Democracy: Communication Politics in Dubious
Times*. Despite much conventional wisdom to the contrary, McChesney argues persuasively that the Internet will not "set us free." Rather, Internet
content will be subject to the same corporate control and consolidation that
exists in the "real world."

> Aside from the notion of Internet content per se, the notion that the
> Internet is a democratic medium—that it will remain or become avail-
> able to the public on anything close to egalitarian terms—seems du-
> bious at best. A market-driven digital communications system seems
> just as likely to accentuate widening class divisions as to lessen them.
> In the eighteenth century, Thomas Paine wrote that "The contrast of
> affluence and wretchedness continually meeting and offending the
> eye, is like dead and living bodies chained together." In the digital
> age, the affluent can increasingly construct a world where the
> wretched are unchained and out of sight—a communication world
> similar to the gated residential communities to which so many millions
> of affluent Americans have fled in the 1990s.[3]

Democracy depends on relative equality among all citizens, at least in their access to information. If the Internet fails in this regard, then journalism online cannot hope to provide a significant countervailing force.

Transforming Programming and Production

More than one hundred pages in length, the complex Telecommunications Act of 1996 raises a variety of issues that affect not just the structure of the communications industry and how it is regulated but the nature of news programming and production, as well. The act permits and promotes direct competition among all telecommunications providers, including terrestrial broadcasters, direct broadcast satellite providers, mobile communication services, cable providers, and the regional Bell telephone companies. Further, the act specifically targets two forms of programming: violent or sexual programming and interactive services. It also opens up new opportunities in radio station ownership, and this has produced a series of mergers and acquisitions at a record pace since 1996. Most important, however, the next decade will see a rapid rise in the production and direct-to-home delivery of video programming, including news and information, created not by traditional programming providers but by corporate organizations, advertisers, direct marketers, public relations firms, and even political strategists, all interested in reaching the U.S. and international markets directly, without going through the traditional news programming gateway. Increased channel capacity, increased bandwidth availability, and the growth of video delivery through multiple media are all driving this shift, which is directly fueled by the provisions of the Telecommunications Act, which not only remove competitive barriers across industries but support the development of new video services.

Fostering competition or building a cartel?　　Although reaffirming the licensing requirement of broadcasters to serve in the public interest, convenience, and necessity (see section 203), the 1996 act is designed foremost to foster competition and to increase the competitiveness of U.S. players in the international arena. The preamble of the act states that it is intended "to promote competition and reduce regulation in order to secure lower prices and higher quality services for American telecommunications consumers and encourage the rapid deployment of new telecommunications technologies."[4]

Will this be achieved? Yes, but not without a cost. U.S. companies will become more competitive in the international arena. New telecommunications technologies will continue their rapid diffusion in the marketplace. At the same time, however, there will be a major increase in the concentration of ownership, not just among program providers but especially among those who own the media of delivery. And where merger and acquisition do not drive concentration, cross-industry alliances will drive the formation of new media cartels. The act puts no limit on the number of television stations a single person or organization may own in the United States, as long as the combined reach is no more than 35 percent of U.S. households. This, too, will spur greater concentration of ownership. Moreover in 1999 the FCC ruled that for the first time a single company may own two television stations in a single market, perhaps increasing the potential for profitability (through greater economies of scale) but absolutely decreasing the level of local competition and diversity in news and other forms of programming. As a result of these regulatory, economic, and technological trends, observers Eli Noam and Robert N. Freeman point out, we are witnessing unprecedented programming diversity (including news and public affairs) at the national level and ever-dwindling diversity at the local level.[5]

Further, we are witnessing in 2000 a major shakeout in the new media industry, with bigger players taking control, such as AOL's proposed acquisition of Time Warner, Viacom's acquisition of CBS, AT&T's acquisition of the broadband Internet service @Home as well as the well-known Web browser Netscape, and the acquisition of Continental Cablevision by U.S. West, which will enable a major Bell company to take advantage of complementary core competencies, including packet switching, high bandwidth, ubiquitous service, and video programming. The act enables this development by permitting phone companies to enter the cable television business, as well as permitting them to offer long-distance phone service and vice versa (and long-distance providers to enter the local phone market). This furthers the erosion of diversity of journalistic voices as well.

Perhaps the easiest entry into the local and long-distance market will be via wireless, mobile, personal communications services. The act states that providers of commercial mobile services are exempt from certain requirements of other common carriers, such as cable television providers or telephone service providers. For example, section 332 specifies that providers of mobile services will be exempt from the general requirement to provide equal access to common carriers for the provision of telephone toll services.

More importantly, the recently completed FCC auction of radio spectrum for the delivery of personal communication services (PCS) will drive this even further. By 2005 PCS will be capable of delivering wireless video to mobile or stationary television/computer receivers. Although the $10.22 billion spectrum auction was intended to open doors to entrepreneurial small businesses, just five companies bid more than $8 billion for spectrum covering more than two-thirds of the U.S. population.[6] Four of the companies are backed by Korean and Japanese investors. The largest single bid came from Nextwave Communications, Inc., which bid more than $4 billion for a service area covering more than 40 percent of the U.S. population. Nextwave is backed by Japan's Sony Corporation, four Korean companies, and the government of South Korea.[7]

All these changes open up new possibilities for news delivery to mobile devices and the consumers who carry or wear them. News services for pagers and other devices are common, and CNN.com is even planning a new video news service delivered directly to cellphones equipped with small, flat-panel displays.

Direct-to-home satellite services (also known as Direct Broadcast Satellite, or DBS) may similarly prove a viable means for distributing multimedia programming, including news. Such services are also exempted from certain sections of the act, such as the general requirement to provide effective competition on rates. In addition, the act exempts DBS providers from any taxes or fees imposed by local taxing jurisdictions (see section 602). This exemption reflects the technical design of DBS as a national or regional service, not a local service, although in late 1999 DirecTV began transmitting local signals. Although not all local markets are served, most of the major ones are, including New York, Los Angeles, and dozens of others. The inability of DBS to deliver local programming had been the sole barrier blocking direct competition between cable and DBS. Removal of this barrier only fosters direct DBS-cable competition, but in the context of provisions of the Telecommunications Act of 1996, it gives DBS a significant tax advantage over cable.

DirecTV also offers a remarkable array of national and international news services. The All News Channel, CNN, and MSNBC are just a few of the English-language news services available on DirecTV. Univision and Telemundo, the two leading Spanish-language television programmers in the United States also deliver programming, including news, via DirecTV.

Future of the networks.   What can we forecast about the future of the television networks, which have traditionally set the standards for broadcast news? Two patterns are clear. First, because the 1996 act eases the barriers prohibiting telephone companies from providing video services, the phone companies will enter the programming business. Despite their great resources, research, and reach, however, the phone companies lack the necessary tradition, infrastructure, and culture to create quality television programming. The television networks, on the other hand, while committed to producing quality programming, have no great tradition in producing interactive programming. Thus telephone companies will seek partnerships or alliances with the television networks and other program producers to create interactive programming for the emerging broadband infrastructure both domestically and internationally. We are seeing these alliances in the way of partnerships with Internet and cable companies that will bring additional national news and other video programming to the consumer via the Internet. We are also seeing many alliances between the networks and Internet companies. For example, CBS has acquired more than a half dozen Internet companies, such as MarketWatch and HealthWatch.

Second, the networks, as well as other traditional providers of television programming, including local broadcasters, will face increasing competition from providers of video on the Internet, especially the World Wide Web. Today, the primary obstacles to providing broadcast quality video on the Internet are bandwidth and connectivity. Bandwidth refers to the amount of electromagnetic spectrum available for use by broadcasters or other telecommunication service providers (see table 10.1). It is typically translated into the amount of information, data, or video programming that can be transmitted per second via a particular medium or channel. Text requires the least bandwidth; audio somewhat more; still images, graphics, and animations still more; and video, motion pictures, and virtual reality the most. Bandwidth is rapidly growing, and advances in compression and new software tools are increasingly making it possible to deliver full-motion video in real time over the Internet. Pixelon, Digital Bitcasting, and others were by 1999 delivering full-motion, full-screen video in real time over the Internet to a worldwide audience.

Connectivity refers to the proportion of individuals and households in the United States and around the world who have access to a communication service, such as broadcast television, radio, telephony, or the Internet. In April 1996 some 11 percent of U.S. homes were connected to the Internet (i.e., they had a home computer, modem, and online service with Internet

TABLE 10.1 The Meaning of Bandwidth

Bandwidth refers to amount of electromagnetic spectrum available for transmission of information; designated in terms of transmission speed of medium.

Medium	Transmission speed	Text capability	Multimedia
Phone modem	14.4/28.8 kbps	1 story in *New York Times*	Internet/online/ no video/slow still pix/graphics/ CUSeeMe/ VDOLive/RA
ISDN	128 kbps	1 page of NYT	H.320 video conference/fast/ hi-res pictures
T1 4-wire copper	1.5 mbps	4 pages of NYT	VHS video
Cable modem	4 mbps	1 section of NYT	MPEG2
ADSL	6 mbps	2 sections of NYT	Multichannel/ MPEG2
Low-power radio*	25 mbps	2 days of NYT	Near broadcast quality video
T3 Optical, copper, coaxial cable	45 mbps	4 days of NYT	Near BQV
Optical Fiber			
ATM	155 mbps	1 week of NYT	Broadcast Quality VOD
Commercial	2.5 gbps	26 weeks of NYT	Multichannel
BQVOD			
Laboratory (Fujitsu Ltd.; Nippon Telegraph and Telephone; AT&T Research and Lucent Technologies)	1 tbps	300 years' worth of Virtual Reality NYT in one second	

*Low-power radio is under consideration by the Federal Communications Commission (FCC) and would allow short-distance high-bandwidth transmission; this wireless medium can link many users to a single high-speed phone line to the Internet.

TABLE 10.1 *(continued)*

Key:
ADSL: asymmetric digital subscriber line
ATM: asynchronous transfer mode
BPS: bits per second
  k: 1,000
  m: 1,000,000
  g: 1,000,000,000
  t: 1,000,000,000,000
CUSeeMe: Cornell University's Internet video conferencing software
H.320: commercial video conferencing standard
ISDN: integrated services digital network
modem: modulate/demodulate
MPEG2: digital video standard/VHS standard (Motion Picture Experts Group)
RA: RealAudio
T1: T-carrier (AT&T, Bell); 24 channels of audio, 64 kbps
T3: 28 T1 lines
VDOLive: "streaming" video on the World Wide Web (WWW)
VOD: video on demand

Source: Prepared by John V. Pavlik, executive director, Center for New Media, Columbia University Graduate School of Journalism

access). By February 1998 the percentage had reached 25 percent (with 62 million people online in the United States). In August 1999 it reached 37.5 percent. In February 2000 a study conducted by researchers at Stanford University found that Internet penetration in the United States had reached 55 percent (although other research suggests the 50 percent level was not reached until June 2000). Cable modem services are rapidly introducing broadband connectivity for Internet and "streaming" video (i.e., real-time video) on a mass scale. Among the companies developing cable modem technology are Intel, Cablevision, and TCI.[8]

The advent of widespread connectivity and broadband capability means consumers will have access to viable alternative sources of video. These sources will become increasingly capable of providing interactive programming, greater viewer control, and full audience participation.

Will the television networks continue as the preeminent provider of quality video programming to most Americans? The answer depends not only on their response to the changing competitive climate fostered by the Tele-communications Act of 1996 but also on how effectively they integrate in-creasingly interactive technologies into their programming and production processes. The three traditional commercial networks once dominated tele-vision viewership, with 90 percent of television households watching their programming. Today, the big four commercial networks, ABC, CBS, FOX, and NBC typically reach just 42 percent of television households. Research fore-casts predict their share of the audience will erode to less than 30 percent in another ten to fifteen years. Beyond that, television's share of the American mind is eroding, with new media, especially the Internet, capturing increas-ing amounts of viewers' time (the 2000 Stanford study shows television view-ership, readership, and even forms of face-to-face interaction are all decreas-ing because of Internet usage).

Who will be the major television programming providers, especially in the news and public affairs arena, a decade from now? Topping the list will be some traditional players and networks, including Disney/ABC, Rupert Murdoch's NewsCorp, Viacom/CBS, AOL/Time Warner, and ATT/@home/TCI, as well as some new companies and some cross-industry alliances, es-pecially Microsoft/NBC. The most interesting forms of programming, how-ever, will emerge from some unexpected enterprises, such as Jones Digital Century, a new media company out of Englewood, Colorado, where they are testing new forms of interactive storytelling and have enough capital backing (from parent Jones Intercable) to market their programs successfully. Studios, independent producers, and others will have increasing opportu-nities in the multichannel new media environment, as well. Such entrepre-neurial efforts will produce some of the programming highlights of the post–Telecommunications Act world. How much of this will be news and public affairs, and what will be the quality? The answer to the first half of this question is, probably a great deal, as digital broadcasting opens up channel capacity, especially for local programmers, who will often be drawn more to the multicasting capability of compressed digital television than to the high-definition/bandwidth-intensive opportunities: they will need cheap content (i.e., news) to fill their new-found airwaves and return a profit or at least a significant audience (in the case of public broadcasters).

The answer to the second half of the question (to do with quality) is, probably not very high. Much of the content will be similar to C-SPAN, but on a local level, which, although it may serve a limited public interest, doesn't have much added journalistic value. Moreover, much of the new content is likely to come from sources such as video news releases (VNRs) produced by public relations firms. New technology now makes it possible for PR firms not only to produce broadcast quality programming but to customize it to the particular programming formats preferred by different stations in different markets, thus enabling a station to air VNRs that look exactly like other news programming that it regularly produces. The Telecommunications Act does not require local stations to identify the source of a VNR for its viewers; that is only an ethical mandate.

Two cases to watch in the digital twenty-first century are the online start-ups *foreigntv.com* and *space.com*. *Space.com* was founded by Lou Dobbs, an award-winning, veteran financial news anchor formerly with CNN. Dobbs, who staked out the *space.com* domain name, is building an online news service featuring streaming video news about space and especially stories about Earth as reported from space (e.g., using remote-sensing satellite images and other technology). He is opening bureaus in cities around the country, including New York and Houston, and staffing them with top-quality journalists, among them, Glen Golightly, a former editor of the *Houston Chronicle*'s online newspaper.

Foreigntv.com is an online news venture specializing in video news streamed from all around the world and offering an alternative voice to the traditional news providers. One of the founders of the site is Peter Arnett, another award-winning veteran journalist from CNN, who earned his fame from covering the Persian Gulf War live from inside Baghdad in 1992.

Fostering Interactive Services

Recognizing the development of interactive services in broadcasting and telecommunications, the 1996 act promotes the further growth of interactive services through what it calls individual and family empowerment. Section 509 of the act states that it is the policy of the United States:

1. to promote the continued development of the Internet and other interactive computer services and other interactive media;
2. to preserve the vibrant and competitive free market that presently exists for the Internet and other interactive computer services, unfettered by federal or state regulation; and,

3. to encourage the development of technologies that maximize user control over what information is received by individuals, families, and schools who use the Internet and other interactive computer services.

As a result of this policy, there will be continued albeit slow growth in the amount of programming produced by individuals. One study, for example, suggests that in the early days of the Web as a medium of mass communication nearly a third of the sites were created by individuals (i.e., seventy thousand of the roughly two hundred thousand Web sites in May 1996, or about one in three sites), not organizations.[9] The next three years saw the portion developed by individuals drop off dramatically; by 1998 roughly one million of the eight million Web sites were created by individuals, not organizations.[10] Individually produced programming will take many forms, including text, audio, and image and video communications, some of it what we would call news. Neighborhood-level news and entertainment programming produced by individuals will grow during the next decade, although not at the rate of corporate-produced Web content. Although some individual citizens will use camcorders and other new media tools to produce local programming, media companies will play an important role in editing and packaging this programming for commercial use, much as *America's Funniest Home Videos* derives most of its programming from the video clips submitted by viewers across the United States. One interesting example is *BNNtv.com*'s CameraPlanet. Formerly the Broadcast News Network, an award-winning New York City television production company that produced wide-ranging quality programming, including documentaries and programs such as MTV's *Real World*, *BNNtv.com* launched in 2000 CameraPlanet as an interactive online channel. CameraPlanet places cameras in the hands of viewers and lets them use video technology to tell their own stories. *BNNtv.com* won three CINE Golden Eagle awards for 1999 productions: *Baby Beauty Queens*, shown on A&E; *Crimes in the Name of God*, shown on Court TV; and *Generation H: National History Day*, shown on the History Channel.

Individually produced programming, however, may ultimately deliver little more than the public access television on today's cable. Much ballyhooed in the 1970s by companies vying for local cable franchises, public access channels were championed as a forum for public debate and discourse on a variety of levels and subjects. Instead, most have delivered an abundance of low-quality, often sexually oriented programs and little more. Even on the Internet's hyperactive World Wide Web, there had begun to emerge by 1999 a pattern in which individual-produced sites were being overwhelmed by corporate sites and sites produced by major programming providers ranging from newspapers companies to television networks. As a result, the Web today is in many ways an engine of public relations and marketing. Tomorrow's million-channel digital video universe may follow a similar pattern. With some notable exceptions (*BNNtv.com*), most programming will likely be produced by major players with the resources to create broadcast-quality programming, whether interactive or traditional TV.

A growing amount of programming, however, will not flow through traditional news or new media gatekeepers. Rather, as bandwidth and connectivity grow, the World Wide Web and other video delivery systems will become increasingly important media for interactive, multimedia programming produced by nontraditional program providers seeking to reach the U.S. market without going through a journalistic filter. Corporations, political strategists, and marketers will make programming available for direct access by consumers interested in on-demand, targeted information or entertainment. This represents the greatest challenge for traditional news program providers: to preserve their role as sense makers in an increasingly networked environment, news providers will need to adapt in fundamental ways. One avenue for adaptation will be to develop specialized program reviews that evaluate the quality of programming produced by corporate providers. More important, news program providers will need to develop synergistic links between the their television-based news programming and other forms of news delivery, to help to keep viewers, even when away from their television sets, somewhere within that programmer's news environment. Branding will grow dramatically in importance in an increasingly fragmented programming marketplace.

Because the Telecommunications Act eliminates the legal barriers preventing telephone and television companies from competing in the areas of telephone and video services, consumers will see an increased array of alternative service providers, at least initially. Similarly, we will see an increase in the range of both phone and video services, including video, news, advertising on demand, and transaction-based services.

More important, however, program producers will create highly targeted, real-time information produced in an increasingly competitive environment. Driven by the urgency of digital technology, consumers will demand and get more information with ever less delay between the occurrence of an event and its reporting (i.e., unfiltered, real-time reporting). Some of this will happen with live robotic cameras positioned around communities providing nonstop traffic (more than two hundred cities in the United States have live traffic weather cameras available online), weather, and event reports with viewers able to use wireless keyboards to operate the robotic camera and select the view they prefer. One Web site extends this model to twenty-four-hour monitoring of Internet traffic.[11]

Consider the rapidly coming so-called million-channel viewing environment enabled by the broadband cable modem and the advent of combined television and computer devices. The Gateway 2000 Destination personal computer, for example, combines computer and television capability in a single device accessed through a wireless keyboard and mouse and viewed on a thirty-one-inch screen. Similarly, Zenith has marketed a television set equipped with both a high-speed modem and an Ethernet connection that will make high-speed Internet access possible without using a personal computer. Motorola has begun shipping its CyberSurfer cable modem, which provides data at 30 million bits per second, or roughly one thousand times the speed of telephone-based computer modems. In response, regional Bell telephone companies (RBOCs) have begun rolling out their comparable high-bandwidth service, known as aDSL, or asymmetric digital subscriber line. Together, these technologies will enable viewers to obtain real-time, on-demand video programming. Moreover, they will spur the growth of interactive video services. Although programmers have sought the holy grail of interactive TV for at least four decades, they will finally find it in the coming decade, although it will prove to be no panacea. The technologies described above will enable full interactive TV services, but they will not by themselves change hardened viewer habits. Nor will they eliminate the high cost of producing quality interactive programming, including news and entertainment. Still, as today's youth become tomorrow's prime market segment, interactive TV will become a major portion of prime-time television viewing. But it may not be interactive TV anymore but instead simply interactive video programming.

The act also calls for the development of competitive schemes for navigating in the online world. One notable clause prohibits operators of open video systems (OVS) "from omitting television broadcast stations or other unaffiliated video programming services carried on such systems from any navigational device, guide, or menu" (section 653). Open Video Systems is a new medium the act introduces for telephone company participation in video programming and delivery. Section 653 is analogous to the "must-carry rule" in today's video programming environment that requires cable providers to, sometimes reluctantly, carry the programming of local over-the-air broadcasters. The act extends the must-carry notion to any provider of video that uses a radio-based system or otherwise acts as a common carrier to provide video programming to subscribers using radio communication (section 651).

Consumer Access

Consumer access to programming will change dramatically, as well, but not just in the planned-for fashion. As has been widely discussed, the act seeks to give parents greater control over their children's viewing of violent and sexual programming (section 551). It begins by summarizing research findings that show:

- "children exposed to violent video programming at a young age have a higher tendency for violent and aggressive behavior later in life than children not so exposed, and that children exposed to violent video programming are prone to assume that acts of violence are acceptable behavior";
- the average American child watches twenty-five hours of television a week; and
- "parents express grave concern over violent and sexual video programming and strongly support technology that would give them greater control to block video programming in the home that they consider harmful to their children."

Based on this evidence, the act states that the government has a compelling interest to provide "parents with timely information about the nature of upcoming video programming and with the technological tools that allow them easily to block violent, sexual, or other programming that they believe harmful to their children." Thus the act calls for the development of an "apparatus designed to receive television signals that are shipped in interstate commerce or manufactured in the United States and that have a picture screen 13 inches or greater in size (measured diagonally), that such apparatus be equipped with a feature designed to enable viewers to block display of all programs with a common rating of video programming that contains sexual, violent, or other indecent material about which parents should be informed before it is displayed to children."

Broadcasters have developed a rating system for the so-called v-chip, or violence chip, the common name for the apparatus to enable parents to block selected programming based on its sexual or violent programming, which is now being installed in all new television sets sold in the United States. Exempted from the v-chip rules is all news programming, on a First Amendment basis (i.e., that Congress shall make no law abridging freedom of speech or of the press).

The issues at stake relate not only to the First Amendment but also to whether this clause will act as a deterrent for companies seeking to enter video services, since they will not be able to provide a full range of services to compete with cable. More fundamentally, the obscenity clause undermines the entire premise of the act, which was to bring federal law up to date with technology, in which distinctions among media, telecommunications, and computing have faded.

Most troubling, however, is the likely failure to deliver significant increases in public access to public records, the records kept by government. Historically, these records were once kept exclusively on paper; now they are stored electronically and accessible and searchable via computer. Journalists have traditionally mined these public records for news stories. The rise of the Internet has made it increasingly possible to make these electronic public records available online, not only to journalists but to the public at large.

On its face, this is a major breakthrough: it is now possible for government to become increasingly accountable and for all citizens to have full access to what is ostensibly the public's information. Unfortunately, it is not this simple. Although some data are being made available electronically, such as the campaign contributions at the Federal Election Commission Web site (www.fec.gov) or the census data at the Web site of the U.S. Department of the Census (www.census.gov), many agencies not only have been slow to put their data online but have formulated congressionally mandated policies not to do so.

Especially troubling is the case of the Environmental Protection Agency, whose data on chemical facilities were scheduled to go online in 1999. The proposed plan was formulated as a safeguard to the public to prevent a reoccurrence, especially domestically, of the tragic chemical spill that killed thousands in Bhopal, India, in the 1980s. Congress ordered the EPA in 1990 to take appropriate steps, but just as it was about to implement its plan via the Internet, industry groups and law enforcement agencies intervened, claiming that posting information about the location and nature of chemical plants around the nation would make it easy for terrorists to formulate effective plans of their own. Summing up the opponents' viewpoint, House Commerce Committee chairman Tom Bliley (R-Va.) described the EPA plan as "a reckless plan to put the data at every terrorist's fingertips . . . easily searchable from Boston to Baghdad, from Los Angeles to Libya." As Lawrence K. Grossman notes, "Since Gutenberg invented the printing press, authorities have greeted every major advance in information technology with fear and suspicion. The Internet is no exception." Although there may be merit to the concern that the chemical plant information might fall into the wrong hands, the fact is most of the information is already publicly available on the Internet. Grossman conducted his own online search of sites created by such industry leaders as Dow Chemical, Exxon, and Union Carbide and found extensive data on the products the companies make, the locations of their major chemical facilities, and even more details. The Environmental Defense Fund's Web site (www.scorecard .org) presents color-coded maps indicating the precise location of every U.S. chemical plant ever to experience a leak. But because of irrational fear of the new medium of the Internet, the EPA has been forced to redesign its plans. Grossman reports that staff members of the House Commerce Committee suggested the following alternative information distribution plan: "The EPA could put the data on a CD-ROM that people can read but not reproduce. The agency could make the information available in library reading rooms and government offices without printers; people would be prohibited from copying any of it by hand."[12]

Where will it end? Will the public have reasonable electronic access to important public records such as those the EPA tried to make available? Had the EPA's original plan been simply to publish the data in printed form, it is unlikely any industry groups or law enforcement agencies would have complained. "As new technologies have acquired the functions of the press, they have not acquired the rights of the press," observed MIT media scholar Ithiel de Sola Pool in his classic book *Technologies of Freedom*.[13]

Libel, Pornography, and Censorship

Libel and pornography represent two other major areas of freedom of expression in the online arena yet to be settled. Although the Communications Decency Act of the Telecommunications Act of 1996 was overturned by the U.S. Supreme Court, there are resurgent federal attempts and numerous state legislative efforts to restrict the flow of online adult content, including some that might be considered news or public affairs.

Libel may one day prove to be an online nightmare for journalists, especially freelance journalists who often operate on a shoestring budget and without the safety net of libel insurance. Although there have been several libel cases involving online journalists (e.g., the Brock Meeks case), the case to get the most attention to date involves online gossip columnist Matt Drudge. Drudge, who broke the story of the Clinton-Lewinsky affair, also published an unflattering report about White House aide Sidney Blumenthal, who subsequently filed a $30 million defamation suit against Drudge. Although few may feel much pity for Drudge, who admits that as much as 20 percent of what he has reported at this site is unsubstantiated gossip, the danger is that a reporter (Drudge does not claim to be a journalist; just a reporter) operating online who is sued for libel or defamation by a senior White House official may result in a chilling effect on online free speech globally.

Censorship is in many ways a very different issue in the networked, digital age. To understand it, consider this seven-part censorship question, modeled after political scientist Bernard Cohen's fifty-year-old media effects question: who says what to whom through what channel with what effect? Today consider: (1) what is said (obscenity, political speech), (2) by whom (consider the so-called two faces of anonymous online speech, which protects Kosovars threatened by bodily harm, death, or imprisonment for speaking out during the 1999 war but also permits online hate speech, as in the case of the "Asian hater" email to University of California Los Angeles students with "Asian-sounding" last names),[14] (3) to which audience (such as children), (4) through which medium (print vs. electronic/online), (5) censored by whom (such as ICANN, the new domain registration body that refuses to register "obscene" or "indecent" domain names, such as those identified in comedian George Carlin's famous "Seven Dirty Words" monologue and ruled on by the U.S. Supreme Court in *FCC vs. Pacifica* (the words are *shit, piss, fuck, cunt, cocksucker, motherfucker,* and *tits*; Carlin admits some of these are compound words and really shouldn't be counted but points out that some of the compound words when separated into their component parts would not be objectionable), (6) using which tools (increasingly automated via computerized filters in the online domain), and (7) to prevent what harmful effect? Consider sociologist W. Philip Davison's third-person effect model of communication, which has been tested in many studies to show that a communication will often exert a significant influence, but not on the purported audience; rather the communication may influence a third party to the communication who anticipates a significant effect on the purported audience and therefore acts preemptively.[15] This was apparently the case in World War II when the Japanese dropped propaganda leaflets on black troops stationed on islands in the South Pacific. The leaflets urged the troops to surrender and be treated well by their Japanese captors, because the Japanese did not consider WWII a war against them but rather a war against the imperialist whites of the United States. The leaflets had no apparent effect on the soldiers' morale, but the white commanding officers had them immediately transferred to new locations in the Pacific theater. Why? Davison explains that the commanding officers fell victim to the third-person effect of communication. They believed the leaflets would affect the soldiers' morale and acted preemptively. The same principle may apply to many other instances of censorship, such as in the movies, where film censors seek to avoid negative influences on viewers.

There is a significant flip side to the consequences of the Internet for censorship. Although The Internet is resistant to centralized efforts to censor unwanted content because of its openness and uncontrollability, it might simultaneously lead to a diminution of voices from minority groups, espousing unpopular views or representing unempowered citizens. Consider the free speech observations of Andrew L. Shapiro, legal scholar and author of *The Control Revolution: How the Internet Is Putting Individuals in Charge and Changing the World We Know*: "The control revolution is changing the ground rules of free speech and, consequently, of civil society. Even as new technology gives individuals the ability to speak without fear of institutional censorship, it gives all of us a new ability to avoid speech we don't want to hear. The result, in the aggregate, is that the speech of certain individuals—especially marginal speakers—may well be lost in cyberspace."[16]

Other Consequences: Rule Making by the FCC

The consequences of the 1996 act are not limited to the terms of the act itself. The FCC is charged with developing and implementing a new set of rules based on the act. The commission's schedule for rule making includes relaxing the broadcast ownership limits, relaxing cross-ownership rules to permit ownership or control of a network of broadcast stations and a cable system, extending broadcast license terms, Open Video System rules that exempt from certain requirements of the act system operators who provide equal access for all video programmers, cable indecency scrambling, and the elimination of filing requirements for telephone companies wishing to distribute video.

Building on the television industry tradition of providing closed captioning for the hearing impaired, the act mandates that the Federal Communications Commission undertake a study to evaluate the use of video descriptions on video programming in order to provide accessibility of video programming to people with visual impairments. Video description refers to the insertion of audio descriptions of a television program's key visual elements into natural pauses within the program's dialogue. Such video description has been used extensively in live theatrical productions and tested in video trials. The art of audio description is explained by Joel Snyder of the National Endowment for the Arts. He observes that in audio description you make the visual oral and aural. For example, you don't say "He is angry" or "She is sad" but rather "He's clenching his fist" or "She is crying." With an estimated thirteen million Americans legally blind, audio description will serve as an empowering tool in the next generation of television programming, especially in the context of news and public affairs. Audio description is also available in online content through streaming media players such as Real Networks.

Another important item for the FCC's future agenda will be the definition of universal service, a long-cherished notion central to the 1934 act and vital to the effectiveness of video journalism in a democracy. The act does not goes so far as to provide a definition of universal service but merely states that "universal service is an evolving level of telecommunications services that the Commission shall establish periodically under this section" (section 254). It identifies six principles central to this evolving notion of universal service. They are to provide:

1. Quality services at reasonable and affordable rates.
2. Access to advanced telecommunications and information services throughout the United States.
3. Access in rural and high-cost areas.
4. Equitable and nondiscriminatory contributions to the preservation and advancement of universal service.
5. Specific, predictable, and sufficient federal and state mechanisms to preserve and advance universal service.
6. Access to advanced telecommunications services in elementary and secondary schools and classrooms, offices of health care providers, and libraries. Despite this, however, a February 15, 2000, report by the U.S. Department of Education shows that the digital divide continues to exist, with public schools in predominantly poor economic regions having significantly less access to the Internet, both in terms of an installed base of computers and online, broadband connectivity, than do schools in higher income regions.[17]

The likely outcome of this evolving notion is a new model of universal service. In one scenario, this model would make fully interoperable high-bandwidth two-way communication service the twenty-first-century equivalent of "plain old telephone service" (POTS) mandated in the 1934 act. This would create a powerful network engine to drive a new information infrastructure linking wired and wireless technologies and empower the development of fully interactive, multimedia communications. An alternative paradigm, however, would simply mandate that all homes, public schools, and libraries have access to at least two communication service providers capable of delivering both traditional and new media services (including the Internet), with low-income households receiving the equivalent of information stamps, as once proposed by media mogul Ted Turner.

Tomorrow's TV Programming: A Vast Interactive Wasteland?

Newton Minow observed in a 1991 presentation marking the thirtieth anniversary of his famous "vast wasteland" speech that he had hoped his first speech as FCC chairman to broadcasters would be remembered for two words, but not those two words. His goal was to put "public interest" into the forefront of television programming in the 1960s.[18] As we enter a new millennium, will television programming finally move beyond the dark shadow of the vast wasteland? Or will it become a vast *interactive* wasteland?

The competitive environment fostered by the new telecommunications act will propel television programming along the same trajectory it has followed for most of the previous half century. Programming will continue to be driven by commercial, not public, interests. News and public affairs programming will be of generally high quality at the network level but will likely follow the "if it bleeds, it leads" model in most local markets. The allure of international markets will draw even more U.S. programming dollars. Programming for children will continue to languish, especially news and public affairs prepared for children. Interactive services will develop slowly, but a decade from now they will be a familiar, though small, part of the television landscape.

Programming specialization will increase, however, and will provide the best opportunity for quality programming, especially in the arena of news and public affairs. Programs such as *C/Net*, which is offered as both an online service and a television program, will gain momentum and quality through the synergy of combining the best of both media. Conversely, ownership will continue an ever-greater pattern of concentration, with cross-industry alliances making for both strange bedfellows and oligarchic cartels. More than a footnote to the act, Open Video Systems (ovs) will permit telephone companies to become major players in video programming and delivery, ensuring that the telephone companies will emerge as an important force in this cartel.

Although not the sole catalyst for this coming transformation of programming, the Telecommunications Act of 1996 has unleashed the forces making it possible. The public interest will be served, but as a secondary by-product of the forces of the commercial marketplace. Those program providers who find a healthy balance between commercial and public interests, as well as a comfortable synergy between both old and new media, will discover a programming landscape offering profits and promise.

11   Implications of Intelligent Agents for Journalism: Ghosts in the Machine

In the age of the Internet, ubiquitous information has become both a blessing and a curse. For journalists as well as anyone who is a news consumer, this is especially true. With more than five thousand newspapers and other news sources online, it is possible to enjoy more access to information than at any other time in history. But at the same time, information overload has become an ever-present fact of life.

This chapter examines the rise and role of intelligent agents as information filters, personal editors, and news summarizers in the digital age.[1] How might agent technology transform both the practice of journalism and the news itself, for better or for worse? Although intelligent agents have the potential to serve as valuable tools in reducing information overload, they raise a variety of ethical concerns as well. Paramount among these concerns are implications for privacy. This chapter revolves around four questions about the implications of intelligent agents for journalism:

1. How do intelligent agents affect the way journalists do their work?
2. What are the implications of intelligent agents for the content of news?
3. How will intelligent agents affect newsroom or news industry structure?
4. What are the implications of intelligent agents for the news audience?

How Do Intelligent Agents Affect the Way Journalists Do Their Work?

Journalists today are flooded with an increasing amount of information to sort, sift, and process. That information comes mainly in either of two forms: primary or secondary. Primary is original reporting, which can come from interviews, direct observation, or analysis of public records and may be audio, text, video, or data. Secondary is typically information obtained off the Internet or from other publications or newscasts.

In either case, tools for processing this information efficiently and effectively are vitally needed and traditionally have been very limited. Intelligent agents, a branch of artificial intelligence in which software robots act autonomously on another entity's behalf (typically a person, but it could be another agent), offer a potentially significant advance in this area of news production.[2]

A basic ethical consideration in this regard is whether the use of agents could lead to the replacement of newsroom personnel, such as librarians, whose primary function today is to conduct background research. Although this is possible, it is unlikely. Agents will enable journalists to delegate certain lower-level functions to software robots who can act as drones tirelessly searching vast collections of data for the occasional gold nugget and liberating the journalist, or the librarian, to focus on more analytic functions. It would be a mistake, contends virtual reality pioneer Jaron Lanier, to believe that agents have the capacity to perform the higher-level analysis that human information agents, or journalists, perform.[3]

Information access and management represent an area of great activity in intelligent agents research and are vitally important to journalists, given the rising popularity of the Internet and the explosion of data available to reporters. Intelligent agents are helping journalists not only with searching and filtering—through both Web-based news articles and *Usenet* newsgroup discussions—but also with categorizing, prioritizing, selectively distributing, annotating, and collaboratively sharing information and documents. This collaborative journalism represents a paradigmatic shift in the traditions of modern journalism.

Agents also can be useful to journalists by partially or fully screening, filtering, sorting, or otherwise managing a reporter or editor's email. This is increasingly important for journalists who work for media with large audiences, since they can be flooded with email responses to something they have reported. Adaptive agents can also facilitate the handling of a journalist's email by inferring filtering and sorting rules by observing the journalist's behavior (i.e., how he or she responds to email), finding patterns, and then basing agent email handling rules on those patterns. For example, if an agent observes that the journalist typically responds most quickly to messages from her or his editor, it will set the highest priority on any future incoming messages from that editor.

Much current research is being conducted on separate agents, such as mail agents, news agents, and search agents. These represent the first step toward more integrated applications, where individual agents are can be used as building blocks for more sophisticated, multifunctional integrated agents. A likely model for an integrated master agent is that it will delegate subtasks and queries to other single-function agents. The master agent will serve in a managerial role, coordinating the subagents' activities and then serving as a single point of liaison with a human master, or journalist.

An important set of ethical considerations arises from the ability of agents to learn, especially from other agents, and thereby to adapt their behavior. This type of agent is called an adaptive agent. Consider the following scenario: The news is about the unusual, so a reporter programs an agent to scour the Internet for anomalies in patterns of data. Along the way, the agent encounters another agent that has been programmed to unlock encrypted files illegally. In observing this robot at work, the first agent learns how to unlock encrypted files and begins to use this newly found skill to uncover a very unusual pattern in data at a major banking institution. It immediately reports back to its journalist master, and the journalist strikes out hot on the trail of a major story about financial irregularities at the banking institution.

Clearly a crime has been committed. An encrypted computer system has been illegally hacked into by an intelligent agent. Who is responsible? The agent? Its human master? Have any ethical standards been breached? Do the ends (i.e., the story) justify the means (i.e., hacking into the bank's computer network)? If not, who is responsible for the ethical violation? Can the journalist be held responsible for the acts committed by an agent he did not intentionally program to commit illegal or unethical activities? If this scenario seems implausible, consider the forecast of coming computer technology as outlined by futurist Ray Kurzweil in his book *The Age of Spiritual Machines*.[4] Kurzweil has determined that the computing power of machines has actually been growing exponentially the entire twentieth century; in fact, even the exponential growth curve is growing exponentially: In the first part of the twentieth century, computing power was doubling every three years. By midcentury, it was every two years. Now it doubles every eighteen months. Kurzweil predicts that a $1,000 computer in the year 2020 will have the processing power, or intelligence, of a human brain. And by 2060 a single $1,000 computer will have the intelligence of all human brains combined. But, because computers have the ability to share their knowledge, they will be far more intelligent than humans. Is it really too much to imagine two agents sharing their knowledge and capabilities in this environment, where technology races ahead far faster than humans can comprehend, command, or even control?

What Are the Implications of Intelligent Agents for the Content of News?

One of the most significant implications of intelligent agents for news content has already become a reality: by 1999 agents were being used to create increasingly customized, often highly specialized content for individual audience members. A know-bot or spider usually does this by selecting individual news items from any of a number of places that it identifies as of interest to its master. A variety of Internet intelligent agent products perform this function by reviewing *Usenet* newsgroups, mailing services, Web-based news reports, and other online content. Among the most popular newspaper-built software agents is the Nando News Watcher, one of the first such agent-based news applications.[5] Others are offered by online news services such as the *Wall Street Journal Interactive Edition*. The *New York Times on the Web* is also using agent technology to deliver customized local content in its New York Today feature. Here, user profiles are analyzed to identify items of potential interest, such as performances, restaurants, and films. These items are then downloadable either to the desktop or to a personal digital appliance such as the Palm Pilot.

Other effective news agents include *Free Agent News and Mail Reader* and *NewsFerret*, which read and sort *Usenet* newsgroups.[6] *NewsPage* (now called *Individual.com*) uses Individual's SMART (System for the Manipulation and Retrieval of Text) agent technology (developed at Cornell University) to sort through up to twenty thousand news stories daily from more than six hundred sources.[7] Relevant news articles are sorted into twenty-five hundred news topics and displayed in a customizable, hierarchical structure. The SMART system does not rely on Boolean search technology dependent on keyword and string matching but instead uses content-based analysis based on plain English queries. Another example, developed at Carnegie Mellon University, is *AGENT_CLIPS*, a multiagent/single-agent tool that each user customizes and implements for different applications.[8] It uses a rule-based expert system that scans newsgroups and Web pages. News sources are also increasingly using agents to perform electronic tracking of when their organization or industry is mentioned in online news stories or newsgroups. *Excite NewsTracker*, for example, offers a free clipping service.[9]

Many news organizations host chat sessions and other online forums to enable readers to discuss stories that have appeared in their news products and to bring readers and reporters together online. Such news organizations will also find agent technology useful for monitoring these chat and other online discussions and identifying possible story ideas, potential sources, and even unacceptable comments, such as cursing and flaming.

Censorship is the dangerous flip side of agent filtering technology. Whether in governments, libraries, or schools, agents and filters are increasingly being used to censor Internet access to content. One recent case involved the government of Hong Kong, which used an agent-based filter to block residents access to the Web site run by Smartics, a popular sweet-and-sour candy. For some reason, the filter classified the site as pornographic, which is illegal content in Hong Kong. Useful filtering tools for parents or governments, such as *Cyber Patrol* or *Netnanny*, represent an effective, non–agent-based alternative (i.e., real people classify sites) to censorship of Internet content.

Agents do present an opportunity to assess certain aspects of online news content effectively. For example, an agent could be employed to identify and authenticate the source of a news story, video, or audio clip quickly, if that content has been encoded with source information. Furthermore, it is a relatively simple task for agents to compare news stories and identify points of similarity or difference. This could be useful in a number of ways, including identifying plagiarized copy and noting key disagreements in different news reports about the same event. For example, readers, editors, and policy makers might find it very useful to get a summary of news reports about the death toll from a tidal wave in the south Pacific as reported by the

AP, the BBC, and Reuters. In fact, a system under development by Professor Kathy McKeown, chair of the computer science department at Columbia University, uses intelligent agent technology to do just that. Called the *Columbia Digital News System* (*CDNS*), the system uses natural language processing and text generation to analyze and create summaries of textual news reports about terrorism, stock market statistics, and medical information. An online demonstration of the system is available at http://www.cs.columbia .edu/~hjing/sumDemo/multiGen/.

Next steps in the *CDNS* research will incorporate a variety of digital video tools developed by Professor Shih-Fu Chang, including *WebSEEK*, *WebClip*, and *VideoQ*, all of which employ intelligent agents in the form of spiders to classify visual content automatically according to not only textual descriptions but also video characteristics themselves. These characteristics include low-level features (beyond pixels) of color and texture and higher-level features such as patterns and shapes, as well as motion. This content-based approach will ultimately include semantic-based tools that sort video by its inherent meaning, face recognition, and other advanced characteristics. Collaboration with the Center for New Media at Columbia's Journalism School will evaluate the utility of *CDNS* technology in news content and journalistic reporting.

Based on such an approach as *CDNS*, agent technology could be used to develop a variety of content measures and characteristics and build a multidimensional matrix assessing news accuracy, timeliness, comprehensiveness, source diversity, and attribution. One of the most interesting dimensions would be the ability to measure the amount of new content a news site publishes, suggests Andras Szanto, a former research associate at the Freedom Forum Media Studies Center and now associate director of the National Arts Journalism Program at Columbia University. It would be a relatively straightforward process to use agent technology to identify in a dynamic, temporal sense how much redundancy or repetition occurs in stories on the same subject (throughout the day or across days or weeks) published at a specific news site and in comparison to other news sites published elsewhere on the Web. A site that routinely publishes a high percentage of new content, or content not previously published elsewhere, would score more highly than a site that largely repackages wire copy and content obtained from other secondary sources.

Such an agent-based content-quality matrix could be created for individual stories, beats (or topical domains), news products, different news media, and ultimately for the news industry as a whole. A reliable content-quality matrix could be a useful antidote to the spate of media gaffes and errors in recent months, ranging from the stunning retraction of CNN's Vietnam nerve gas story to the *Boston Globe*'s firing of a celebrated columnist who fabricated sources and interviews, all of which has contributed to the continuing downward spiral of media credibility.

One area where this type of agent application had found a role by 1998 is *Profnet*, the online news source locater service.[10] When a reporter submits a request to *Profnet*, the service identifies from a database of more than two thousand participating institutions (mostly universities) potential expert sources for that reporter to interview. *Profnet* then uses agent technology to track the utility and efficiency of its matches by identifying the corresponding news stories where its sources have been quoted.

How Will Intelligent Agents Affect Newsroom or News Industry Structure?

On a relatively basic level, agents can help facilitate the management of an online newsroom. Agents can schedule meetings and appointments, book travel arrangements, and otherwise act as tireless secretaries for harried journalists. For many online news operations that employ large numbers of freelancers, agents can be especially helpful in coordinating virtual newsrooms that include an ever-changing cast of characters assembled on an as-needed basis. Agents are also proving useful at a variety of newspapers with significant online publications. The *New York Times on the Web*, for example, uses agents to automate site subscription and registration, user notification of site registration, password confirmation, site updates, and the like.[11] Other online newspapers do the same.

Carnegie Mellon University (CMU) has developed an approach that emphasizes agents that are adaptable, flexible, and reusable. The multiagent system *RETSINA* creates intelligent agent applications for personal productivity and organizational integration (called *PLEIADES*), financial portfolio management (*WARREN*), information extraction (*DVINA*), Web browsing and searching (*WebMate*), commerce, airfare monitoring, and meeting scheduling.

Systems and network management, one of the earliest areas to be enhanced using intelligent agent technology, is also relevant to newsroom management, where the growth of Web publishing and the movement to client/server computing has intensified the complexity of systems being managed, especially in local and wide area networks. Mobile computing and wireless communications, other technologies transforming the newsroom, can also benefit from agent technology. Mobile agents that reside in the network rather than on the users' personal computers can address the needs driven by mobile computing by persistently carrying out user requests despite network problems.

Agents can prove especially useful in managing the complex e-commerce systems now developing. As buyers and sellers of products and services need to find each other, as specialized, niche marketing moves to the level of one-on-one sales, as consumers need to find detailed product information (such as technical specifications, system configurations, etc.), all parties need automated systems for handling their electronic commerce. Intelligent agents can be used for such tasks as shopping for an airfare, looking for the best price, and delivering an electronic product to the consumer's desktop. Their use may be critical to the future financial success and viability of online news organizations. However, it also raises potentially troubling privacy concerns, which play out very differently in the United States, Europe, and elsewhere in the world.

Research shows that most sites, including news sites, routinely gather a great deal of personal information about the people who visit their sites, such as a visitor's email address, type of computer, Web browser, e-commerce preferences, address in the physical world, age, gender, and more.[12] In the United States, the Clinton administration favors letting electronic commerce industries regulate themselves and set their own standards for protecting consumers' privacy. In contrast, European governments favor enacting laws to protect consumer privacy online. The European Union (EU) has the European Privacy Directive, which restricts the ability of businesses to collect private information about individuals without their permission. An EU committee has issued a report criticizing both the Privacy Preferences Project (P3P) and the Open Profiling Standard (OPS), sets of standards currently being considered by the Internet standards group, the World Wide Web Consortium, that are intended to give users the tools to determine how much personal information they are willing to make available at a Web site. The EU committee has blasted these proposals as inadequate and possibly in violation of European laws.

What Are the Implications of Intelligent Agents for the News Audience?

A fundamental ethical question agent technology raises for the society at large is, will audiences become increasingly fragmented because of more and more specialized content? There is considerable evidence that agents are especially effective at delivering highly customized news and information to individual audience members. I believe audience fragmentation is inevitable but that social disintegration is not. Although people want customized content, especially for business and investment purposes, health, and sports, they still want to know what is going on in the world. Some specialized tracking is thus likely (e.g., of investments, such as via *Stock Symbol Agent*, *StockVue*), but most users will still want the general scanning function. There is great reason to believe that many users will employ agents to keep them informed of important developments in the world at large, not just in areas of special interest. People, especially younger people, value the diversity of information sources available via the Web and the resulting variety of perspectives those sources provide. Agents can enhance this richness by helping users find sources with different points of view on the same subject or event.

To this end, readers may use agents to compile news from a variety of sources and may not be overly concerned with whether the source is a traditional news provider or another organization that provides online content, as long as the content meets certain criteria of timeliness, reliability, and the like. In this sense, agents may play an important role in transforming the relationships among news organizations, audiences and other content providers, individuals, and organizations that in the past may have been news sources.

Computer user interfaces were transformed in the 1980s by the development of graphical user interfaces (GUIs); intelligent agent technology has the potential to transform them even further. As the user population grows and diversifies, an important area of agent application is to learn user habits and preferences and adapt each computer interface to the individual user. Intelligent agent technology can monitor an individual user's actions, develop models of user preferences and actions, and provide instantaneous and automatic assistance when problems arise. When linked to speech recognition and synthesis technology, intelligent agents will enable computer interfaces to become even more user-friendly, especially for the physically challenged, making the potential journalistic uses all the more compelling.[13]

Intelligent agent technology offers a potential solution to the information overload so many journalists and members of the news audience are facing in the digital age. By acting as a personal assistant or editor, an agent can filter, sort, and organize Web-based news content, *Usenet* newsgroup discussions, and electronic mail. Agents can also help news organizations re-establish their credibility by creating the tools to measure the accuracy, timeliness, and comprehensiveness of their news content.

At the same time, agents pose serious ethical questions for the modern newsroom. How do editors and news organizations compete responsibly in the information age when everyone from Microsoft to *Yahoo!* is in the content business, trying to attract as much attention as possible? Will news organizations utilize intelligent agents to acquire profiles of every reader or visitor to a site and then sell that well-known reader to hungry advertisers? What steps should news organizations take to protect reader privacy? What balance should be struck between protecting reader privacy and maintaining profitability?

Agents also pose challenges to the very fabric of society. By facilitating the creation of the ultimate in customized news—what Nicolas Negroponte once dubbed "The Daily Me"[14]—will the agent-based media continue to be the glue that holds society together by providing a shared experience?

These questions have no easy answers. In a free and open marketplace, however, it is imperative for industry and academic leaders to discuss these issues and work to formulate standards for the ethical, responsible, and effective application of agents to journalism. This is an opportunity too important to leave to government regulators.

12 New Media and Journalism Education: Preparing the Next Generation

In journalism, no matter how much the world changes, some things should never change, among them, checking facts rigorously; relying on reputable, known sources; presenting facts impartially; asking tough questions; and adhering to the highest ethical standards. But some things must change, or will inevitably change, for better or worse, things like the tools of the modern journalist. In today's e-world, the tools of modern journalism are being transformed in a fundamental way in five broad areas: (1) news gathering and reporting; (2) information storage, indexing, and retrieval, especially multimedia content; (3) processing, production, and editorial; (4) distribution or publishing; and (5) presentation, display, and access. These functions are frequently intertwined and integrated into single technical devices. For example, Nokia of Finland is investing in a Silicon Valley start-up company to integrate GPS technology into the next generation of cellular telephones.

This chapter provides a brief conceptual roadmap to the new media landscape and speculates on some of the implications of new media for journalism and mass communication (JMC) education. It also examines some of the key resources and issues relevant to JMC educators attempting to keep up with the ever-changing new media scene and provides a technology checklist for those planning or upgrading new media JMC educational facilities.

Technology Overview

News Gathering and Reporting

The tools for news gathering are changing in dramatic ways. Among the most relevant are a variety of software tools, especially Internet search tools (e.g., *Yahoo!*, which provides both search and directory services, including tools for finding people, both online and off) and browsers (e.g., *Netscape Navigator, Microsoft Internet Explorer*), news databases (e.g., *Lexis/Nexis*), electronic mail (e.g., *Eudora*), virtual communities (e.g., chat rooms, listserves, *Usenet* newsgroups), telnet applications and file transfer protocols (FTP). For a detailed report on the status of many of these technologies in journalism, see the annual "Media in Cyberspace" study by Dan Middleberg and Steve Ross (http://www.middleberg.com). See also a special report on Internet search tools, "Greatest Hits," written by *CBS News* producer and technologist Dan Dubno (http://www.cbs.com/network/htdocs/digitaldan/).

Another extremely useful resource is *Bare Bones 101: A Basic Tutorial on Searching the Web* (http://www.sc.edu/beaufort/library/bones.html), created by Ellen Chamberlain, head librarian at the University of South Carolina at Beaufort. The site provides a series of practical lessons, including: "Search Engines: A Definition"; "Meta-Searchers: A Definition"; "Subject Directories: A Definition"; "Library Gateways and Specialized Databases: A Definition"; "Evaluating Web Pages"; "Creating a Search Strategy"; "Basic Search Tips"; "Searching with Boolean Logic and Proximity Operators"; "Field Searching" (e.g., title, host or site, domain, URL, and link); "Troubleshooting"; "Alta Vista: A Closer Look" (http://www.altavista.com, "one of the largest search engines on the web. Developed by Digital Equipment Corporation in December 1995, it has powerful features [e.g., translation] and is easy to use"); "Excite: A Closer Look" (http://www.excite.com/, "launched in late 1995. It is not one of the largest search engines but it has many extra features [e.g., concept searching]. Today it functions as both search engine and commercial portal"); "Fast Search: A Closer Look" (http://www.alltheweb.com, "originated in Norway. Launched in May 1999, it is one of the newest, largest and fastest of the search engines. Its stated goal is to index all the web that's publicly available"); "Google: A Closer Look" (http://www.google.com, "created in the winter of 1998 by graduate students at Stanford University and . . . officially launched in the fall of 1999. This is a straightforward engine that doesn't support advanced search syntax, making it very easy to use. It returns pages based on the number of sites linking to them and how often they are visited, indicating their popularity"); "HotBot: A Closer Look" (http://www.hotbot.com, "launched in May 1996 by Wired Digital. It is a large database offering a sophisticated interface with powerful advanced searching options"); "Infoseek: A Closer Look" (http://www .go.com, "launched in early 1995 and . . . now part of Disney's GO Network, which also functions as a commercial portal. Both the portal page and basic search page [under the GO Network heading]; and the advanced search page [with the Infoseek name]; are powered by the Infoseek engine"); "Northern Light: A Closer Look" (http://www.northernlight.com, "launched in August 1997 and . . . one of the largest search engines on the web. It offers some interesting features [e.g., natural language searches]; as well as fee-based access to online versions of published articles"); and "Yahoo!: A Closer Look" (http://www.yahoo.com, "launched in early 1995 . . . a human-compiled subject directory and commercial portal. It is the oldest major directory on the web, launched in late 1994, and is a good starting point for information of general appeal").

Also important are a wide range of devices for gathering visual information. Digital still cameras now routinely provide megapixel resolution much closer to the resolution of 35 mm film. Cameras such as the Kodak DC290 Zoom Digital Camera offer 2.1 megapixel resolution and for a price less than $1,000. Digital video (motion) cameras such as the Canon Elura capture broadcast quality video for less than $2,000. Modern digital technology is also making possible a variety of new video formats. Among them are cameras that shoot 360-degree panoramic photos and panoramic motion video in either near or full broadcast quality. In the case of one company, Remote Reality, the 360-degree imaging system involves nothing more complicated than attaching a parabolic mirror to the lens of an off-the-shelf still or motion camera and continuing to shoot. Also available are cameras such as one from MetaCreations that shoot images in three-dimensional format.

The end of the cold war has also provided a powerful imaging resource for journalists, remote sensing satellite imagery (images taken by satellites in orbit some four hundred miles above the earth). Although there are ongoing First Amendment battles between the civilian sector and the federal government (i.e., the Defense Department) over what is called shutter control (i.e., military control of when satellite images are available), remote sensing is already opening up important vistas for journalism. This is especially true for journalists interested in gaining access to remote locations or obtaining large-scale views.

Other imaging tools include unmanned air vehicles (UAV) that can capture visual information from relatively low altitudes and thermal-imaging cameras that can shoot pictures within smoke-filled burning buildings. Also emerging is an entirely new class of more experimental sensors that may transform news gathering. At Columbia University one professor has developed a robot that can travel the streets of Manhattan, scan buildings using a laser, and then render the buildings in precise 3-D format. Another Columbia collaboration has led to the development of a mobile journalist workstation (MJW) with a built-in GPS that can automatically encode each image or sound recorded with the precise longitude, latitude, and altitude where the image or sound was observed. One off-the-shelf camera, the Kodak Digital Science 420, comes similarly equipped with a GPS receiver. Linking GPS-encoded imagery to geographic information system (GIS) data makes it even more powerful.

Audio recording is also being transformed. Among the most important tools are digital audio tape (DAT), digital audio disk, and 3-D sound capture. These tools not only replicate all the capabilities of analog audio recording technology but add a variety of important capabilities such as time codes or annotation (i.e., the reporter can easily annotate sections of the audio recording during an interview, for example, to mark questions).

Storage, Indexing, and Retrieval

Once acquired, the raw material of news content must be stored and indexed for later retrieval and processing or editing. In the analog world, storage devices were usually specifically designed for the specific type of content being acquired, or at least for the modality of that content. For example, words were stored on paper, written often by hand by the journalist conducting an interview or attending a press conference and taking notes. A photographer captured images on film, a videographer motion images on film and later on magnetic videotape. Audio was similarly recorded on magnetic tape, sometimes synchronized with motion images. All this material had to be indexed and filed manually, and later retrieval was done either by referring to the index or reviewing each item in the file, picture, or audio clip. Needless to say, this last was a slow, ponderous, and expensive (in people hours) process and meant that a lot of historical context was never provided in news, especially at the local level.

All this has begun to change in the digital age. Raw news material gathered today is typically stored on digital media that are increasingly independent of the specific types of content or modalities involved. (Video requires more storage capacity than words, but the basic magnetic or optical storage devices are essentially the same.) Moreover, indexing can be increasingly automated, with information such as the subject, date, or location electronically encoded into each piece of information or data acquired. The intelligent agents described in chapter 11, such as the video search tools developed by Professor Shih-Fu Chang and others, also make retrieval ever more efficient.

Today's journalist increasingly works in a variety of media formats, including text, audio, images, graphics, and motion video. Working in these various formats requires ever greater amounts of digital storage. Where once a computer with 256 kilobits of storage was a lot (say, in 1982), today's computers come with hundreds of megabits of random access memory and hard drives with hundreds of gigabits of storage. It will soon be standard for the typical journalist workstation to have terabit or even petabit storage capability, amounts necessary to handle some of the very large, high-resolution files being created. Fortunately, digital storage capability has grown exponentially in recent years, just as its cost has fallen precipitously, so much so that many online services now provide fifty megabits of storage to any user for free. Digital storage offers a variety of significant advantages over analog storage, including automatic indexing (i.e., labeling of content), random access for easy and fast retrieval of content stored anywhere in the file, and advanced search capabilities for audio and video. For example, it is now possible to search audio and video not only based not only on keyword descriptions but on features of the content itself, and not just low-level features such as color, texture, or shapes but also faces, voices, or scene changes. Such capability can be especially useful to the journalist on deadline. A variety of news organizations are already employing these tools, including CNN, PBS, and ABC News. Powerful portable storage devices such as the Iomega Jaz 2 gb drive are increasingly common.

Although digital storage promises to assist journalists in placing current news reports into greater historical context, there is a flip-side danger: digital

storage media tend to become technically obsolete very rapidly, making retrieval of the content impossible. In contrast, analog media almost never
become obsolete and may not require more than a human eye or ear to
retrieve.

Production, Editing, and Design

In 1965 Gordon Moore, former chairman of Intel Corp., the world's
largest manufacturer of computer chips, offered his now famous observation
that the number of transistors that can be placed on a single microchip
doubles every eighteen months. Now known as Moore's Law, this trend has
continued for more than thirty years and means that computers have doubled in processing speed every year and a half. The mainframe computer of
the 1950s that used to fill an entire room has less processing power than a
two-dollar calculator you can slip into your pocket today. Accordingly, journalists have migrated from minicomputers to desktop PCs to laptops to handheld devices like the Palm, which is in effect a fully functional computer.
I'm writing this chapter on my Palm, in fact, which I've inserted into my
Stowaway keyboard, a full-size keyboard that collapses like an accordion to
fit into a pouch about the size of my Palm, which is itself about the size of
a wallet. Once I've finished writing in the Palm "memo" pad, I'll simply
synchronize with my office computer, perhaps even beam what I've written
to another device (a printer, for example), or email it to my publishers using
a wireless modem. Using *Visto.com*, I can also synchronize my Palm (or
other applications such as MS Outlook Express) with an automatically gen-
erated and secure Web site to which only I can gain access, using a unique
user name and password. In addition, I can use *Visto* to build automatically
a "guest" Web site with as much or as little information as I wish visible,
and I can password protect this guest site as well.

The next generation of journalists will rely increasingly on wearable
computer devices. These are likely to involve devices no bigger than a
pager that will clip to one's belt. Users will be able to enter data either by
voice recognition or a hand-held keyboard. Futurist Ray Kurzweil, one of
the pioneers of speech recognition, even forecasts that in less than twenty
years computer processing power will far exceed that of humans and will
have been so miniaturized that microchips will be biologically inserted into

people, giving them access to vast repositories of knowledge and internal computing power.³ Is this part of the future of journalism in the twenty-first century? It's not as far-fetched as it may seem. Microchip technology is already being designed for use in aides to the blind or hearing impaired, in some cases successfully restoring sight or hearing.

Regardless, a variety of new processing and production tools are already available and widely used by journalists not only in central newsrooms but in the field. Among the most common and important are tools for editing HTML, such as Allaire Homesite (v. 4.5), for designing and producing Web sites, such as Macromedia Dreamweaver (v. 3), and for working with dynamic or d-HTML, and XML (which permits layering of data into HTML documents). Other important tools include those for editing digital video. Expensive high-end professional hardware-based systems such as Avid are rapidly being replaced by simpler, far less expensive software-based systems such as Adobe Premier 5.1 (with versions that run on Mac, Windows, and Unix/Linux operating systems) or Final Cut Pro 1.2, which runs on a Power Mac G4. Equipped with FireWire (version 2.2.2) with 400 mbps transfer capability, this option offers near-broadcast-quality postproduction capability. Similar tools are available for editing digital still images. Popular packages for still image processing include Adobe Photoshop (v. 5.01). Experiments have also demonstrated the compatibility of image processing on a Palm. Graphics packages include Adobe Illustrator (v. 7.0). Audio production tools include Digidesign Protools (v. 2.0).

On a more experimental level, software tools for creating professional 3-D images and graphics are now available. Once only possible on costly and complex high-end Silicon Graphics workstations, high-quality consumer-friendly 3-D imaging programs are available from companies such as MetaCreations, whose Canoma program has been used by CBS News and others to produce useful 3-D views of a variety of objects, such as sculptures in an art report or historical artifacts in an archaeological report. Using MetaStream these 3-D objects can be easily streamed to a viewer accessing the Web site using a 28.8 modem. Tools for creating Web-based animations are also increasingly simple to create and effective in reporting a variety of news stories. Java, Flash, and other tools have been used by reporters at news organizations from CNN to the New York Times. Even mundane applications such as word processing and spreadsheets, extensively used in computer-assisted reporting (CAR) are being transformed. Today's state-of-the-art tools can maintain detailed records of every change made to a document, enabling reporters and editors to retrace its evolution, a process sometimes useful in fact checking. Increasingly, these tools are available to run on low-cost, portable devices that enable journalists and other communication professionals to work in the field or in virtual newsrooms. Consider the Project Candide, in which five new media journalists have used a variety of digital tools to report from remote locations in East Africa and China.[4]

Object-oriented multimedia represents perhaps the next generation in production, editing, and design technology. Work at IBM (e.g., Hot Video) and Columbia University (Professor Alex Eleftheriadis's Zest) illustrate the nature of object-oriented multimedia. In most static Web pages, content is made up of clickable objects that contain additional information, synthetic elements (e.g., graphics, animations), multimedia (e.g., streaming video), or links to other Web pages; for this reason, object-oriented multimedia, or video, is made up of clickable, interactive objects. In contrast to traditional analog video, digital programming created using Zest (which is compatible with both Web browsers and MPEG-4, the next standard for digital television, and similar to virtual reality modeling language, or VRML, which is used to create 3-D Web content), every element in a video can contain additional content. For example, in a ninety-second video report about President Clinton and Monica Lewinsky, the images of Clinton, Lewinsky, and Kenneth Starr might contain additional content—such as brief synopses of their roles in the controversy—available on demand using a mouse or a remote control or even through voice command. This will enable journalists to layer in much greater context and information than is currently available on television.

MovieBuilder, software from iMove (www.imoveinc.com) released in 2000, allows video editors to seam together multiple video streams of the same event into a single video package, allowing viewers to cut back and forth between multiple views of the same event. In the past, multiple views of the same event were rarely retained, much less provided to the viewer, except when separate clips were edited together into a single linear narrative or replayed for viewers of sporting events. Tomorrow's digital video will permit viewers to observe the same event from multiple angles and perspectives. Although this may not always be important, under some circumstances it might help reveal the fuller truth of an event. This would especially be the case in videos depicting such complex events as a shuttle launch or a medical procedure.

Distribution

Perhaps no part of modern journalism has been more visibly transformed than how news is distributed or published. The rise of the Internet and its World Wide Web in the 1990s brought news online, on demand, and onto a global stage as never before. With more than five thousand newspapers, television and news operations, magazines, and Internet-original news services (including many Web-zines) available for free to anyone with a computer and access to the Internet, journalism from all parts of the world has become universally available. The Internet makes it possible for virtually anyone to own a digital printing press capable of reaching a worldwide audience. The cost of the cheapest Internet server has now fallen to less than a dollar, and with many service providers offering free Internet service, it doesn't take a mathematician or an accountant to understand why millions of people around the world have created their own personal Web pages, many of them, like cybergossip Matt Drudge's, published under the guise of news.

The Internet continues to evolve. Some of the most important recent developments have dramatic implications for journalists and journalism. The delivery of audio and video on demand—streaming, in Internet parlance—has made it possible for virtually anyone to launch a radio or television station, with or without news. The growth of broadband (i.e., high-speed) telecommunications services via cable modems, digital subscriber lines (DSL), direct broadcast satellite, and various terrestrial wireless technologies promises to bring even more change to journalism in the next decade and beyond. Dial-up modems with speeds as slow as 28.8 or 56 kbps are being rapidly replaced by 300 kbps services or even faster T1 or Ethernet services. These broadband services make delivering broadcast-quality video or audio on demand via the Internet increasingly common. Real Media Player G2, Windows Media Player, Digital Bitcasting, and Pixelon now deliver full-screen, twenty-four-frames-per-second, VCR-quality–resolution video on demand to Internet users with a broadband connection. Technology for delivering high-quality audio is also available, including the WinAmp player, which can deliver CD-quality audio. An increasing number of traditional news and media organizations are beginning to see the possibilities presented by this technology.

Other network technologies are also transforming journalism. File transfer protocol (FTP) is used to move large files, such as images or video, across the Internet easily and are extensively used by journalists today. Electronic mail, or email, is used not just for communication but as a means of interviewing sources who may live thousands of miles away. Increasingly sophisticated journalists prefer to have their email reside on the server (the computer that routes incoming and outgoing data traffic), using a technical protocol called "imap" that keeps the mail on the server but permits the user to download mail from any computer anywhere in the world, as long as it is equipped with a Web browser such as *Netscape*. A variety of related tools are enabling journalists to create virtual newsrooms that they can access from any place at any time, with full access to all their work. For example, a Palm can be synchronized to either a desktop or a network, including the Internet, making it possible to have one's address book, schedule, email, and more all accessible from either the Palm or any other device with Internet access. Using *Avantgo.com*, synchronizing when connected to the Internet enables the Palm to download virtually any Web site, from the *New York Times* to the *Wall Street Journal*, for later reading. The Visor, which also runs on the Palm operating system, has a growing number of plug-ins, ranging from GPS to MP3. The BlackBerry handheld similarly offers many of the Palm functions but adds fast email capability anywhere in the United States.

Journalists increasingly participate in online discussion forums known as mailing lists and bulletin boards that deal with specialized topics of any and all types. Research by Middleberg and Ross indicates that reporters frequently find not only story ideas on such forums but also sources and leads.[5] One popular online forum, *egroups.com*, not only hosts threaded discussions and mailing lists (where members receive via email a copy of each message posted to the group) but automatically builds a searchable Web site of the entire history of the forum and permits members to upload files into an archive known as the "vault"; it also provides folders of relevant links or URLs.

Poised to transform journalism even further is the beginning of digital broadcasting, both audio and video. Direct broadcast satellite has demonstrated the potential of digital broadcasting, and other satellite systems for digital radio broadcasting and terrestrial digital broadcasting of video will roll out over the next half dozen years (according to the law under the direction of the Federal Communications Commission). These services will enable vastly personalized, on-demand news and entertainment services in audio and video, as well as the multiplexing of signals to expand greatly the specialization and possibly localization of news and information, not to mention marketing and e-commerce.

Access and Display

For journalism, function has often followed form. Julius Caesar's Acta Diurna in 59 B.C. was possible only because of the existence of parchment. The first daily newspapers published in the 1600s were possible only because of the invention of both paper and the printing press. Real-time news over great distance became possible only in the 1800s with the invention of the electric telegraph. Broadcasting of first audio and then motion-picture news reports developed only in the first half of the twentieth century with the invention of radio and television. The Internet today is continuing to lead a reinvention of how news is accessed, displayed, and presented to an increasingly global public. Through the World Wide Web news can be presented not only in text, audio, or video format but interactively as well. News is also increasingly being delivered to a variety of portable devices continuously connected through wireless communications to the Internet. Internet cellular telephones, pagers, and other devices now provide everything from breaking news to stock alerts and sports scores. One network, CNN, is now experimenting with the delivery of video news to cellular telephone displays.

Display, access, and presentation technology is continuing to evolve. By the end of the next decade or two the media of news delivery may have as little in common with the media of today as modern media do with the town crier. Many Internet users now get much of their news delivered via a cathode ray tube (CRT), the basic technology used in a typical television set. But the flat-panel display is already familiar to anyone with a laptop computer, a Palm, or a cellular telephone. Already available in prototype form, something called "e-ink" promises to bring even more change to news display devices. E-ink, or electronic ink, is essentially a virtual replacement for traditional printing paper. It is a computerized laminated paper product that already can display text information and in the future perhaps images and video—with the resolution of ink on paper. It is fully reusable and operates with a minimal electrical charge. In many ways, it promises to be a viable electronic medium for the daily newspaper, and it is environmentally much friendlier than today's newspapers.

Also being tested are a variety of wearable display devices, such as prescription eyewear that can also display video, text, or other images. If this sounds far-fetched, check to see how many devices you or the person sitting next to you are already wearing: cellular telephone, pager, and so on.

Speech synthesis and recognition are also poised to transform journalism. AnaNova, a Max Headroom—like Internet personality in the United Kingdom, already delivers personalized news as a virtual anchor. More seriously, speech synthesis tools are already widely used by the visually impaired to listen to computerized readings of virtually any news text. Increasingly sophisticated speech recognition tools are also being used by video indexing services such as Virage to classify video news automatically.

Implications for Journalism and Mass Communication Education

New media technologies have important implications for journalism and mass communication education. These implications fall into four broad areas: (1) how new media are transforming how we teach and research journalism and mass communication, or how educators do their work; (2) how new media are transforming the content of what we teach; (3) how new media are transforming the structure of journalism and mass communication schools and departments, as well as universities and other institutions of higher education; and (4) how new media are transforming the relationships between journalism educators and a variety of publics, including students, funders, competitors, and others.

What are some of the potential implications of new media for journalism education, both good and bad? The following discussion is not meant to be comprehensive but rather provides an example or two in each area to illustrate the implications of new media for journalism education. Although not driven by a technological determinist perspective, this chapter argues that new media developments are enabling the transformation of journalism and mass communication education. Although some would contend that new media are inherently value laden or at least predetermined in their outcome, this contention is untenable, at least in some of the most important cases. The Internet grew in large part from a U.S. Defense Department initiative, but its value depends largely on how people use it. It can be used as a vehicle for distributing online pornography, pedophilia, and hatred or simply to foster commercial culture and communications. But it can also be used to promote understanding, communication, and learning.

The Way Journalism Educators Do Their Work

Just as new media are transforming how journalists and other communication professionals do their work, they are changing how journalism educators perform their work as teachers and scholars. Among the most obvious examples are email and presentation software. Email greatly facilitates communication among work and research teams, especially those involved in international collaboration, where asynchronous communication is a boon to productivity and the low-cost nature of email is a blessing to budgets already stretched too thin. Email is also transforming how many faculty communicate with their students, enabling twenty-four-hour access. Other areas that are in somewhat earlier stages of adoption and diffusion are online journalism courses (e.g., see the author's *Exploring New Media Online* Web site.[6] In addition, a variety of free online resources such as *Free: The Freedom Forum Online*, the *Columbia Journalism Review*, the *American Journalism Review*, and the *Online Journalism Review* published by the University of Southern California Annenberg School) are available to journalism educators for use in their teaching and research.[7]

The Content of What We Teach

Many journalism educators are increasingly relying on presentation software (such as Microsoft Powerpoint) not only to transform how they teach but to enrich the content of their lectures with multimedia graphics and illustrations. These applications are enabling educators to create more dynamic, multimedia content to help their students understand complex concepts more easily and completely. In my own teaching, for example, I use Powerpoint presentations to supplement my lectures with everything from screen shots of relevant Web sites to charts and diagrams illustrating important ideas.

Although some would contend that there is a downside to using such presentation software (i.e., once you start using a Powerpoint presentation, it's hard to shift focus), the truth is that if you are experienced with the features of the software, it is relatively easy to skip slides, pause or miniaturize a presentation, and launch a discussion in an entirely unanticipated direction. Even so, such tools are not necessarily useful for every teacher or every subject and must be reviewed on an individual basis.

More important, some are envisioning new media as a catalyst for a fundamental restructuring of the basic JMC curriculum. This restructuring is playing out in dramatic fashion at the University of Minnesota. As reported in the University of Minnesota's newsletter *Brief*, planners of a new media initiative have decided a stand-alone curriculum would be a mistake. Instead, Dean Stephen Rosenstone has reported, new media will be built into several disciplines. The journalism curriculum "is prepared for a major overhaul," director Al Tims adds. All new hires will be people with experience in new media. Employers have said, "We will beat a path to your door," if the university produces graduates who combine new media skills with an understanding of how to use them in context, Tims notes.[8]

Kathleen A. Hansen, associate professor and director of the Minnesota Journalism Center, elaborates on this curricular transformation and explains the importance of integrating new media into the entire JMC curriculum:

> I think an important example here for journalism educators has to do with how new media concepts and skills are taught. Al Tims and I spoke with many new media practitioners in visits around the country this summer. A common theme in every one of our conversations was the issue of "stand-alone" vs. integrated models for new media education. Many schools and departments have added one or two courses on "new media" or have started separate enterprises where new media issues are examined. Our discussions with industry folks have led us to believe that is a mistake. We are intending to offer an integrated curriculum that incorporates new media technologies and issues in every course. We envision an editing course, for instance, that would incorporate skills for editing in print, video, online and many other delivery formats. The format of delivery is not the issue—the conceptual and technical skills of editing content for an audience are. In sum, because new media are transforming the content of what we teach in some basic, fundamental ways, journalism educators are being forced to rethink their entire curriculum. We either incorporate this in a piecemeal fashion, or we look for an integrated approach that encompasses all of the technologies and transformative processes and skills.
>
> (personal email, September 19, 1998)

The Structure of Journalism and the Institutions That Teach It

A growing number of universities are offering entire online degree programs. In the summer of 1998 Stanford became the first major university to offer an entire graduate degree program online, a master's degree in electrical engineering. International University is a cyberuniversity entirely online, the first to be accredited (not without controversy). Its offerings include courses in new media and telecommunications, as well as more traditional areas of learning. It won't be long before entire journalism and mass communication curricula are commonly offered online. It may also not be long before we in journalism and mass communication education begin to reexamine the very notion of what constitutes a classroom and what represents the best way to teach our discipline. For example, is the notion of a course built around a physical classroom, a time period defined in terms of a semester or quarter, and a narrowly defined body of knowledge the most effective and efficient way to teach our field in an age of new media?[9] Some JMC programs in 1999 were heavily involved in long-distance education — for example, the University of Memphis (formerly Memphis State University) offers a degree program entirely via the Web—and many educators routinely offer courses via satellite and other distance technologies. The definition of *classroom* had thus evolved significantly by the time of this writing in 2000.[10]

The Relationships Between Educators and Their Publics

Perhaps most important, the relationships between JMC educators and their publics, especially their students, are undergoing a transformation enabled by new media. At one level, the transformation is relatively simple and straightforward: more and more classes are being supplemented by online discussions, bulletin boards, chat rooms, and email, giving students and teachers an unprecedented level of interaction.

On another level, the transformation is more paradigmatic. Throughout most of the twentieth century in the United States, JMC education has been dominated by a very traditional model of learning. The instructor is in the role of omnipotent bearer of knowledge, who imparts as much knowledge about JMC in one semester as possible to as many students as is feasible. New media, especially the Internet and the World Wide Web, have made this traditional model obsolete. With knowledge, especially journalistic knowledge, available at an unprecedented level, the role of the JMC educator is undergoing a transformation from omnipotent teacher to experienced and critical guide. The role of the student is changing from absorber of facts to discoverer, interpreter, and synthesizer of knowledge. The implications for JMC education are profound and suggest that it is time not only to revisit the substance of what we teach but also how the JMC curriculum is structured.

13 Job Prospects in Online Journalism

Although graduates of traditional journalism programs enter a diminishing job market, those who are comfortable with technology and have some experience producing new media content have a brighter future. Despite the retrenchment of some major news organizations in their new media endeavors (e.g., the online venture initiated by Rupert Murdoch's News Corporation and MCI), the new media market still represents the best opportunity for growth.

This discussion takes both a short- and long-term look at:

- where the jobs are in new media;
- the necessary skills for landing and succeeding in a new media job;
- opportunities for those trained in traditional areas of journalism to transfer to new media;
- the salary range in new media; and, perhaps most important,
- the future: will the next generation of journalists, those especially trained or educated to work in a new media environment, produce an improved form of journalism?

Where the Jobs Are

Jobs in online journalism today increasingly have to do with content creation. Not too long ago (e.g., 1995–1997), most were largely involved in

coding HTML and in repurposing the writing of other journalists for online
distribution and access.[1] By 2000, although many positions still entail a significant amount of such work, more new media journalists are creating original content for online news publications and occasional new media products
delivered on fixed media, such as DVD. A good example is *Cloakroom.com*,
an online publication launched in 1998. *Cloakroom's* journalists report extensively on campaign activity at both the national and local level, creating
new content for online delivery.[2]

All types of traditional news organizations are developing or offering new
media news products: an estimated 4,925 newspapers around the world
maintain Web sites, many including original news content (www.ajr.com).
In the United States alone, more than 1,000 daily newspapers and hundreds
of weeklies now have online offerings.[3] Dozens of online original news publications, as well as hundreds of specialized online news offerings in trade
areas, also offer journalism employment opportunities. Some eight hundred
U.S. television stations and all major networks offer Web sites, although most
local stations in 2000 do not provide news content. Many cable companies
have a Web presence as well. Cablevision, for example, has launched a
neighborhood news service via the Web, featuring streaming video, or real-
time video content delivered via the Internet.[4]

The annual cyberspace survey by Steve Ross and Don Middleberg confirms this growth pattern:

> Original content on Web sites grew enormously in 1998. Only 22
> percent of newspaper respondents with Web sites said their sites had
> less than 5 percent original content. This compares with 39 percent
> of the respondents in 1997—a huge cut in one year! For magazines,
> the drop was from 27 percent to 11 percent—nearly three-fold. Thus,
> 1998 marks a historic moment—news organizations have now clearly
> broken away from their tendency to use on-line technology (Web sites
> usually, but not always) as a distribution device more than as a new
> medium.[5]

The Ross and Middleberg study also indicates that many new media jobs
are for online magazine products.

Particularly significant among the developments in the new media marketplace are the joint ventures of some major communication industry play-

ers. These ventures include the multimillion dollar Microsoft-NBC alliance, MSNBC, which had a 1996 debut and has spawned many new media positions producing interactive news content.[6] Another interesting joint new media venture is the Alternative News Network, Inc. (ANNI), a partnership of Cummings Multimedia Entertainment and Internet Video Services, a Internet service provider based in Sunnyvale, California, that specializes in video storage and distribution. Launched in 1996, ANNI now has its base in Australia and provides twenty-four-hour coverage of local, state, national, and worldwide news aimed at young adults.[7] The full-time staff of more than two hundred professional journalists from around the world is supported by stringers including university and college journalism students.

Many of the most interesting new media journalism jobs involved in content creation are for specialized publications, such as publications in the worlds of computing, medicine, and science. *Medscape* is an example of one growing online medical news and information service.[8]

Finally, a broad category of new media jobs often overlooked is in financial news services, including the big three of Reuters, Dow Jones, and Bloomberg, as well as smaller niche providers such as *TheStreet.com, Raging Bull, CBS Marketwatch,* and *Motley Fool* that providing extensive coverage of the financial markets.[9] Specializing in financial news and information, although featuring general news products as well, these companies offer commercial real-time, multimedia news information at a premium price (with some basic services available for free), distributed via the public telecommunications network and designed for delivery via the Web. Growth in this industry sector has been extraordinary. Each of the major players has introduced new online news services or features over the past several years and has sought new editors and reporters. As the global economy, especially the Internet sector, continues to grow, with day trading and twenty-four-hour markets expanding at an almost exponential rate, the growth of these financial news and information services shows little sign of slowing.

Geographically, the greatest concentration of U.S.-based companies looking for people to fill positions in new media content creation are headquartered in the greater metropolitan areas of New York (the *New York Times,* the major television networks, MSNBC, ESPN, and others) and San Francisco/ San Jose (Knight-Ridder/Mercury Center, C/Net, and others). The picture is somewhat less sharply focused in the online news arena, however, where major players are also based in Atlanta (e.g., CNN), Chicago (e.g., the Tribune Co.), Boston (e.g., *Boston.com*), Dallas (e.g., the *Dallas Morning News*), Los

Angeles (e.g., the *Los Angeles Times*), and Seattle/Redmond (e.g., the *Seattle Times* and Microsoft).

An early Bay Area Multimedia Partnership study of new media employment in the San Francisco area found that twenty-two hundred Bay-area new media companies employed some 62,000 workers in 1995. Although the number of firms has not increased dramatically since then (with some new firms entering the market, but some others disappearing, either through attrition or mergers/acquisitions), the number of employees had more than doubled by 2000.[10] A comparable 1995 study by the accounting firm Coopers and Lybrand showed that more than forty-two hundred New York–area new media companies employed some 71,500 full-time employees, up from 28,500 in 1992.[11] Subsequent editions of this study have shown a steady increase in the number of new media employees, many of them working in online journalism, with an estimated 105,000 in 1998 and some 130,000 in 2000. The study indicates that so-called Silicon Alley, the Manhattan home of many new media companies, employs an estimated 39,000 full-time workers, more than the numbers estimated to be working in Manhattan in television broadcasting (16,914), book publishing (13,466), newspapers (12,226), or cable television (6,784) in 2000. Of course, not all these are new media journalists.

For more on trends and developments in Silicon Alley, as well as the Digital Coast (the new media or dot com industry of southern California, especially Los Angeles and Hollywood's entertainment industry), see the *Silicon Alley Reporter* and *Digital Coast Reporter*, two publications offered by Rising Tide Studios (RST).[12] Rising Tide was founded in the 1990s by Jason McCabe Calacanis and has grown into a premier provider of intelligence on the growing new media sectors on both the East and West Coasts.

Because of the nature of new media, these employment data don't mean that living in New York or San Francisco is necessarily a requirement. Many new media journalism positions involve freelancing, and this can be done from almost anywhere in the world, wherever the story may be. One interesting example is *Tamnet*, the second online daily in Louisiana, a joint project of two community newspapers in St. Tammany Parish, a suburban parish north of New Orleans, but staffed and maintained by the *News Banner* in Covington. The site's Web master in 1998 was Eric Ulken, a native of the St. Tammany Parish and full-time student in the School of Journalism at the University of Missouri. Ulken conducted his duties as Web master remotely via the Internet. Although it was not an ideal working arrangement, it worked. "The most difficult part about working from several hundred miles away is coordinating efforts on anything," Ulken admits (personal email, September 26, 1998). Notably, the actual Web site is uploaded through an Internet server in Houston.

A number of online services offer extensive job listings in journalism and new media, including the *American Journalism Review*, the *Columbia Journalism Review*, and the *Online Journalism Review* (where a visit on February 21, 2000, revealed more than two hundred job openings in online journalism; an April 2000 market correction triggered later job cuts at a number of dot-com news sites, however).

Necessary Skills for New Media Journalists

Although the most fundamental skills required for a new media journalist are good reporting, writing, and editing, it is also essential to understand the capabilities and aesthetics of new media. This includes developing an appreciation for the interactive nature of digital, networked media and learning to think in new ways for nonlinear or multilinear storytelling. At Columbia University, all students in the Graduate School of Journalism learn to report and tell stories with these new media capabilities in mind. Students also learn reporting and storytelling capabilities that transcend the specific tools of today's new media environment (visit the Graduate School of Journalism Web site or the Center for New Media for details and examples).[13] See also the *Online Journalism Review*'s "Guide to Online Journalism Programs," where a look on February 21, 2000, provided reviews of some two dozen programs in online journalism education.[14]

Certain specific skills are useful in obtaining and succeeding in a new media job. Foremost is comfort with using a computer to go online, in particular to navigate the Internet and the World Wide Web. A prerequisite to getting a job in new media is having and using an email address, knowing how to transfer files electronically, and building and maintaining your own Web site. Although creating a Web site means having some facility in HTML, the development of Pagemill and virtual communities such as *TheGlobe.com* (which offer Web page design templates) and other software authoring tools for the Web is making this less critical. It is not necessary to know how to create so-called Dynamic-HTML pages, Shockwave-enhanced pages, or how to use Macromedia's popular Web design package Dreamweaver, but the well-trained journalist who does understand the capabilities of these tools certainly has an advantage. An eye for multimedia design and knowing how to launch an online publication are also increasingly a requirement for landing a position in online journalism. This includes understanding everything from Web page layout and graphics, to the selection of fonts and use of streaming media tools such as RealPlayer or Windows Media Player for streaming video delivery, to being experienced with the Java programming language and managing online forums and electronic databases. As digital television comes into place over the next decade and as broadband capabilities (i.e., high bandwidth) transform the Web, it will become increasingly useful for all journalists to understand the basics of visual and aural storytelling. Mastering the basics of producing and editing audio and video in a digital environment (such as knowing how to work with a nonlinear editing tool like Adobe Premier) will fashion an increasingly employable and effective cross-media-trained journalist. This is in fact a core component in the new media curriculum at Columbia's Graduate School of Journalism.

Here are some of the requirements and preferred skills noted by some new media employers in 1999:

- two to five years of experience in journalism, print, or broadcast, including reporting, copyediting, and handling multiple feeds;
- experience on a major online service and facility with HTML, Java, and World Wide Web site design;
- strong attention to details;
- excellent written and verbal communication skills, solid experience with a PC and MS Office software (e.g., word processing, spreadsheet use);
- experience in business journalism;
- at least two years of experience as a sports editor/writer in the newspaper or magazine industry, along with fantasy sports knowledge;
- exceptional motivation, strong interest in news, and knowledge of personal computers and the World Wide Web;
- a strong work ethic, a willingness to pursue original stories aggressively, and experience in computer reporting; and
- the ability to submit a résumé via email.

Opportunities for Those Trained in Traditional Journalism

As even a cursory reading of the above requirements makes clear, the most important requirement for a position in new media is experience in reporting, writing, and editing, especially under deadline pressures, where stress is the ultimate test of a reporter's mettle. Web experience and skill follow as a close second and third but clearly lag behind sound skill as a journalist. Many positions in new media are senior or at least not entry level, thus giving those with solid journalism experience an upper hand, especially if they can complement their reporting experience with HTML and Java skill, perhaps obtained through a professional training seminar on Web design. An additional skill often valuable in new media is a specialized knowledge base in an area of coverage, such as sports, financial, or fashion reporting. Knowing what works well in an online publication is also important, as is an eye for graphic design.

Salary Range for New Media

Jobs in new media are generally better paying than comparable positions in traditional news organizations. Many job postings indicate that salaries are competitive and commensurate with experience, with a typical beginning salary in 1999 in the mid-$30,000s to $40,000s. Graduates of the Columbia University Graduate School of Journalism with a concentration in new media have obtained in 1999 and 2000 positions in new media with starting salaries averaging roughly $40,000, nearly double their print and broadcast counterparts. The graduates have been hired at a wide range of companies, including *New Jersey Online*, *MSNBC.com*, and *ABCNews.com*.

The Future

These patterns in the new media journalism marketplace are likely to shift somewhat during the first decade of the twenty-first century, as some news companies downsize their new media efforts and there is some consolidation among online news operations. But the overall patterns are likely to continue: job growth, content creation emphasis, and competitive salaries in new media ventures. Those entering the market should keep their focus on quality journalism and quality content but be sure to envision the creative opportunities afforded by new media, especially nonlinear, interactive storytelling and multimedia content. Those attracted by the nonlinear world of cyberspace will be particularly rewarded as pioneers on the frontier of new media journalism.

Afterword

Contextualized Journalism:
Implications for the Evolving Role of Journalists
in the Twenty-first Century

This book has argued that new media technology is enabling the emergence of a new form of news perhaps best described as contextualized journalism. Contextualized journalism incorporates not only the multimedia capabilities of digital platforms but also the interactive, hypermedia, fluid qualities of online communications and the customizable features of addressable media. It may help reengage an increasingly alienated and mistrusting news audience often frustrated by some traditional journalists' overuse of anonymous sources (e.g., even at distinguished news operations, veteran journalists reporting on independent prosecutor Kenneth Starr's investigation of President Clinton frequently attributed insights and allegations to unknown sources), unsubstantiated rumors, and quotations and other materials taken out of context.

Contextualized journalism also raises serious questions about the evolving role of journalists in an increasingly electronic world. The role of the journalist in an analog world has traditionally been dominated by three objectives: (1) to survey the world and report the facts as they are best understood; (2) to interpret those facts in terms of their impact on the local community or society at large; and (3) to provide opinion or editorial guidance on those facts, thereby helping to shape public opinion on matters of civic importance and to set an agenda for public discourse.

How is the role of the journalist changing as a result of an increasingly networked world? I believe change is happening in three fundamental ways. First, because of the ubiquitous nature of news and information in today's online environment and the positioning of contextualized journalism next to other forms of online content, the journalist needs to become much more than just a teller of facts. Just as educators are seeing their role change from omnipotent bearer of knowledge in the classroom to guide to a continually changing knowledge landscape where students are often as much teacher as learner, journalists need to adjust to being in the role of guide as well. Journalists in the twenty-first century will no longer be the sole or frequently even the primary provider of much news and informational content on current events. Today, it is just as easy for a news consumer to get the "facts" from any of dozens of sources, whether corporate, governmental, or other aggregated on *Yahoo!* Moreover, it is increasingly practical to observe news directly as it unfolds through Webcams and other new media tools that are the digital counterpart to cable TV's familiar congressional window, C-SPAN. The journalist of the twenty-first century will need to become a much more skillful storyteller, one who can not only weave together the facts of an event or process but connect those facts to a much wider set of contextualizing events and circumstances. She will need to place a premium on helping the reader sort through the myriad of Web sites and other forms of online content that provide news and commentary on events around the world or at home and establish which forms are reliable. This process of accrediting content, contends Raph Kasper, associate vice provost for research at Columbia University, will be essential in an online news environment where virtually anyone can publish and content is easily manufactured or manipulated (personal communication, October 1998). Echoing this view is Tom Goldstein, dean of the Columbia University Graduate School of Journalism, who contends that the avalanche of information available on the Internet has moved modern society from a state of information scarcity to information abundance and has resulted in a "scarcity of attention" among members of a sometimes overwhelmed public.[1] The impact on journalism is an increasing need for journalists who can sort through this avalanche of information and placing editing skills at a premium. Many journalists are under intense pressure to produce short news bites for an online audience with an increasingly short attention span. It is necessary to produce news abstracts that will provide the essential facts, but it is also critically important to produce the full exposition of the facts in context. It is this balancing of the public's need to know quickly with the need to know fully that will fundamentally challenge journalism in the twenty-first century.

Second, the journalist's role as interpreter of events will be much expanded and somewhat changed. Audiences will place a premium on understanding why certain information is important and what its significance or impact may be, so journalists will need to develop their role as sense makers of events and processes. This role will be facilitated by the use of hypermedia and object-oriented content that allows seamless integration of content developed by a variety of information providers. But it will also require journalists to think in new, more fluid fashions and will require new forms of journalism education and training that emphasize integrated thinking and storytelling. Furthermore, the journalist will add value by searching and sorting through increasingly large electronic information haystacks to find the single needle of significance. This will become increasingly important as information overload—"data smog," as one writer calls it[2]—overwhelms us and the news consumer's patience erodes. Intelligent software agents will support journalists in this process, but only human intelligence will be able to evaluate effectively when something new is important, especially in relation to a seemingly unrelated fact, process, or circumstance.

Finally, online journalists will play a central role in reconnecting communities. This online form of civic journalism will not only encourage more citizen participation in public life but help improve journalism, both online and off, by connecting local journalism organizations more to the institutions and processes they cover. Journalists, and journalistic organizations, will need to become much more responsive to their audiences. Journalists will need to be comfortable reading and answering email from audience members who in many cases will not only be smarter but more well informed on a subject than the reporter him- or herself. This humbling reality is something journalists will need to get used to. In the networked world, readers respond by email to reporters and other readers sometimes within seconds of a report's publication, typically with special intensity when a mistake has been made. The networked world requires journalists to be even more attentive to detail and accuracy because feedback can be swift, hard-hitting, and self-correcting.

This changing role of the journalist will help to maintain the business health of the institution of journalism by keeping audiences large and growing and building new revenue streams to support quality news reporting. More important, it will help ensure the larger role served by journalism in society as the mechanism by which citizens in a democracy stay informed.

Notes

Introduction

1. James W. Carey, "The Internet and the End of the National Communications System: Uncertain Predictions of an Uncertain Future," *Journalism Quarterly* 75, no. 1 (spring 1998): 28.

1. Transforming Storytelling

1. Jeri Clausing, "Hurricane-Watchers Clog Weather Web Sites," *The New York Times on the Web*, August 26, 1998, http://www.nytimes.com. The address of the Weather Channel's Web site is http://www.weather.com; the address of the National Hurricane Center's informational site is http://www.nhc.noaa.gov.
2. http://www.learntech.com (September 12, 1999).
3. http://www.nightkitchen.com (September 12, 1999).
4. http://bagpipe.cs.columbia.edu (September 10, 1999).
5. http://www.remotereality.com; http://www.behere.com; http://www.imoveinc.com; http://www.ipix.com (September 12, 1999).
6. http://www.ipix.com (May 15, 2000).
7. http://www.cs.columbia.edu/CAVE/ (September 15, 2000).
8. http://www.cpj.org/pubs/attacks97/killed97.html (October 10, 1998).
9. "Injured Journalist Ian Stewart Making Steady Recovery," Canadian Journalists for Free Expression, http://www.cepj.ca/ (February 4, 1999).
10. http://www.suc.org/news/b92/archive (February 1, 2000).

11. http://rex.opennet.org/cyberex/Kosovo/klecka.htm (February 15, 1999).
12. http://www.popstudios.com/film/CINERAMA_1.html, p. 1 (September 14, 2000).
13. www.ctr.columbia.edu/~laitee/NewsLab/Omnicamera/.
14. Eric S. Fredin and Prabu David, "Browsing and the Hypermedia Interaction Cycle: A Model of Self-Efficacy and Goal Dynamics," *Journalism and Mass Communication Quarterly* 75, no. 1 (spring 1998): 35.
15. The global positioning system was developed by the U.S. military to provide precise locational information about objects anywhere on earth using a constellation of twenty-four satellites orbiting the earth.
16. A. J. Liebling, "The Wayward Press," *The New Yorker*, quoted in *1,911 Best Things Anybody Ever Said*, ed. Robert Byrne (New York: Fawcett, 1998).
17. Carl Bernstein, February 1998, quoted in Ted Pease, TODAY'S WORD ON JOURNALISM, March 9, 1999, tpease@cc.usu.edu.
18. The film is available at http://member.aol.com/n0tch/HOME/JFK/8mm-Zapruderfilm.html.
19. Walter Lippmann, "The World Outside and the Pictures in Our Heads," *Public Opinion* (New York: Macmillan, 1922), p. 3.
20. Trevor Butterworth, *NewsWatch* associate editor, "The Ultimate Distortion" March 2, 1999, http://www.newswatch.org/spotlight/990302f1.htm (March 2, 1999).
21. Michael Gartner, *Daily Tribune* (Ames, Iowa), 1998, quoted in Mark Lisheron, "The Mentor," *American Journalism Review*, January/February 1999, p. 1, http://ajr.newslinkorg/ajrmarkjan99.html (September 14, 2000).
22. http://www.freedomforum.org/technology/1999/3/1katz.asp.
23. Thomas L. Friedman, "FOREIGN AFFAIRS: KillingGoliath.com," *New York Times*, March 9, 1999, sec. 1, 16.

2. Assessing the State of Online Journalism

1. "World Online Markets, Jupiter Communications, 1996," http://www.nua.ie February 2, 1999.
2. http://www.msnbc.com.
3. http://www.money.com.
4. Bernard Berelson, "What 'Missing the Newspaper' Means," in *Communications Research*, ed. P. F. Lazarfeld and F. N. Stanton (New York: Harper and Brothers, 1948–49), 111–128.
5. I introduced this concept in "The Future of Online Journalism: Bonanza or Black Hole?" *Columbia Journalism Review*, July/August 1997: 30–34, 36.
6. http://www.clarin.com.ar.

7. http://www.frecuenciaweb.com.ar/.

8. *CNN.com*, February 22, 1999, http://www.altavista.com (February 22, 1999).

9. http://www.psu.edu/ur/NEWS/news/kosovohelp.html.

10. Adam Clayton Powell III, "Balkans-Related Sites Offer Images, Online Analysis," http://www.freedomforum.org (April 2, 1999).

11. http://www.fas.org (February 15, 1999).

12. Mark Rinzel, "Between Propaganda and Talking Heads: Wartime Journalism in the Internet Age," special report to the *Silicon Alley Daily*, April 14, 1999, http://www.SiliconAlleyreporter.com.

13. http://www.egroups.com (March 26, 1999).

14. http://www.nytimes.com.

15. http://www.washingtonpost.com.

16. http://www.time.com.

17. http://www.cnn.com.

18. http://www.abcnews.com; http://www.usatoday.com.

19. http://www.mercurycenter.com.

20. http://www.chicago.tribune.com.

21. http://www.orlandosentinel.com.

22. http://www.boston.com.

23. http://www.nando.com.

24. http://www.northscape.com.

25. http://www.dallasnews.com; http://www.nj.com.

26. http://www.reuters.com;   http://www.wsj.com;   http://www.bloomberg.com; http://www.thestreet.com; http://www.fool.com.

27. http://www.cnnfn.com.

28. http://www.businessweek.com.

29. http://www.cnet.com.

30. http://www.zdnet.com.

31. http://www.techweb.com; http://www.infoworld.com.

32. http://www.hotwired.com.

33. http://www.theatlantic.com.

34. http://www.netlynews.com.

35. http://www.salon.com.

36. http://www.slate.com.

37. slate.msn.com/Assessment/97-05-03/Assessment.asp.

38. http://www.stale.com.

39. http://allpolitics.com; http://www.cloakroom.com.

40. http://www.aol.com (keyword: George).

41. http://espn.go.com/; http://www.cnnsi.com; http://www.sportsline.com.

42. http://www.sportsnetwork.com.

43. http://www.golf.com.

44. http://www.onwis.com/packer/.
45. The People and the Press, Pew Research Center, Washington, D.C., 1996, http://www.people-press.org/.
46. Pew Research Center, 2000, http://www.people-press.org/.
47. Kevin Featherly, *Guide to Building a Newsroom Web Site* (Washington, D.C.: Radio-Television News Directors Foundation, 1998).

3. New Tools for News Gathering

1. http://www.ctr.columbia.edu/advent/demos.
2. Forsyth's Naked People Finder at the Digital Library Project at Berkeley (http://cs.berkeley.edu/daf/people.html); MIT's Imagen; IBM's QBIC; and Photobook.
3. Roger Fidler, *Mediamorphosis* (Newbury Park, Calif.: Sage, 1998).
4. http://www.cross-pcg.com/products/crosspad/pad.html.
5. Steven Feiner, Blair MacIntyre, and Tobias Hollerer, "A Touring Machine: Prototyping 3D Mobile Augmented Reality Systems for Exploring the Urban Environment," *Proceedings of ISWC '97* (San Francisco: IEEE, 1997).
6. Peter Lewis, "Mega-pixel Camera Review," *New York Times*, June 11, 1998, C1.
7. http://www.wearcam.org.
8. http://www.pbs.org/newshour/convention96/.9. http://herndon1.sdrdc.com.

4. A Reporter's Field Guide to the Internet

1. *Silicon Alley Reporter Daily*, August 28, 1998.
2. Robert Zakon, maint., "*Hobbes*' Internet Timeline," http://www.isoc.org/guest/zakon/Internet/History/HIT.html (March 29, 2000).
3. CERN, maint., http://cern.web.cern.ch/CERN/.
4. Dan Middleberg and Steve Ross, maint., "Media in Cyberspace," March 2, 2000, http://www.middleberg.com/sub_cyberspacestudy.html (March 29, 2000).
5. Dan Middleberg and Steve Ross, maint., "Media in Cyberspace," May 1999, http://www.middleberg.com/studies/broadcast/execsummary.cfm (February 17, 2000).
6. *Columbia Missourian*, maint, University of Missouri, Columbia, "Missourian Guidelines for Using Information on the Web," March 29, 2000, http://www.missouri.edu/jschool/missourian/guide.htm (March 29, 2000).
7. "The Spider's Search Engine: How to Use Web Search Engines," http://www.monash.com/spidap3.html.
8. Bob Jensen, maint., "Index to Bob Jensen's Web site," http://www.trinity.edu/rjensen/.

9. *Yahoo*, maint., http://www.yahoo.com.
10. *Web Crawler*, maint., http://www.webcrawler.com; *Alta Vista*, maint., http://www.altavista.com; *Infoseek*, maint., http://www.infoseek.com; *Lycos*, maint., http://www.lycos.com; *Hotbot*, maint., http://www.hotbot.com; *Excite*, maint., http://www.excite.com; *Northern Light*, maint., http://www.northernlight.com.
11. http://excellent.com.utk.edu/~mmmiller/vbpro.html; http://www.gsu.edu/~wwwcom/content/csoftware/software_menu.html.
12. For children and families, contact listserv@umdd.umd.edu; for the environment, contact Society of Environmental Journalists, maint., "Environmental Journalism Homepage" http://www.sej.org; for higher education, contact National Education Writers Association, maint., "EWA," http://www.ewa.org; for international reporting, contact majordomo@true.net; for police and courts, contact majordomo@reporters.net; for religion, contact majordomo@iclnet93.iclnet.org; and for science writing, contact majordomo@nasw.org.
13. L Soft International, maint., "CataList, the Official Catalog of LISTSERV Lists," http://www.lsoft.com/lists/listref.html.
14. "Majordomo FAQ," http://www.cis.ohio-state.edu/barr/majordomo-faq.html.
15. http://tile.net/news/; LC&D Internet Publishing, maint., "Cyberfiber Newsgroups," http://www.cyberfiber.com.
16. National Press Club, maint., "2000–2001 Directory of News Sources," http://npc.press.org/sources/.
17. The Reporters Committee for Freedom of the Press, maint., "The Fully-Automated Fill-in-the-Blanks FOI Letter Generator," http://www.rcfp.org/foi_lett.html.
18. Student Press Law Center, maint., "Fully Automated, Fill-in-the-Blanks State Open Records Law Request Letter Generator," http://www.splc.org/ltr_sample.html.
19. U.S. Census Bureau, maint., "Uncle Sam's Reference Shelf," http://www.census.gov/stat_abstract/; U.S. Census Bureau, maint., "Census Bureau News," http://www.census.gov/pubinfo/www/news.html; U.S. Census Bureau, maint., "Search the Census Bureau," http://www.census.gov/main/www/srchtool.html; U.S. Census Bureau, maint., "Census State Data Centers," http://www.census.gov/sdc/www/.
20. *Lexis-Nexis*, maint., "Lexis-Nexis Academic Universe," http://www.lexis-nexis.com/universe.
21. Nua Ltd, maint., "Nua: New Thinking for the Digital Age," http://www.nua.ie/.
22. eMarketer, maint., "Transforming Information Into Intelligence," http://www.emarketer.com/estats/welcome.html.
23. U.S. Government Printing Office, maint., "Database List," http://www.access.gpo.gov/su_docs/db2.html.

24. U.S. Government Printing Office, maint., "Federal Register," http://www
.access.gpo.gov/su_docs/aces/aces140.html.

25. Inspector General's (IG) office, maint., "Internet_.for the Federal IG Community," http://www.ignet.gov/.

26. Library of Congress, maint., "The Library of Congress," http://lcweb.loc.gov/.

26. Library of Congress, maint., "Legislative Information on the Internet," http://
thomas.loc.gov/.

27. General Accounting Office, maint., http://www.gao.gov/.

28. Right to Know Network, maint., http://www.rtk.net/.

29. Steve Ross, maint., "Media and Academic Resource List," http://moon.jrn
.columbia.edu/j-news/ross/main.htm.

30. For public opinion polls, see the Gallup Organization, maint., http://www
.gallup.com. For business directories, see Companies Online, maint., http://
www.CompaniesOnline.com/; Business Wire, maint., http://www.businesswire
.com/; and PR News Wire, maint., http://www.prnewswire.com/. For nonprofits,
see http://www.guidestar.org; for the Securities and Exchange Commission, see
Securities and Exchange Commission, maint., "Search the EDGAR Database,"
http://www.sec.gov/edaux/searches.htm. For workplace health and safety, see
Occupational Health and Safety Administration, maint., http://www.osha.gov.
For health and medical data, see Centers for Disease Control and Prevention,
maint., http://www.cdc.gov. For searchable full-text medical articles, see Medscape, maint., "Today on Medscape," http://www.medscape.com/. For health
organizations and drug information, see HealthTouch, maint., http://www
.healthtouch.com/. For the Mayo Clinic online, see Mayo Clinic, maint.,
"Mayo Clinic Health Oasis," http://www.mayohealth.org/. For Supreme Court
legal references and directories, see Emory Law Library, maint., http://www
.law.emory.edu/FEDCTS/; and Legal Information Institute, maint., http://
supct.law.cornell.edu/supct/. For grand juries, see www.udayton.edu/~granjur/.
For state and local governments, see Global Computing, maint., http://
www.globalcomputing.com/govern.html.

31. Investigative Reporters and Editors, maint., "Campaign Finance Information
Center," http://www.campaignfinance.org.

32. Federal Election Commission, maint. "Campaign Finance Data and Reports."
http://herndon1.sdrdc.com.

33. http://www.fec.gov (September 14, 2000).

34. Center for Responsive Politics, maint., http://www.tray.com/fecinfo.

35. Columbia University, maint., "Subject Guides and Internet Resources," http:
//www.columbia.edu/cu/libraries/indiv/dsc/dsc.html.

36. Federal Communications Commission, maint., http://www.fcc.gov.

37. Jim Martindale, maint., "Martindale's: The Reference Desk," http://www-sci
.lib.uci.edu/martindale/Ref.html.

38. Bartleby.com, maint., "Familiar Quotations: A Collection of Passages, Phrases, and Proverbs Traced to Their Sources in Ancient and Modern Literature," http://www.columbia.edu/acis/bartleby/bartlett/.

39. Mark Olsen, maint., "ARTFL Project: ROGET'S Thesaurus Search Form," http://humanities.uchicago.edu/forms_unrest/ROGET.html; Wordsmyth Collaboratory, maint., http://www.wordsmyth.net/; Mark Olsen, maint., "ARTFL Project: 1913 Webster's Revised Unabridged Dictionary," http://humanities.uchicago.edu/forms_unrest/webster.form.html; Merriam Webster, maint., "WWWebster Dictionary," http://www.m-w.com/dictionary; Oxford English Dictionary, maint., http://oed.com/ (March 15, 2000).

40. Integrated Media Systems Center, maint., http://imsc.usc.edu.

41. John Pavlik, maint., "Exploring New Media," http://members.theglobe.com/exnm.

42. *Columbia Journalism Review*, maint., http://www.cjr.org/; *American Journalism Review*, maint., http://ajr.org; *Editor & Publisher*, maint., http://www.mediainfo.com.

43. Poynter Institute, maint., http://www.poynter.org.

44. Rich Meislin, maint., www.nytimes.com/library/tech/reference/cynavi.html.

45. Asian American Journalists Association, maint., http://www.aaja.org/; South Asian Journalists Association, maint., http://www.saja.org/; National Association of Black Journalists, maint., http://www.nabj.org; National Association of Hispanic Journalists, maint., http://www.nahj.org; National Association of Minority Media Executives, maint., http://www.namme.org; National Lesbian and Gay Journalists Association, maint., http://www.nlgja.org; Medill School of Journalism, maint., http://www.medill.nwu.edu/naja/.

46. Visit the Center for Democratic Technology privacy site at http://www.cdt.org, and click on the CDT Privacy Demo button. Read the results, and consider the privacy implications.

47. BMI, maint. http://www.bmi.com.

48. Harvard RSI, maint., "Harvard RSI Action Home Page," http://www.eecs.harvard.edu/rsi/.

50. http://www.emergency.com/1999/bnldn-pg (July 25, 1998).

5. Journalism Ethics and New Media

1. I discussed this in a speech at Marist College, Poughkeepsie, New York, April 28, 1997.

2. For a detailed list of the ethical issues raised by new media, see Tom Cooper, "50 Ethical Issues Raised by Communication Technology," *Media Ethics* 10, no. 2 (spring 1999): 1.

3. Transactional Records Access Clearinghouse, maint., "Your Source for Comprehensive, Independent, and Non-Partisan Information on Federal Law Enforcement," March 26, 2000, http://trac.syr.edu/index.html (March 26, 2000).

4. Don Tomlinson, "Computer Manipulation and Creation of Images and Sounds: Assessing the Impact" (monograph) (Evanston, Ill.: Annenberg Washington Program, Communications Policy Studies, Northwestern University, 1993).

5. Martha L. Stone, "Print to Web: It Takes Teamwork," July 10, 1999, p. 8, www.MediaINFO.com.

6. ASME Guidelines for New Media, June 24, 1997, http://asme.magazine.org/guidelines/new_media.html (June 24, 1997).

7. A. J. Liebling, *The Press* (New York: Ballantine, 1975), p. 32.

8. Matt Drudge, maint., *The Drudge Report*, January 17, 1998, http://www.drudgereport.com (January 17, 1998).

9. Lawrence Grossman, *The Electronic Republic: Reshaping Democracy in the Information Age* (New York: Penguin USA, 1994).

10. Melvin Mencher, *Basic Media Writing* (Madison, Wisc.: Brown and Benchmark, 1993), p. 74.

11. Jeremy Iggers, *Good News, Bad News: Journalism Ethics and the Public Interest* (Boulder, Colo.: Westview, 1998).

6. Newsroom for a New Age

1. I first discussed the issues covered in this chapter in a speech at an IFRA seminar held November 18–19, 1997, in Darmstadt, Germany. On the tendency to create separate online newsrooms, see Paul Farhi, maint., "The Dotcom Brain Drain," September 1997, http://www.ajr.org (September 15, 1997).

2. *Wall Street Journal*, maint., http://www.wsj.com.

3. *MIN's New Media Report*, September 29, 1997: 1.

4. Dan Middleberg and Steve Ross, maint., "Media in Cyberspace," March 2, 2000, http://www.middleberg.com/sub_cyberspacestudy.html (June 5, 2000).

5. Amy Virshup, "The XY Files," *Salon*, February 8, 1998, http://www.salonmagazine.com/21st/feature/1998/08/25feature.html (March 26, 2000).

6. Robin Goldwyn Blumenthal, "Woolly Times on the Web," *Columbia Journalism Review*, September/October 1997: 34–35.

7. Rob Fixmer, seminar on exploring new media held at Columbia University, September 30, 1997.

8. David Barboza, "Reporters Try on Many Hats in Chicago News Experiment," March 15, 2000, http://www.nytimes.com/library/financial/031500tribune-chicago.html (March 15, 2000).

9. Adam Clayton Powell III, "Portable, High-Tech Reporting System: Journalism, Anyone?" November 4, 1999, http://www.freedomforum.org/technology/1999/7/29urbanjunglepack.asp (July 15, 2000).

10. James Ryan, ojr contributor, "Mobile Reporting with the Palm VII," *Tools of the Trade,* July 15, 1999, http://ojr.usc.edu/ (July 15, 1999).

11. Radio and Television News Directors Foundation (RTNDF), "News of the Future Project" (Washington, D.C.: RTNDF, 1995).

12. Adam Clayton Powell III, "Getting the Picture: Trends in Television News Reporting," ch. 13 in *Demystifying Media Technology,* ed. John V. Pavlik and Everette E. Dennis (Mountain View, Calif.: Mayfield, 1993), pp. 81–86 (Benjamin is quoted on p. 82).

13. Paul Sagan, "The Network Economy" (New York: Center for New Media, Columbia University, 1997).

14. Les Brown, "Les Brown's Encyclopedia of Television," 3d ed. (Detroit: Gale Research, 1992), p. 209.

15. The Computer Museum, maint., http://www.tcm.org/html/history/timeline/years/1952.html.

7. Digital Television and Video News

1. First discussed in John V. Pavlik, "Television News: A Crisis of Opportunity," *Television Quarterly* 28, no. 1 (1996): 21–29.

2. Comments at the annual meeting of the Association for Education in Journalism and Mass Communication, August 4, 1999, New Orleans.

3. Ibid.

8. Audiences Redefined, Boundaries Removed, Relationships Reinvented

1. Howell Raines, "The High Price of Reprieving Mike Barnicle," *New York Times,* August 13, 1998, editorial page.

2. Andrew Schneider, "The Downside of Wonderland," *Columbia Journalism Review,* March/April 1993: 32.

3. Shyam Sundar, "Effect of Source Attribution on Perception of Online News Stories," *Journalism and Mass Communication Quarterly* 75, no. 1 (spring 1998): 55–68.

4. Comments at the annual meeting of the Association for Education in Journalism and Mass Communication, August 4, 1999, New Orleans.

5. Quoted in Paul Sagan, "News.com," *Columbia Journalism Review,* July/August 1997: 37.

6. Pew Research Center, "Internet News Takes Off" (Washington, D.C.: June 8, 1998), 1.

7. Quoted in Frank Newport and Lydia Saad, "A Matter of Trust," *American Journalism Review*, July/August 1998: 30–33.

8. Paul Lester, *Photojournalism: An Ethical Approach* (Hillsdale, N.J.: Lawrence Erlbaum Associates, 1991), p. 97.

9. Joseph Pulitzer, "The College of Journalism," *North American Review*, May 1904.

10. Pew Center for Civic Journalism, maint., http://www.pewcenter.org (September 12, 2000).

11. North Jersey Community, maint., May 1998, http://www.njcommunity.com.

12. North Jersey Community, maint., May 1998, http://www.njcommunity.com.

13. Project Vote Smart, maint., http://www.vote-smart.org.

14. Steve Silberman, maint., "Mapping Anarchy on Usenet," March 5, 1998, http://www.wired.com/news/news/culture/story/10724.html (March 5, 1998).

15. *Editor & Publisher*, maint., "Web Trend Watch," http://www.mediainfo.com/ephome/news/newshtm/webnews/webtrend.htm#a1.

16. Nielsen Media Research and *CommerceNet* study, as reported by the Associated Press, August 26, 1998; research memorandum, Office of Research, International Broadcasting Bureau, U.S. Information Agency, Washington, D.C., August 18, 1999.

17. "FIND/SVP Internet Usage Study," 1997, http://www.findsvp.com/.

18. http://www.jupiter.com (September 15, 1999).

19. *Science*, 1997, http://www.sciencemag.org/.

20. John Carey, "The First 100 Feet for Households' Consumer Adoption Patterns," http://www.ksg.harvard.edu/iip/doeconf/carey.html (March 24, 1997).

21. Egil Juliussen and Karen Petska-Juliussen, *The Internet Industry Almanac* (Glenbrook, Nev.: Computer Industry Almanac, 1999).

22. http://www.gslis.utexas.edu/lis312/LIS312f97/lectures/pres2.htm (must access http://www.gslis.utexas.edu/lis312/LIS312f97/lectures/ and then click on pres2.htm).

23. Robert W. McChesney, *Corporate Media and the Threat to Democracy* (New York: Seven Stories, 1997), p. 13.

24. Clarice Olien, George Donohue, and Philip Tichenor, "Community Structure and Media Use," *Journalism Quarterly* 55 (1978): 445–55.

25. Everette E. Dennis, Martha Fitzsimon, John Pavlik, Seth Rachlin, Dirk Smillie, David Stebenne, and Mark Thalhimer, *The Media and Campaign '92* (New York: Freedom Forum Media Studies Center, 1992).

26. http://www.vallone98.com; see also New York City, maint., http://www.council.nyc.ny.us/council/qs_val.htm.

27. New York State, maint., "Office of the Governor," http://www.state.ny.us/governor.

28. http://www.geocities.com/CapitolHill/Lobby/5500/rcheck.html.
29. *Shetland News*, maint., http://www.shetland-news.co.uk; *Shetland Times*, maint., http://www.shetland-times.co.uk.
30. Software Piracy Association, maint., "SPA Report on Global Software Piracy," 1998, http:// www.spa.org.
31. Nullsoft Inc., maint., "Nullsoft Winamp," http://www.winamp.com.
32. Worldwide Piracy Initiative, maint., http://www.piracy.com.

9. Business Models for Online Journalism

1. First discussed in John V. Pavlik, "Finally, a Peek at Profits," *Columbia Journalism Review*, November/December 1998: 14–15.
2. Capital Newspapers Division of the Hearst Corporation, maint., "Times Union," http://www.timesunion.com; Channel 4000, maint., http://www.wcco.com; *Motley Fool*, maint., http://www.fool.com.
3. Peter M. Zollman, maint., "The Numbers Racket," July 1998, http://www.mediainfo.com (August 15, 1998).
4. http://www.timesunion.com/aboutus/edgieaward.stm (January 15, 2000).
5. *Fort Worth Star-Telegram*, maint., http://www.star-telegram.com; *Hartford Courant*, maint., http://www.courant.com; homearts.com; *Internet Broadcasting System*, maint., http://www.ibsys.com; *KLAS-TV8's Las Vegas Online*, maint., http://www.klas-tv.com.
6. Cable News Network, maint., http://www.cnn.com.
7. NetNoir, maint., "The Black Network," http://www.netnoir.com.
8. *Wall Street Journal*, maint., http://www.wsj.com.
9. Dan Middleberg and Steve Ross, maint., "Media in Cyberspace," March 2, 1998, http://www.middleberg.com/sub_cyberspacestudy.html (April 5, 1998).
10. Dan Middleberg and Steve Ross, maint., "Media in Cyberspace," March 2, 1999, http://www.middleberg.com/sub_cyberspacestudy.html (June 5, 1999).
11. Microsoft Corp, maint., "Home Advisor," http://homeadvisor.msn.com.
12. *Owners.com*, maint., http://www.owners.com.
13. Martha L. Stone, maint., "Papers Face Serious Classified Threats," August 1, 1998, http://www.mediainfo.com (August 1, 1998).
14. MyWay Corp, maint., http://www.zip2.com.
15. Margaret Johnston, maint., "Web Design Guru Predicts Demise of Site Ads," August 21, 1998, http://www.infoworld.com/cgi-bin/displayIcommerce.pl?/980821.eiwebads.htm (August 21, 1998); Jakob Nielsen, maint., "useit.com: Jakob Nielsen's Website," http://www.useit.com/.
16. Ralph F. Wilson, maint., "Using Banner Ads to Promote Your Web Site," June 22, 1996, http://www.wilsonweb.com/articles/bannerad.htm.

10. Long-Term Consequences of the Telecommunications Act of 1996

1. First discussed in John V. Pavlik, "Competition: Key to the Communications Future," *Television Quarterly* 28, no. 2 (1996): 35–44.
2. Lawrence K. Grossman, "An Outbreak of Internet-Phobia," *Columbia Journalism Review*, September/October 1999: 15–16.
3. Robert W. McChesney, *Rich Media, Poor Democracy: Communication Politics in Dubious Times* (Urbana: University of Illinois Press, 1999), pp. 183–84.
4. The Telecommunications Act of 1996 is available online in a number of locations, including the Web site of the Federal Communications Commission, at http://www.fcc.gov/telecom.html, as well as via the Web site of the U.S. Library of Congress, http://thomas.loc.gov/.
5. Eli Noam and Robert N. Freeman, "Global Competition," *Television Quarterly* 29, no. 1 (1998): 18–23.
6. Edmund L. Andrews, "Asians Win F.C.C. Bidding for Licenses," *New York Times*, May 7, 1996, Technology Section, p. 1.
7. It is not surprising the Japanese have great interest in mobile communications. Mobile communications is booming in Japan. As of December 1999, Japan's NTT DoCoMo had 27,636,000 Personal Digital Communications (PDC) cellular subscribers, up some 513,000 users in a single month, and 1,375,000 Personal Handyphone Services (PHS) cellular subscribers, up some 20,000 in a single month (http://www.nttdocomo.com/num.htm [February 21, 2000]).
8. http://www.nua.ie (March 1, 2000).
9. Ibid.
10. The number of Web pages is far greater than the number of sites. Google indexes more than one billion Web pages (http://www.google.com [September 13, 2000]).
11. http://www.internettrafficreport.com.
12. Lawrence K. Grossman, "An Outbreak of Internet-Phobia," *Columbia Journalism Review*, September/October 1999: 15.
13. Ithiel de Sola Pool, *Technologies of Freedom* (Cambridge: Harvard University Press, Belknap Press, 1983), p. 250.
14. See the online journal *Information Society* at www.slis.indiana.edu/tis/.
15. W. P. Davison, "The Third-Person Effect of Communication," *Public Opinion Quarterly* 46: 1–15.
16. Andrew L. Shapiro, *The Control Revolution: How the Internet Is Putting Individuals in Charge and Changing the World We Know* (New York: Century and Markle Foundations, 1999), p. 126.
17. The report is available at http://nces.ed.gov/pubsearch/pubsinfo.asp?pubid 000086.
18. Newton Minow, "The Vast Wasteland Revisited," speech presented May 15,

1991, at the Freedom Forum Media studies Center, Columbia University, New York.

11. Implications of Intelligent Agents for Journalism

1. I first discussed this in a speech delivered at the Foundation for Intelligent Physical Agents (FIPA) convention, Dublin, Ireland, July 15, 1998.
2. Jeffrey Bradshaw, maint., "Software Agents" (Cambridge, Mass.: AAI press/MIT press, 1997), http://agents.umbc.edu/introduction/01-Bradshaw.pdf (January 10, 1998).
3. Jaron Lanier, speech presented on October 21, 1997, at the Center for New Media, Columbia University Graduate School of Journalism, New York.
4. Ray Kurzweil, *The Age of Spiritual Machines* (New York: Viking Penguin, 1999).
5. *Nando Times*, maint., http://www.nando.net.
6. Forte Inc., maint., http://www.forteinc.com/agent/index.htm; *ZDNet*, maint., "Ferret Soft," http://www.ferretsoft.com/netferret/index.html.
7. *Individual.com*, maint., http://www.newspage.com or http://www.individual.com
8. http://www.cs.cmu.edu/afs/cs/project/ai-repository/ai/areas/expert/systems/clips/agent/0.html.
9. *Excite*, maint., "News Tracker," http://nt.excite.com.
10. *Profnet*, maint., "ProfNet's Experts Database," http://www.profnet.com/ped.html.
11. *New York Times*, maint., http://www.nytimes.com.
12. John Markoff, "Differences Over Privacy on the Internet," *New York Times on the Web*, maint. *New York Times*, July 1, 1998, http://www.nytimes.com (July 1, 1998).
13. Bjorn Hermans, maint., "Intelligent Software Agents on the Internet," http://www.firstmonday.dk/issues/issue2_3/ch_123/.
14. Nicolas Negroponte, *Being Digital* (New York: Random House, 1995).

12. New Media and Journalism Education

1. John Markoff, "Deals to Move Global Positioning Technology Toward Everyday Use," maint. *New York Times*, August 10, 1998, *http://www.nytimes.com* (August 10, 1998).
2. This chapter is adapted from John V. Pavlik and Adam Clayton Powell III, "A 'White' Paper," originally prepared for the Task Force on Journalism and Mass Communication Education at the Millennium for the Association for Education in Journalism and Mass Communication, September 1999.

3. Ray Kurzweil, *The Age of Spiritual Machines* (New York: Viking Penguin, 1999).

4. *Pathfinder.com*, maint., "On-Line in Africa," http://www.pathfinder.com/travel/candide/index.html.

5. Dan Middleberg and Steve Ross, maint., "Media in Cyberspace," 1999, http://www.middleberg.com/sub_cyberspacestudy.html.

6. John Pavlik, maint., "Exploring New Media," http://www.columbia.edu/~jp35.

7. Freedom Forum, maint., "Free: The Freedom Forum Online," http://www.freedomforum.org; *Columbia Journalism Review*, maint., http://www.cjr.org; *American Journalism Review*, maint., http://www.ajr.org; University of Southern California Annenberg School, maint., *Online Journalism Review*, http://ojr.usc.edu/.

8. *Brief* 28, no. 30 (September 16, 1998), http://www.umn.edu/tc/brief/.

9. See, for example, *Lucent Technologies Persyst Virtual Classroom*, http://www.multimedia.bell-labs.com/projects/persyst/.

10. Bell Labs Multimedia Communication Research Department, maint., http://www.multimedia.bell-labs.com/projects/persyst/.

13. Job Prospects in Online Journalism

1. First discussed in John V. Pavlik, "New Media Offer Growing Job Prospects," *Nieman Reports* 50, no. 2 (summer 1996): 26–28.

2. *Cloakroom.com*, maint., "National Journal's Cloak Room," 1998, http://www.cloakroom.com/ (1998).

3. For weeklies, see the *Newspaper Association of America Online*, http://www.infi.net/naa/; *Editor & Publisher*, http://www.mediainfo.com/edpub/; *American Journalism Review*, www.ajr.org.

4. Cablevision Systems, maint., http://www.cablevision.com/.

5. Dan Middleberg and Steve Ross, maint., "Media in Cyberspace," March 1999, http://www.middleberg.com/Keyfindings.htm.

6. MSNBC, maint., 1996, http://www.msnbc.com (1996).

7. Alternative News Network, maint., "ANN—The Cairns Web," http://www.altnews.com.au.

8. Medscape, maint., "Medscape News," http://www.medscape.com/home/news/medscape-news.html.

9. Reuters, maint., http://www.reuters.com/index.html; Dow Jones, maint., "Ask Dow Jones," http://bis.dowjones.com/; *Bloomberg.com*, maint., http://www.bloomberg.com; *Motley Fool*, maint., http://www.fool.com; http://www.thestreet.com; http://www.ragingbull.com; http://www.cbs.marketwatch.com.

10. http://www.bayeconfor.org/bamp3.htm (September 15, 2000).

11. Steve Lohr, "New York Area Is Forging Ahead in New Media," *New York Times*, April 15, 1996, D1.
12. http://www.siliconalleyreporter.com/; http://www.digitalcoastreporter.com/.
13. Columbia Journalism School, maint., http://www.jrn.columbia.edu/; Center for New Media, maint., http://www.cnm.columbia.edu/.
14. University of Southern California Annenberg School, maint., *Online Journalism Review*, http://ojr.usc.edu/.

Afterword

1. Tom Goldstein, "Welcome Address to Class of 1999," speech presented on September 1, 1998, in the lecture hall of the Graduate School of Journalism, Columbia University.
2. David Shenk, *Data Smog: Surviving the Information Glut* (New York: HarperCollins, 1997).

Index